Praise for *Shooting Crows*

'*Shooting Crows* is a meticulously researched and sharply written account of an astonishing series of events. It provides riveting insights into the way in which power can be abused in modern Ireland.'

Noel Doran, former Editor, *Irish News*

'Trevor Birney masterfully lays bare the history of collusion between loyalsist murderers and their British masters. *Shooting Crows* should be taught in every college in the British Isles, and read by all its citizens. Historic work.'

Academy Award winner Terry George

'The deadly murderous campaign by loyalism is chilling enough but the involvement of the British state is absolutely shocking. A remarkable story brilliantly told.'

Denzil McDaniel, former Editor, *Impartial Reporter*

Trevor Birney is an Emmy-nominated film producer, director and journalist who began his career at *The Impartial Reporter* newspaper on the border in Fermanagh. In 2017 he produced the groundbreaking documentary *No Stone Unturned*, about the 1994 murder by UVF gunmen of six Catholics in Loughinisland, Co. Down. Following the film's premiere, the PSNI launched an investigation into the alleged leaking of secret documents and arrested Birney and his colleague, Barry McCaffrey. Police later apologised and paid both journalists significant damages. His first book was the bestselling *Quinn* (Merrion Press, 2022).

SHOOTING CROWS

MASS MURDER, STATE COLLUSION AND PRESS FREEDOM

TREVOR BIRNEY

First published in 2024 by
Merrion Press
10 George's Street
Newbridge
Co. Kildare
Ireland
www.merrionpress.ie

© Trevor Birney Publishing Ltd, 2024

978 1 78537 525 5 (Paper)
978 1 78537 537 8 (Ebook)

A CIP catalogue record for this book is available from the British Library.

All rights reserved. No part of this publication may be reproduced, stored in a retrieval system, or transmitted, in any form or by any means (electronic, mechanical, photocopying, recording or otherwise), without the prior written permission of both the copyright owner and the publisher of this book.

Typeset in Calluna 11.5/16

Cover design by Chris Scott.

Merrion Press is a member of Publishing Ireland.

Contents

Abbreviations	vii
Prologue Executive Action	1

PART I

1	Dressed to Kill	11
2	Troubling Times	19
3	The Way Ahead	35
4	Cross-Pollination	63
5	The Slow Waltz	89
6	A Night in November	113
7	The Black North	135
8	'Fenian Bastards'	149

PART II

9	The Aftermath	169
10	To Annihilate Truth	182
11	How to Define Collusion	208
12	*No Stone Unturned*	219
13	Hear No Evil, Speak No Evil, See No Evil	242
14	Offences	259
15	Shooting Crows	277
16	Truth and Justice	293
Postscript		309
Select Bibliography		313
Acknowledgements		314
Index		318

Abbreviations

ACC	Assistant Chief Constable
CAJ	Committee on the Administration of Justice
CJI	Criminal Justice Inspectorate
DHAC	Derry Housing Action Committee
DSA	Directed Surveillance Authorisation
DUP	Democratic Unionist Party
GAA	Gaelic Athletic Association
INLA	Irish National Liberation Army
IPP	Irish Parliamentary Party
IPT	Investigatory Powers Tribunal
IRA	Irish Republican Army
LPA	Loyalist Prisoners Association
NGO	Non-Governmental Organisation
NIO	Northern Ireland Office
NUJ	National Union of Journalists
OPONI	Office of the Police Ombudsman of Northern Ireland
OSA	Official Secrets Act
PFC	Pat Finucane Centre
PONI	Police Ombudsman of Northern Ireland
PSNI	Police Service of Northern Ireland
RCJ	Royal Courts of Justice
RFJ	Relatives for Justice
RIC	Royal Irish Constabulary
RPOA	Retired Police Officers Association

RUC	Royal Ulster Constabulary
SDLP	Social Democratic and Labour Party
SIO	Senior Investigating Officer
TA	Territorial Army
UDA	Ulster Defence Association
UDR	Ulster Defence Regiment
UFF	Ulster Freedom Fighters
UULF	United Ulster Loyalist Force
UUP	Ulster Unionist Party
UVF	Ulster Volunteer Force

Prologue

Executive Action

My wife, Sheila, is a fitful sleeper and a slave to an alarm, which isn't a great mix for a good night's rest. However, shortly after 7 a.m. on that final bank holiday weekend in the summer of 2018, she was awoken not by an alarm or her own fitfulness, but by the sound of cars in the drive outside our home in East Belfast.

She walked to the window, opened the shutter and narrated the scene in our driveway as I began to stir. 'There's a lot of police in our drive, cars everywhere; what are they doing here?'

Her final words were accompanied by the sound of banging on our front door. Continuous heavy bangs.

Despite the rude awakening, Sheila remained totally unflustered as she closed over the shutter again and came away from the window. While I got out of bed and she dressed, we both remained in the dark.

I mumbled, 'It's about Loughinisland,' as I sneaked a peek through the shutters. It didn't fluster her as she continued to get dressed. She had never experienced anything like this before – neither had I for that matter – but she met it head-on, like she had been dealing with such situations all her life. In that moment, before we left the bedroom, her self-possession set a distinct tone for what lay ahead – we can deal with this, it assured.

Next door to our room there were three kids in the one bed – our youngest daughter Freya, along with her cousins Gabriel and Liv, who, along with Sheila's niece, Sarah, and Sarah's husband, James, had arrived at our home the evening before to spend the long weekend with us. We'd had other sleeping arrangements for Gabriel and Liv, but in the excitement of being together again, they had all ended up bunking in together. Upstairs, was our eldest Ella and middle daughter Mia, with James and Sarah in the room at the top of the house. None of them seemed to have heard the commotion that had woken Sheila.

Speaking of my wife, she was now armoured in a sweatshirt and jogging bottoms and left our room to confront whoever was trying to break our front door down. I held back, still fumbling about in the dark to find clothes, while at the same time trying to get hold of the one person in the world who would understand the position that was quickly dawning on me: my solicitor, Niall Murphy. He had warned us that this day could come.

No answer. It was 7 a.m., after all. He would still be asleep at his home across the city in Glengormley, if he hadn't already left to spend the weekend in his happy place: Donegal.

I could hear Sheila downstairs. By now, she had opened the front door. Disjointed and disordered male voices were echoing up the stairs from our hallway.

Mia, our sixteen-year-old, appeared in the bedroom. No one who has ever come across Mia will be surprised to learn that she was the first to respond. Since she was no height – well, she still is no height, having inherited such status from my side of the family – she has built a reputation for managing not only her own affairs, but the family's too, and at times even our film productions, all with an attitude of serious intent that borders on the hint of a threat.

'Get hold of Murph, tell him the police are here,' I said.

Mia raised her phone to her ear; she didn't have to ask questions. For whatever reason, she already had Niall's number in her phone book (which might go some way to explaining her reputation). She understood the task. Niall wasn't going to get any more sleep that morning.

I made my way downstairs, safe in the knowledge that no matter what was about to reveal itself, Mia's tenacity and Niall's legal experience would soon come to bear on the situation. By the time I reached the hallway, there was what seemed like an army of police officers dressed in blue boiler suits, revolvers holstered by their side, coming through the front door. There was no time to take it in.

Sheila was already in the kitchen, at the back of the house, remonstrating with a tall, moustached officer, who, at first glance – maybe because he was holding a clipboard – seemed to be the one in charge. There was no doubt he was the one getting the full force of Sheila's frustration. I went into the kitchen to join them and, having realised I was there, the officer turned away from Sheila and introduced himself to me. With the noise and the chaos around us, I could hardly take in what he was saying. I heard his name and rank but was largely distracted by what the rest of his colleagues were doing as they continued to flow into the ground floor of the house.

I quickly wheeled back as he laid out a piece of paper on the stainless-steel island. He brushed it flat with his hand and began to explain what he was doing in our kitchen at 7 a.m. on a Friday morning. I heard *No Stone Unturned* for the first time that day, confirming my suspicions and laying to rest the niggling fear that I had somehow brought all this on my family for some legitimately criminal reason that had simply slipped my mind. He said he was investigating matters relating to the aforementioned documentary, and they were here to search the house for documents that were protected under the Official Secrets Act (OSA).

I reacted to this with both relief and incredulity. I wasn't going to tell him, but there were no documents whatsoever in the house that had any connection to the film. The tall officer – who had a hint of a North Antrim accent, I thought – was still talking, but I'd heard all I needed to hear for the moment.

My mind was racing. So they were going to search the house. Okay, we could handle that, although it wasn't going to be much fun for the small kids. But they had clearly gone to all this bother to search the house for a document we had made no secret of having in our possession. We had plastered the bloody thing all over the documentary, which had been released to the world over a year earlier. This didn't make much sense. So what was it really about?

By then, some of the kids had begun to appear. Sheila moved to comfort them and lead them into one of the other rooms, away from the police. James, who had pulled on a blue jumper and shorts, was also there.

Seeing his face, I realised just how shocking the scene must be. He had grown up in Kent, after all, a world away from the conflict in the North of Ireland. He had likely never had much cause to have any interaction with a police officer. Now he was surrounded by them. His puzzlement and bemusement were sketched all over his face. He looked at me in a way that screamed in an out-of-place south-of-England accent, 'What the hell is this all about then?'

Out of the sea of blue-uniformed officers, a small, somewhat burly man appeared in the kitchen beside me: Detective Constable Andy Allen. He was there for one thing only, I was soon to discover.

Andy was in plain clothes and spoke in a quiet, almost apologetic manner. 'Can I talk with you in the living room?' he asked, while also introducing a female colleague who was in charge of the operation. Her surname immediately struck me. I remembered a very senior detective in the Royal Ulster Constabulary (RUC) who shared the same name. The big guy with the Ballymena accent stepped back. I didn't understand what the arrival of the guy in plain clothes meant, but I could see that this had all been rehearsed.

I followed Detective Allen through the armed police and into the living room at the front of the house, seeing for the first time the full force of the law that had come down upon us, the driveway full of marked and unmarked police vehicles. Beyond them, I could see Land Rovers out on the street. It was going to be an interesting morning for my neighbours.

Andy was keen to get on with the real business of the day: 'I'm arresting you,' he said. He then proceeded to read what journalists would regard as a pre-prepared statement, listing the offences of which the Police Service of Northern Ireland (PSNI) believed I was guilty.

So they aren't here just to search the house then, I thought.

I would later discover that police had been planning for this day for over a year. Operation Yurta, as they called it, was set up to find the source that had leaked a top-secret document to my friend and colleague Barry McCaffrey, who had led our investigation into the Loughinisland massacre at a pub in Co. Down in 1994, when six men were shot dead by loyalist paramilitaries. Barry had produced several stories for our investigative website *The Detail* on the massacre and had been centrally involved – indeed, played a pivotal role both on and off screen – in the film on the subject, *No Stone Unturned*, which I had produced, and the New-York-based, Academy-Award-winning Alex Gibney had directed.

After the film premiered at the New York Film Festival in October 2017, the PSNI had contacted an English police force, Durham Constabulary. Not to reopen the investigation into the Loughinisland massacre, which the documentary was about, but to go after our source. The PSNI had previously called Durham in to examine the leaking of a secret Police Ombudsman of Northern Ireland (PONI) report into the murder of female RUC Constable Colleen McMurray in Newry in 1992. Now they had the team behind *No Stone Unturned* in their sights.

Darren Ellis was the top cop in charge at Durham and, judging from documents that would later be disclosed to us, he had been pushing for our arrest with nothing less than a myopic zeal. 'Executive Action' was how he had described it, as he appealed to his superiors to green light the operation. Ellis had ordered PSNI officers to arrest Barry, too; in fact they were doing just that at that very moment, five miles from my home. And in the centre of the city, more armed police were storming through the doors of our offices. All deployed at huge cost to find a journalist's source.

While Andy Allen read out the list of alleged offences, I kept my head down, trying to work through what all this meant for my family. My eighty-year-old mother, who lived alone ninety minutes west in Enniskillen, would already be awake. Mia would have to call her or get hold of my younger brother, so he could tell her about this in person.

My incredulity was also rising. Raiding the house was one thing, but arresting a journalist in front of his family was something else. All because of a piece of A4 paper in a documentary? What the fuck was going on?

My phone was sitting on the coffee table in front of me. I could see my bank alerting me about direct debits due to be debited from my account on the last working day of the month. Today. It would have distracted me twenty minutes earlier; now my personal finances were the least of my worries.

I picked up the phone, hoping to at the very least spare myself the embarrassment of two detectives seeing my banking details, but Detective Constable McVicker reached out to prevent me from using the phone.

This caused a moment. Not a stand-off, exactly, but I certainly paused for a beat to take in what she had done. A journalist's phone is a very sensitive device, holding numbers of and communications with contacts and sources, as well as all the other detritus of a digitally connected lifestyle.

We looked at each other as Andy Allen explained that I would have to hand over the phone. I set it back down on the coffee table. It was in that moment that I realised that I was no longer in control of my home, or, seemingly, my possessions. The calm but bewildered tone that Sheila had set was being overtaken by the first sparks of anger.

One of them asked me for the phone's pin code. Caught off guard, I stepped back to think. Should I comply or not? I had a split second to weigh it all up.

I gave them it. I had nothing to hide and had done nothing wrong, so I decided why give them a chance to say that I had been uncooperative? Now, I would act differently, but then it felt like the right thing to do.

Given the sudden storm of their arrival, I had only thrown on a T-shirt and trousers, so I asked if I could dress properly before they took me to wherever they were going to take me. They granted the request, though a young officer was told to escort me upstairs to keep an eye on me. He watched me dress and brush my teeth before ensuring that I came back down into the hall, where Detective Allen was waiting.

Sheila was there, too, and I could see James sitting at the kitchen table, his face failing to hide his shock. I tried to lighten the mood, shouting to him something about how this is what happens if you make a documentary in Belfast. Sheila had returned to remonstrating with the moustached search officer. She was seething. I gave her a quick kiss and then, less than fifteen minutes since the police had arrived, I was led out of my front door to a waiting squad car.

Two officers were already in the front seats. Another uniformed officer opened the back passenger door and told me to get in. Andy Allen came around the car and joined me in the back.

As we drove away, my anger broke. 'Are you arresting Ronnie Hawthorne this morning? Or are you only interested in journalists?' I asked the detective.

He remained silent.

I shut up. There was no point shouting at them.

What I didn't know was that Darren Ellis had in fact sent police to see Hawthorne, the chief suspect in the Loughinisland massacre. Not to question him, mind you, but to take the complaint that had helped Ellis and his colleagues find their way to arresting myself and Barry McCaffrey.

PART I

1 | Dressed to Kill

The neighbouring villages of Clough and Loughinisland in rural Co. Down are little more than five minutes apart, sitting at opposite corners of a geographic triangle with the historic town of Downpatrick to their east. Running between the two villages is a straight, wide road that facilitates locals and foreigners alike as they travel south for the beaches, golf courses and mountains of South Down.

On the summer evening of 18 June 1994, a red Triumph Acclaim car sped north out of Clough on this very road. The three occupants knew the car was somewhat unreliable, but they didn't have a choice. It was a vehicle that had been supplied for this journey: a murderous journey.

The terrorists had chosen this long, warm Saturday evening for their attack, knowing the vast majority of their fellow people on the island of Ireland were gathered in homes, bars, clubs – really, wherever there were heavy-tube televisions – to watch a football match. The men were dressed to kill, in workmen's blue boiler suits and woollen, black balaclavas. For one of the men in the Triumph in particular, the act of killing had become the core focus of his life. It was a life steeped in the sectarian hatred that over recent decades had come to mark and score this most beautiful and culturally rich landscape. Their victims were unknown to them, but their target was set. A two-roomed country pub that would be jammed to the doors. To the inhabitants of the car, it didn't matter who they were or why they had made the choice to be in the pub; all that mattered was that they were Catholic.

Despite all the technological advances that paramilitaries in Ireland had embraced over the previous thirty years, the loyalist paramilitary killing machine had failed to evolve beyond shooting unarmed innocents, usually in the back. An explanation for that lack of sophistication was typified by the man sitting in the front passenger seat of the Triumph, a pathological serial killer who had been travelling the roads of the Mourne County for many years, knowing he had total and complete impunity. He hadn't needed to develop his tactics, hone his methodology or his ability to avoid prosecution. In his personal war on his neighbours, near and far, he was rewarded for his action by the very fact that he was free to do so, to carry on killing at will.

He was likely unaware, as he sped north, that his campaign of violence would end here, with a savage and brutal massacre of his close neighbours. What he was aware of, however – or what he would have felt, at least – was that he was part of a loyalist tradition that stretched back over a hundred years, to the time of Home Rule.

***

South Down has been a British parliamentary constituency since 1885, which, at the outbreak of the Troubles, took in the towns of Banbridge to the west and Newry to the south, while the boundary ran east to Warrenpoint and along the northern side of Carlingford Lough and up the Irish Sea coastline to the village of Kilclief.

Downpatrick, ten miles west of Kilclief, is the historic and political heart of the constituency. When the seat was established, it was first held by John Francis Small, a member of the Irish Parliamentary Party (IPP) at Westminster, the official party for Irish MPs in the British House of Commons. The IPP would lead the push in Parliament for Home Rule, or self-government, for Dublin.

Prime Minister William Gladstone introduced the first Government of Ireland Bill, or Home Rule Bill, in 1886, but it was defeated in the House of Commons. A second attempt in 1893 was defeated in the House of Lords. In 1912 the Liberal Party Prime Minister, Herbert Asquith, brought a third Home Rule Bill before parliament. Jeremiah MacVeagh, the MP for South Down at the time, was at the centre of the debate and produced a book titled *Home Rule in a Nutshell*, which had an introduction by Winston Churchill, also a supporter of Home Rule. The two men would witness the Home Rule Bill gain Royal Assent in September 1914, even if its enactment was simultaneously delayed until after the First World War.

Still, the gaining of that Royal Assent was enough to cause a storm in unionist Ulster, one that had been building in the preceding years.

***

The three men in the Triumph Acclaim car on their way to Loughinisland in June 1994 were speeding irrevocably towards violence. These men were convinced that they were members of the modern-day iteration of the Ulster Volunteer Force (UVF), which first emerged as a 'militant expression of Ulster Unionist opposition' to the Third Home Rule Bill, according to historian Timothy Bowman in *Carson's Army: The Ulster Volunteer Force, 1910–22*.

Unionists were undoubtedly preparing for conflict in the event of Home Rule. The son of an East Belfast whiskey distiller and former soldier, James Craig became one of two hard-line MPs who would lead unionism through this turbulent period. Craig had served in the British Army in South Africa and returned home to become an MP for East Down in 1906, later forming the Ulster Unionist Council, which would oppose any notion of Home Rule. With his military background and organisational skills, Craig was able to harness unionist opposition and, indeed, create a paramilitary force that would be prepared to fight should the need arise.

In 1912, with Asquith pushing his bill forward, the 'Ulster Volunteers' emerged, with its membership drawn from the Ulster Clubs, formed in the 1880s in reaction to the first Home Rule Bill, and the Orange Order. If Craig was the controlling military mind of unionism, its intellectual leader was Lord Edward Carson. Born in Dublin, he would become known as the 'Uncrowned King of Ulster'. In February 1910 Carson became leader of the anti-Home Rule Irish unionists, effectively committing himself to the Ulster unionist cause. Prime Minister Asquith and the Irish nationalists now had a devoted adversary determined to oppose any attempt to introduce Home Rule.

Under Craig and Carson, unionists embraced the 'show of strength', a tactic that would become a defining feature of their character throughout the rest of the century, embraced by loyalist paramilitaries as a reason for sectarian murder. In September 1911 a 'monster demonstration' attended by over 50,000 at Craig's East Belfast home was a catalytic moment for unionism, which believed that the large numbers and fiery speeches would send a clear signal of intent to London. At one such gathering, Carson told his listeners, 'Ulster sees in Irish nationalism a dark conspiracy, buttressed upon crime and incitement to outrage, maintained by ignorance and pandering to superstition.'

On Easter Tuesday, 9 April 1912, as Asquith was making the final preparations for his Home Rule Bill and a crew on board the *Titanic* were readying for their maiden voyage, there was another huge demonstration of unionist opposition to Asquith's plans, with over 100,000 members of the newly established Ulster Volunteers marching through central Belfast to Balmoral, in the south of the city, where the newly elected leader of the Conservative Party, Andrew Bonar Law, led the platform party. Seventy special trains had been laid on for the demonstrators and several dozen English, Scottish and Welsh MPs were there to hear Bonar Law tell the crowd: 'Once again you hold the pass, the pass for the Empire. You are a besieged city ... The government has erected by their Parliament Act a boom against you to shut you off from the help of the British people. You will burst that boom. That help will come ...'

Two days later, Asquith introduced the Third Home Rule Bill in the House of Commons. In Westminster, Unionist MPs and their Conservative allies fought the bill every step of the way. Back in Belfast, Carson and Craig rolled out another 'show of strength' on 'Ulster Day', 28 September. The leaders wanted to leave Asquith and the Irish nationalists in no doubt of the strength of opposition to Home Rule. On that day, over 470,000 men and women would sign the Solemn League and Covenant and the corresponding women's declaration, pledging to use whatever means necessary to defeat Home Rule.

The Irish News described Ulster Day as a 'grotesque production and political failure, though a comic success'. It told its readers on the Monday morning: 'At last the curtain has been rung down on the Ulster Day farce, and we may hope for, at any rate, a temporary return to the civic pride on which Belfast prides itself so tremendously. The Carson circus having toured North East Ulster gave its final and greatest performance entitled, "Signing the Covenant", in Belfast on Saturday, and wound up its fantastic career in a paroxysm of flag waving and noise, emblematic of the meaningless nonsense of the whole grotesque scheme from start to finish. The stage lost an actor manager when the law and politics claimed Sir Edward Carson. His unfailing instinct for theatrical effect was never better exemplified than on the Saturday in his "state" progress from the Ulster Hall to the City Hall. Something was expected from him as the central figure in the "historic" scene and he rose to the occasion splendidly.'

According to Timothy Bowman, the term 'Ulster Volunteer Force' 'appears to have been used publicly for the first time by a former British Army Colonel Robert Sharman-Crawford when addressing Bangor Unionist Club on 22 December 1912'. The following month, on 13 January 1913, the UVF was formally established. Historians have debated the actual purpose of the organisation and whether Edward Carson really believed it would take on the British Army in the event of Home Rule. Professor Paul Bew of Queen's University Belfast wrote that Carson created the UVF to help manage loyalist 'hooligans' in Belfast. There is no doubt it was formed to send a clear signal to London that the speeches and military drilling were now backed up by a private army determined to protect the Ulster Protestant tradition in the north-east corner of Ireland.

Eoin MacNeill, a scholar and cultural activist born in Glenarm, Co. Antrim, who would become a leading figure in the events that led to the Easter Rising in 1916, wrote an article later in 1913 titled 'The North Began' for *An Claidheamh Soluis* (translation: *The Sword of Light*), which advocated for the establishment of an Irish national volunteer force. The Irish Volunteers, armed, drilled and led by MacNeill, would be formed in November 1913 to protect Home Rule should it be achieved. As regards the UVF, MacNeill stated in his address to the inaugural meeting of the Irish Volunteers, 'The more genuine and successful the [UVF] in Ulster becomes, the more completely does it establish the principle that Irishmen have the right to decide and govern their own national affairs. We have nothing to fear from the existing Volunteers in Ulster, nor they from us.'

The actions of the UVF, however, contradicted this claim. The organisation was intent on arming the thousands of unionists joining its ranks. In June 1913 the British government seized 7,000 Italian rifles destined for the UVF in Hammersmith in West London. The man behind the purchase of the weapons was Frederick Crawford, a former major in the British Army. Crawford had signed the Solemn League and Covenant in his own blood and was appointed as the UVF's director of ordinance. He would later say he was ashamed to call himself an Irishman, saying, 'I am an Ulsterman, a very different breed.' He made no secret of his belief in armed resistance to Home Rule and had been involved in previous attempts to smuggle arms. In *Carson's Army*, Bowman describes how Crawford had set up a 'front firm', John Ferguson and Company, with Sir William Bull MP, and successfully purchased Vickers machine guns at the significant cost of £300 each and 'thousands of rifles'. The Hammersmith Inn, where the rifles were found, had been rented to the company owned by Bull and Crawford, who had written to arms manufacturers in Austria and Germany seeking to purchase 20,000 rifles and one million rounds of ammunition.

Around the same time, Durham Police Constabulary – which many years later, somewhat ironically, would find itself at the centre of the Loughinisland story – seized 150,000 rounds of ammunition destined for the UVF in a raid in the town of Stockton on the banks of the River Tees. In some cases, the unionists showed a degree of ingenuity in arming themselves. It was reported that 175 Martini-Enfield rifles were purchased from Harrods Department Store, destined for the Earl of Erne in Enniskillen.

Crawford's determination to arm the UVF was undiminished by the setbacks in England. Less than a year after Hammersmith, he spent over £45,000 of the UVF's money on the purchase of 25,000 rifles and 3 million rounds of ammunition from a Jewish arms dealer called Bruno 'Benny' Spiro in Hamburg, Germany. On the last day of March 1914, on the Baltic island of Langeland, the weapons and ammunition were loaded onto the SS *Fanny*, which set sail for Ireland. Almost three weeks later, in the Bristol Channel, the shipment was transferred onto the SS *Clyde Valley*, which Crawford had purchased in Glasgow, and made the final part of its journey, north to Larne, where the headlights of 500 vehicles lit up the port on its arrival on 24 April. Over 2,500 UVF men had been mobilised on the North Down coast and 'column after column' of cars were used to disperse the consignment.

Given the scale of the gunrunning, nationalists were convinced there had been collusion between the British state and the UVF. Bowman recorded how one RIC officer told in his memoirs how the guns could have been seized on their arrival in Fermanagh: 'I heard that the arms were to be brought that evening to the house of Mr J. Porter-Porter, of Belle Isle ... I sat on the other side of the road ... after a time along came the cars with their packages in the back. The arms were delivered and there was no interference at any time.'

The gun had been introduced into Irish politics. Carson, Crawford and the UVF had placed between 60,000 and 80,000 illegal rifles, according to estimates, into the hands of unionists across the North.

With the outbreak of the First World War in July 1914, the introduction of Home Rule was put on hold until the end of the conflict. An estimated 30,000 members of the UVF signed up for the newly created 36th Ulster Division of the British Army, where it incurred over 5,500 casualties over two days in the Battle of the Somme. The blood sacrifice would create a new generational bond between Ulster unionists and the British, although it was the 1916 Easter Rising in Dublin that would change the political dynamic between Britain and Ireland forever. As Paul Bew wrote, 'By the end of the war, Republican separatism had replaced the Home Rule movement as the pre-eminent nationalist political force in Ireland. However, the Irish state which Republicans fought to achieve was even less palatable to Ulster unionists than the Home Rule Parliament that nationalists had sought before the war. The First World War, as well as dividing Europe, further polarised the peoples of Ireland. The two sides could not compromise, and the result was the partition of Ireland.'

The UVF had served its purpose, in keeping those six Ulster counties in unionist control. And it was this legacy that those three balaclava-clad killers likely thought they were continuing as they sped along in that red Triumph Acclaim towards Loughinisland.

2 | Troubling Times

In 1965, in a barn on a farm near the village of Pomeroy, Co. Tyrone, a group of forty men from all over the North gathered to swear allegiance to the UVF. Forty-five years after being stood down, the UVF was back.

That was not to say that the preceding half century had been lacking in turmoil – both throughout Ulster and specifically in South Down. Not long after the 'Home Rule Crisis', the Irish War of Independence – or the Anglo-Irish War, as the unionists referred to it – began. One of the most infamous incidents from that period in South Down was an attack by the IRA on Crossgar RIC Station in June 1920. According to the *Down Recorder*: 'The IRA entered a house and ordered the occupants out as they pointed their revolvers. They then sought to tunnel through the dividing wall in order to place explosives which would wreck the interior of the barrack. Once the attack commenced, a guard went into another neighbouring house. From this house and behind a low garden wall, hundreds of shots were fired at the police station. The six officers shot back as best they could from behind sandbags and steel-shuttered windows in both storeys. However, being vastly outnumbered, they were trapped and so shot up flares to illuminate their besiegement in order that help may be sent.'

Overall, the attack was a failure, but for unionists, the violence was worrying. The Anglo-Irish War was largely fought between republicans and British troops in the twenty-six counties, but such attacks showed how the disorder could spill over into the North. It would not be long before unionist concerns led to a violent reaction. Four weeks after the Crossgar attack, an outbreak of sectarian violence in Belfast left nineteen people dead and over 200 injured. Wednesday, 21 July 1920 was the beginning of what came to be described as the 'Belfast pogrom'.

It wasn't simply IRA attacks that led to this reaction. Electoral success for Sinn Féin, which, after the Easter Rising, had won 73 of the 105 parliamentary seats in the 1918 all-Ireland election, paired with the IRA attacks, caused unionists to lash out. Catholics were burned out of their homes and driven out of their jobs in some of Belfast's largest employers – the shipyards and the engineering and tobacco factories.

Banbridge in Co. Down, twenty-five miles west of Loughinisland, also witnessed serious violence. This occurred after the RIC Divisional Commissioner, Lieutenant Colonel Gerald Bryce Ferguson Smyth, called on his men to adopt a shoot-to-kill policy. In a speech to RIC men in Kerry he said, 'If the persons approaching carry their hands in their pockets or are in any way suspicious looking, shoot them down. You may make mistakes occasionally and innocent persons may be shot, but this cannot be helped and you are bound to get the right persons sometimes. The more you shoot, the better I will like you, and I assure you that no policeman will get into trouble for shooting any man.' On 17 July 1920 the IRA tracked down Smyth in Cork and shot him dead. His body was brought back north for burial. In response to this, according to Kieran Glennon in *From Pogrom to Civil War*, in the twenty-four hours after his funeral 2,000 unionists 'went around the local linen mills, chasing Catholics from their jobs. Smyth's mother also announced that the family's two mills would no longer employ Catholics. Over the next couple of days, Catholic-owned pubs and businesses were looted and burned and eighteen Catholic families saw their homes fully or partially burned.'

The war ended when the Anglo-Irish Treaty was signed in December 1921. The Treaty did not end the sectarian tension across Ulster, however; if anything, it exacerbated it. It confirmed the partitioning of Ireland, leading to the creation of the Irish Free State, with the six counties of Northern Ireland remaining under British rule. This caused Catholics in the North to feel abandoned, left in a Protestant state in which they had no cultural identity. 'Insecurity was built into the very foundations of the Northern Irish State,' writes John D. Brewer in *Anti-Catholicism in Northern Ireland, 1600–1998*. 'Although Protestants saw Northern Ireland as a sacred entity, watched over by God, the template was Old Testament Israel, which was continually embattled from external threats and internal disaffection.'

Despite their evident success, Protestants still feared London selling them out; they feared that Dublin would come back for the six counties at some point in the future. But perhaps their greatest fear was the Catholic Church. Brewer recounts how the *Belfast News Letter* regarded the May 1920 beatification of Oliver Plunkett, the seventeenth-century Primate of All-Ireland who was hung, drawn and quartered for treason against the English, 'at which archbishops, bishops and priests supposedly sang rebel songs', as giving encouragement to rebellion. The Northern Ireland Prime Minister at the time, James Craig, said the Education Act, introduced in 1930, would make state 'schools safe for Protestant children'. Many commentators believe the 1930 act created a form of educational apartheid, a system that persists to this day.

Nationalists in the North now harboured a visceral sense of betrayal by Dublin, and the violence of the early 1920s would leave a lasting scar. In Northern Ireland, a 'Protestant Parliament for a Protestant People', as James Craig described it, remained in power for the following five decades. This would see nationalists disengaged politically from the state and, although the gerrymandering of elections excluded the socially disadvantaged on both sides, it was Catholics who were most disproportionately affected. A greatly depleted IRA would continue its activities with the aim of forcing reunification, but with little success. A so-called 'Border Campaign', conducted between 1956 and 1962, failed to meet its objective of igniting a revolt against the Stormont government.

The 1960s would be a tumultuous decade of revolution and change around the world. In Northern Ireland, the Stormont government, with a new prime minister, Terence O'Neill, set out to improve relations between nationalists and unionists but came under sustained pressure from the firebrand Presbyterian minister Ian Paisley, who was gaining support among unionists who feared any form of political compromise.

It was in this charged climate that the men met on that Pomeroy farm and brought the UVF back into being.

***

Home Rule was no longer the enemy for the newly re-formed UVF; this time the threat came from 'physical force republicanism'. In the preceding weeks and months, unionists were picking up rumours that the IRA was about to disrupt an upcoming Stormont election and was planning to resume its Border Campaign ahead of the fiftieth anniversary of the Easter Rising in 1966 (none of which happened). In May 1966 the terror group released a statement to the press in the name of William Johnston, its chief of staff. It read: 'From this day, we declare war against the Irish Republican Army and its splinter groups. Known IRA men will be executed mercilessly and without hesitation. We are heavily armed Protestants dedicated to this cause.'

Two weeks prior to the UVF's verbose pronouncement, the reality of its 'war' had already been visited upon an innocent woman. Matilda 'Tilly' Gould died when two UVF men, one of them described by an eyewitness as having been drunk, threw a petrol bomb into her home on Upper Charleville Street, where she was asleep. The seventy-four-year-old Protestant was crippled with arthritis, which left her unable to descend the stairs. She suffered burns to her face and hands and died several weeks later. Matilda Gould's 'crime' was to rent a home from a Catholic. Reporting on her death, the *News Letter* warned, 'Ulster is in danger of being thrown back into a dark past by sectarian forces which have too long been winked at by many who should know better.'

A week after the statement, twenty-eight-year-old labourer John Patrick Scullion was the UVF's first Catholic victim. Like so many of the UVF's 'targets' in the years to come, Scullion was in the wrong place at the wrong time, returning home from an evening in the pub. He was shot on Oranmore Street in West Belfast on 27 May 1966 and later died from his injuries. Four UVF men had set out to kill a man they suspected of being in the IRA; however, when he wasn't home, they shot Scullion as he staggered from the pub. 'At the time, the attitude was that if you couldn't get an IRA man you should shoot a Taig [a Catholic]; he's your last resort,' said Gusty Spence, a leading member of the UVF, years later.

The same month, the UVF attacks continued, with three Catholics shot outside a pub in Malvern Street, off the Shankill Road. One died, eighteen-year-old Peter Ward. The UVF was 'manufacturing enemies out of their own paranoia, which made them see an IRA man under every bed', wrote Aaron Edwards in his book *UVF: Behind the Mask*.

In the aftermath of Ward's death, the Stormont government proscribed the UVF. In Westminster British Prime Minister Harold Wilson described it as a 'quasi-Fascist organisation masquerading behind a clerical cloak'. That clerical cloak was the Reverend Ian Paisley, who denied being involved with the organisation, although evidence would suggest that he was integral to its evolution.

Spence and two other men were arrested and tried with Ward's murder, being found guilty and sentenced to twenty-five years' imprisonment. Lord Chief Justice MacDermott said the murder had been 'brutal, cowardly and cold-blooded'.

The murders of Tilly Gould, John Patrick Scullion and Peter Ward were the first of over 500 committed by the UVF in the twenty-five-year conflict that engulfed Northern Ireland from the mid-to-late 1960s on. The manner of the murders of the three innocents – conducted by drunks blinded by sectarian hatred who had been stoked up by political leaders – was to become the UVF's hallmark, despite vain attempts to present it as a disciplined, structured organisation at war.

***

The global events of 1968 – the Prague Spring, student riots in Paris and, particularly, the civil rights movement in America – inspired street protests in Northern Ireland. These began in August of that year with a march between Coalisland and Dungannon. One young female protester, Bernadette Devlin – later to become an MP at twenty-one years of age and one of the most important Irish political figures of the later twentieth century – recalled how the friendly atmosphere of the march turned ugly when police stopped the march from entering Dungannon. However, civil rights marchers were not put off from holding more protests.

The Derry Housing Action Committee (DHAC), campaigning against discrimination and gerrymandering in the city, announced it was going to hold a march in the city on 5 October. Although banned by the Minister for Home Affairs, William Craig, the DHAC declared that it would go ahead. 'Derry is a dead city,' recalled Bernadette Devlin, 'about one in five of the men is unemployed and the whole feeling is depressed. But it was electric that day. You could see it on people's faces – excitement, or alarm, or anger. Derry was alive.'

The peaceful protest was met with state violence, the marchers being viciously beaten by police wielding truncheons and using water cannon. Riots erupted in the predominately Catholic Bogside area of Derry, and across the North, as RUC brutality sparked a reaction from nationalists.

Gay O'Brien had been dispatched to the city by RTÉ and captured the violence inflicted on the marchers by police officers from the RUC. His footage went global. 'Never has sixty seconds of film sparked such a change,' said the civil rights campaigner Eamonn McCann. 'I remember when I came home everyone was saying it was on the news; it was the first item on the BBC news,' he told *The Irish News*. McCann knew that the images of the police baton-charging the protesters were hugely significant.

Protestants and Catholics had joined the 5 October march but, after it, the sectarian genie was out of the bottle. Afterwards, this date was marked as the day 'The Troubles' began.

Following the 5 October 1968 march, and the pictures emanating from it of RUC brutality, the O'Neill government came under severe pressure from both nationalists, who demanded the prime minister push through reforms on housing and voting rights, and from Paisley, who accused him of being weak. Paisley organised counter-protests, bringing unionists onto the street, thereby forcing confrontations with police, a tactic he would use for the next thirty years.

Paisley was denouncing Terence O'Neill's government both on the streets and in the pulpit, but, according to a BBC documentary, he was also financing the UVF. Paisley had established another loyalist paramilitary group, the Ulster Protestant Volunteers, who worked hand-in-hand with the UVF and were involved in a series of attacks in March and April 1969 that would ultimately lead to O'Neill's resignation.

***

When it was re-formed, the UVF's attacks were largely confined to Belfast, but by the end of the 1960s its terrorism had spread to other areas of the North, including South Down. By then, it had built up a capacity for sourcing and deploying explosives.

Thomas McDowell was from the Co. Down fishing village of Kilkeel, forty minutes south of Loughinisland on the southern side of the popular tourist town of Newcastle. McDowell, a father of ten who was described by his friends as a 'God-fearing and popular man', worked in a Portadown quarry, where he accessed the gelignite explosives he used in a series of UVF attacks that would ultimately cost him his life.

McDowell's accomplice in eight bomb attacks over a six-week period was a man from Newtownards called Samuel Stevenson, who later told police he had been heavily influenced by the oratory of Ian Paisley. Stevenson said he met two men at one of Paisley's rallies in the Ulster Hall who had paid him to organise the bombings. The two men were responsible for bomb attacks on the Silent Valley Reservoir on 20 April 1969 and the water pipeline at Annalong six days later. The attacks were designed to disrupt the water supply into Belfast and in the hope that they would be blamed on the IRA, which Stormont duly did. All of this, they felt, would ultimately topple Terence O'Neill.

David Hancock, a former British Army commander, told the BBC in 2019 that an RUC inspector showed him evidence that the bomb at Silent Valley had been financed by Ian Paisley. An RUC briefing note claimed that the 'Paisleyite' movement and the UVF in 1969 were 'one and the same'. Paisley and the UVF got their wish on 28 April 1969, when Terence O'Neill resigned as leader of the Ulster Unionist Party (UUP) and as prime minister of Northern Ireland.

Another UVF man, who was convicted of killing two innocent Catholics but would play a leading role in the peace process, Billy Hutchinson, wrote of an incident at Stormont's Parliament Buildings many years after the Silent Valley attack. He was in a lift when he heard a booming voice asking for it to be held. It was Paisley. 'I held the button to keep the doors open. As a breathless Paisley went to step into the lift, he looked up and realised that I was inside it. "Go on!" he panted, "I'll not be getting in a lift with a UVF murderer!" There was an awkward pause for a second before I responded: "Well, it didn't worry you too much when you sent Tom McDowell to his death,"' wrote Hutchinson. McDowell had died when a bomb he was planting at a power station across the border in Ballyshannon, Co. Donegal, exploded prematurely.

The truth was that Paisley's relationship with the loyalist paramilitaries waxed and waned during the Troubles, denouncing them when it suited him and courting them when he wanted their support on the streets.

***

Following Terence O'Neill's resignation, the UUP held a leadership election. Former British Army officer James Chichester-Clark defeated his rival, Brian Faulkner, by one vote – a vote cast by his distant cousin and predecessor O'Neill. Despite pledges to introduce reforms, the new prime minister and the Stormont government lost all control.

August 1969 saw a further escalation in the Troubles. The UVF bombed the Dublin headquarters of RTÉ in the south of the city, injuring a security guard and damaging the main studio building. A week later saw the beginning of the 'Battle of the Bogside', when nationalists, opposed to a march through Derry by the loyalist Apprentice Boys, reacted to the RUC coming into their area. The subsequent rioting lasted two days and led to the British government sending troops into Northern Ireland, where they would remain on the streets for another thirty-seven years.

In London, a former British Army brigadier, Baron Hunt, produced a report which proposed that the Ulster Special Constabulary, or B-Specials

– a largely ineffectual police force, built out of the remnants of the UVF in 1922 – should be disbanded and that the RUC should have a Reserve force instead. Hunt also suggested a part-time military force should be established to support policing in Northern Ireland. This would see the formation of the Ulster Defence Regiment (UDR), which would play a very significant role in the loyalist violence in South Down in the years that followed.

The final months of 1969 were turbulent and deadly. In October, loyalists killed the first RUC officer to die in the Troubles, Victor Arbuckle. That same month, the UVF crossed the border again to plant bombs at the grave of Wolfe Tone in Bodenstown, Co. Kildare, and then, on 26 December, at a monument to Daniel O'Connell in the centre of Dublin.

***

The 1970s began where the previous decade had left off: with more bloodshed. In 1970 twice as many people died as in the previous year. The UVF continued to target the Republic of Ireland, bombing an RTÉ radio mast in Donegal in February and an electrical substation in Tallaght, North Dublin, in March. British troops on the streets did nothing to quell the sectarian attacks in Belfast or the violence in Derry. Recruitment began – drawn predominantly from the Protestant unionist community – for the UDR, which began operations on 1 April 1970. The fuse had been lit and the flames of violence were now engulfing the North.

In 1971 over 170 people were killed. The British government introduced internment, but a decision was taken not to include loyalists on the basis that the list of those to be interned, provided by RUC Special Branch, only related to 'IRA members'. Over time, the British Army would round up over 1,800 Catholics and two Protestants (who had republican tendencies) and incarcerate them without trial in makeshift camps – an action which, of course, only led to more violence.

The IRA was killing soldiers, including members of the newly formed UDR, in almost daily attacks. The UVF used its proven bomb-making abilities to attack McGurk's Bar in North Belfast, killing fifteen Catholics. In a gross misrepresentation of the facts, which would inflict decades of pain on the families who lost their loved ones in the attack, the RUC briefed the press that it was an IRA bomb that had exploded prematurely inside the bar. It was a determined blurring of reality by the authorities in a growing propaganda war.

By the dawn of 1972, the unionist government at Stormont was on the brink. The events of the first four weeks of that year would bring about its collapse.

For the first time, too, rural areas, such as South Down, were being drawn into the conflict. On Sunday 23 January, a civil rights march – in support of the estimated 350 men who had been arrested during Operation Demetrius five months earlier and interned without trial – set off from the village of Castlewellan, fifteen minutes south-west of Loughinisland, en route for Newcastle. The previous day British soldiers had been accused by the Derry nationalist leader John Hume of 'beating, brutalising and terrorising' anti-internment protesters who had gathered on the beaches of Magilligan Strand, forty minutes north-west of the city. In South Down, the Castlewellan march faced a similar violent reaction from the security forces. Local newspaper, the *Down Recorder*, reported that soldiers fired plastic bullets at the protesters and forty marchers were arrested.

Localised incidents such as this would inevitably provoke a response from the IRA. In Castlewellan, it came just three days later. Peter McNulty, a leading member of the IRA in South Down for years, along with one of his neighbours, Oliver Rae, targeted Castlewellan's RUC station on the main Dublin Road. Shortly before 3 a.m., the two IRA members approached its perimeter separately on foot. However, as they neared their target, the device McNulty was carrying – which contained 15lb of gelignite – exploded prematurely, killing him instantly. Within seconds, a second device carried by Rae exploded at the western corner of the station. Rae received severe injuries to his arms, leg and face.

Police and emergency services had barely responded when another bomb exploded, this time at the town's Circular Road telephone exchange.

A few minutes later, a fourth explosion followed, two miles away at a Field Study Centre in Bryansford.

Oliver Rae was first taken to Downe Hospital in Downpatrick before being moved under heavily armed guard to the military hospital at Musgrave Park Hospital. Meanwhile, in a follow-up search, police discovered another unexploded bomb in front of the RUC station, which army bomb disposal experts detonated in a field.

Peter McNulty was the first member of the IRA in South Down to die during the Troubles. According to reports, over 2,000 people attended his funeral in St Patrick's church in the village of Bryansford. His coffin, draped with the Irish tricolour, was taken to the church for the funeral Mass flanked by twenty women wearing black scarves, while youths from Na Fianna Éireann formed a guard of honour. As his body was taken into the adjoining graveyard, members of the South Down Brigade of the IRA fired a volley of shots over his coffin.

The following week, on 30 January 1972, the British Army's Parachute Regiment shot dead thirteen unarmed civilians during another civil rights march in Derry. (A fourteenth victim would later die of his wounds.) This tragedy would go on to be called 'Bloody Sunday'. In the fallout from this, with a sense that the situation was completely out of control, British Prime Minister Edward Heath announced the suspension of the Stormont parliament on 24 March 1972, declaring that London 'would take full and direct responsibility for the administration of Northern Ireland'.

***

From the outset of the conflict, there was a blurring of the lines between the loyalist paramilitaries and the security forces. After the outbreak of violence, the RUC's numbers rose exponentially year after year in the early 1970s – by the mid-1980s its size had tripled from the 3,800 full-time officers on the streets in 1971. Virtually every member was from the Protestant community. The UDR was a part-time army regiment until 1976, when a full-time unit was recruited. According to records, 18 per cent of its initial membership was from the Catholic community, but that figure fell away to less than 3 per cent after the introduction of internment.

There were seven battalions of the UDR, six based along county lines, with Belfast making up the seventh. Co. Down had the Third Battalion, with its base at Ballykinler on Dundrum Bay – fifteen minutes south of Loughinisland. Many members of the disbanded B-Specials remained angry at their disbandment and refused to join the newly formed regiment. This was particularly true in Co. Down where the B-Specials adjutant advised his men not to sign up. John Potter, in his book *A Testimony to Courage: The History of the Ulster Defence Regiment, 1969–1992*, writes: 'It was [County Commandant] Woods who faced the greatest problem. From the outset he emphasised the fact that Catholics would be welcome in the UDR. This did not go down well with some of the Specials. He encountered outright opposition from his County Adjutant, an ex-regular soldier.'

The UDR's first colonel commandant was Sir John Anderson, who had served in the 5th Inniskilling Dragoon Guards before joining the Imperial Defence College, where he rose to the rank of commandant. After his retirement in 1968, he returned home to Co. Down, 'to settle in his mother's house at Ballyhossett, between Downpatrick and Ardglass' – eleven miles south-east of Loughinisland.

Anderson had a dream for the new regiment: 'When I was canvassing people, both lay and clerical, Catholic and Protestant, who I thought could help us in the early days, I said that it was well known that Irishmen of all persuasions had served happily together in the British Army for decades. So surely we could make a "go" of it too on these lines. So, to make the new Regiment succeed, and succeed it must, it was essential that both Protestant and Catholic should join it.'

The young Social Democratic and Labour Party (SDLP) leader who had emerged out of Derry, John Hume, supported the regiment and urged Catholics to join. So too did Ivan Cooper, a young civil rights leader from Derry. But after Ballymurphy and Bloody Sunday, all faith in the British Army of any description was gone as far as nationalists were concerned. Those from the Catholic community who did initially join in 1970 left as the violence, and indeed the threat to their own lives from the IRA, increased dramatically.

Those Protestants who joined became immediately attractive to the UVF. In his book, Potter recounts an episode in Co. Down in 1972: 'A [UDR] soldier who worked in his father's bar in Newcastle reported that a customer from the Shankill Road had tried to recruit him into the UVF. He was told he would be given the rank of sergeant and would be required to recruit other soldiers to form a UVF cell within his UDR battalion. To support his credentials, the stranger gave the soldier a UVF lapel badge.'

Perhaps a more attractive alternative to the proscribed UVF was the Ulster Defence Association (UDA), formed in September 1971. It immediately attracted young men angry about the increase in violence from the IRA. Its membership was drawn from right across the North, but particularly from East and West Belfast, and it was estimated to have risen to 40,000 at its peak the year after its formation. Members openly patrolled areas of Belfast, armed with batons and presenting themselves as protectors of their community. However, very quickly they became aggressors, targeting and killing Catholics in purely sectarian attacks. Unlike the IRA and UVF, the British government did not proscribe the UDA, so its members could openly become members of the UDR – and many did.

Unsurprisingly, UDR weapons were routinely 'stolen' in raids by loyalists. After five rifles were taken from a base in Belfast, a lance corporal guard commander was discovered to be a member of the UDA. He was discharged. According to Potter, the leader of the Alliance Party, Oliver Napier, said at the time: 'I have been informed by a number of Alliance members in the UDR that in their group there are men who make no secret of the fact that their joint loyalty is the UDA, not to the United Kingdom. Some of the men boasted that they joined the UDR to receive arms training.'

The word 'collusion' has now become synonymous with the terrorism that was inflicted on the nationalist community in the North, and in the early 1970s it was barely disputed, particularly by British Army officers, who boasted of their close working relationship with loyalists.

The practice of collusion in Northern Ireland was 'consistent with British counter-insurgency operations in other theatres of conflict since the Second World War,' writes author and historian, Margaret Urwin in her book *A State in Denial*. Urwin quotes from the official British record that, in July 1972, noted one such example of the close relationship between the British Army and loyalist paramilitaries: '[The] Army agree that soldiers should set up road-blocks and that UDA should be allowed to patrol the streets behind them.'

The RUC and the RUC Reserve, along with the UDR, attracted many decent men and women who signed up for queen and country – or, in many cases, for the extra cash that came from putting their lives on the line to patrol the streets and country lanes two or three nights a week. They would have had no time for terrorism, wherever it emanated from. However, their commanding officers had a much more nuanced view of the conflict. Urwin, in *A State in Denial*, describes the fundamentals of the security forces strategy: 'Collusion with loyalists was intended to help defeat the IRA by increasing the effectiveness of loyalist groups. The infiltration of agents into the IRA, and ignoring their involvement in murder, had the same goal – weakening and ultimately defeating the IRA.'

Those at the highest levels of government and the security forces had reconciled themselves to the fact that members of their own security forces, along with innocent civilians murdered by the paramilitaries, would lose their lives in pursuit of their strategy of collusion and infiltration.

Take the 1974 bombings of Dublin and the town of Monaghan, which resulted in the biggest single loss of life in the conflict. Coming in the midst of a 'workers strike' by Protestants angry about the Sunningdale Agreement – which, on 1 January 1974, had seen the British government introduce a form of power-sharing at Stormont in a compromise with nationalist demands – a total of thirty-three people and an unborn child were killed when three bombs exploded on the streets of Dublin on the afternoon of Friday 17 May, while five further lives were lost in a car bomb attack at North Road, Monaghan. The bombs had been prepared on the farm of James Mitchell, in the townland of Glenanne, deep in Co. Armagh. Mitchell was the leader of a notorious Mid Ulster unit of the UVF known as the Glenanne gang, and it was from there that the bombs were transported south by a key member of that unit, Robin Jackson, along with several other UVF members from Mid Ulster and Belfast. The townland of Glenanne, deep in Co. Armagh, is an hour west of Loughinisland, but the terrorism orchestrated by a farmer who lived there would bring death and destruction to the Co. Down village.

The Irish government's commission of inquiry into the attack, conducted by Justice Henry Barron, was told by the British security services that they held over 68,000 pages of information that may be relevant to the inquiry. However, the security forces handed over a total of sixteen pages. The UVF, which initially denied being involved, issued a statement twenty years after the bombings to admit responsibility. When it was published in 2003, the Barron Report concluded that 'it was likely that British security force personnel were involved in the bombings'.

The short-lived power-sharing executive collapsed eleven days after the attack, leaving the North to be ruled, or misruled, by British government ministers for twenty-five years.

James Mitchell, a member of the RUC Reserve, would be involved in numerous bomb attacks over the years, including the 1975 Donnelly's Bar bombing at Silverbridge in which three people died: Michael Donnelly, Patsy Donnelly and Trevor Brecknell. Three brothers from the Reavey family were murdered in their home just a few weeks later in January 1976. In 1976 an RUC commander ordered the army to put surveillance on Mitchell's farm, but he still managed to smuggle out a bomb that killed two people at the Step Inn pub in Keady, South Armagh. Yet, despite all of his terrorism, Mitchell was not expelled from the RUC or arrested throughout the 1970s.

In 1980 Mitchell was charged with and convicted of possession of sub-machine guns and bomb-making equipment, being sentenced to a one-year jail term, suspended for three years, meaning he would never see the inside of a prison cell. 'The sentence passed by Lord Chief Justice Lowry ... and his closing comments, were an absolute disgrace and brought shame on the judiciary,' said a spokesman for the Pat Finucane

Centre (PFC) in Derry, which conducted a series of investigations into the Glenanne gang.

The suspicion, of course, is that Mitchell was a member of a protected species, an agent of the security services. Having been behind some of the worst atrocities of the 1970s, his personal licence to kill meant that he could continue to take the lives of innocents for another two decades.

In January 1988, eight years after his sole conviction, a lorry load of tiles was driven through the townland of Glenanne, along the Mowhan Road, past Shaw's Lake and up Lough Road to Mitchell's farm. Contained within the delivery, which had originated in Beirut, Lebanon, was the largest consignment of weapons ever brought into Northern Ireland by loyalist paramilitaries. They would only discover why many years later, but the peaceful lives being pursued in Loughinisland would forever be destroyed by the arms hidden in the plastic containers in the sheds at the back of James Mitchell's farmhouse.

3 | The Way Ahead

For the 200 families living in Loughinisland, the Troubles were generally a somewhat distant experience. They tended to happen somewhere else, not in the country lanes and fields of this corner of South Down. Life was straightforward, comfortable, free of the daily stresses and threats that the people of Belfast or Derry dealt with, living in a virtual war zone.

Saying that, the red light on a dark road that indicated a UDR patrol at night was a reminder that the Troubles were never really far away. 'Keep your head down', 'say nothing to antagonise them' – these were the codes for those country folk who wanted to get on quietly with their lives and not be drawn into confrontation. In reality, it was never that far away, and whether they recognised it or not, it was creeping closer as each year passed, primarily due to a series of events that would eventually destroy their lives in a brutal, murderous fashion.

The annual death toll caused by the violence peaked in 1972 and fell significantly across the latter half of the decade, with deaths caused by republicans in particular dropping off from 263 at their height to half that by 1975.

Ceasefires and political initiatives played out within the cyclical rhythm of death and destruction, all sides drawing on the deep well of anger, betrayal and sectarianism baked into the very tissue of the North. Led by terrorists such as James Mitchell, Robin Jackson, the Shankill Butchers and numerous others, loyalists had shown that there was no limit to their sectarian depravity. However, by the late 1970s, their murder rate had also dropped dramatically, taking the lives of twenty-six, nine and seventeen innocents in the final three years of the decade respectively, whereas in 1975 alone they had killed 123 people.

However, the election of the Conservative Party's Margaret Thatcher as British prime minister in 1979, followed by the republican hunger strikes in the Maze Prison across 1980 and 1981, in which ten men died from starvation, brought a renewed ferocity to the conflict. The RUC and British Army were briefing Thatcher throughout this period that they were keeping a lid on the violence, while also emphasising that a political solution would need to be found to end the conflict. Thatcher herself became a target, the IRA coming close to killing her in a Brighton hotel bomb attack in 1984.

The following year saw the most significant political initiative since Sunningdale: the Anglo-Irish Agreement, which Thatcher signed against her will. A few months prior to the signing of the agreement by Thatcher and her Irish counterpart, Taoiseach Garret FitzGerald, unionists – fearful of the outcome of the talks between the British and Irish governments – took to the streets again. During the summer of 1985 there was trouble in Portadown when an Orange Order march was rerouted away from the Catholic neighbourhood of Obins Street. Street violence by loyalists lasted for ten days, during which dozens of RUC officers were injured and extensive damage was caused to property in the town centre.

Out of the rioting, a new organisation emerged, the Protestant Action Committee, which, within weeks, was rebranded as the United Ulster Loyalist Front (UULF). (Ten years before, the UVF had used a cover name of Protestant Action Force to carry out murders while it was ostensibly on ceasefire.)

Ian Paisley's Democratic Unionist Party (DUP) was making gains in every election, even if the UUP, led by James Molyneaux, was still the main force within unionism. On the ground, there was always a mistrust of elected politicians among loyalists, i.e. those defined as working-class unionists and prone to resort to violence. The IRA was still undefeated and the actions of Bobby Sands and the hunger strikers, in being prepared to die for their cause, struck fear into unionism – if not a certain grudging degree of respect. There was no doubt the lengths republicans would go to in pursuit of their objectives. In contrast, loyalists never believed their leaders would show the same determination in protecting their place within the precious union with Great Britain. Unionists on the ground distrusted their own politicians in Belfast, never mind Thatcher or the Taoiseach.

From his past association with loyalist paramilitaries, Paisley had deep connections with the leadership of the UVF and the UDA. But, unlike Sinn Féin – who made clear its support for the IRA – when it suited him, the DUP denounced the loyalist paramilitaries. At other times, Paisley used them for his own means. For example, in 1981, just weeks before Bobby Sands began his hunger strike, and in response to Margaret Thatcher hosting a warm and cordial meeting with then Taoiseach Charles Haughey, Paisley had invited several journalists onto a bleak North Antrim hillside at midnight to witness his latest dalliance with paramilitarism. The reporters watched as 500 men formed up in military formation and waved what Paisley said were legal gun licences. 'This is only a small token of the many thousands of men who are pledged to me, and I pledged to them to stand together at this time of grave trouble in Northern Ireland,' Paisley told the journalists. 'They were a motley crew,' wrote Ed Moloney in his biography of Paisley. 'There were sallow-faced teenagers and plump prosperous farmers, there was not a gun to be seen anywhere.'

Loyalist paramilitaries scoffed at his bluster, knowing that Paisley would not be around if a shot was fired in anger. By now, they knew he used the paramilitaries for his own political leverage. They were, and would be again, supportive of the 'big man', but were suspicious of his true motivation, which they believed to be always in his own self-interest.

In contrast, the UULF had the support of the paramilitaries, particularly the UDA Brigadier John McMichael, who had displayed some political nuance compared with his contemporaries. The UULF's leader was Alan Wright, a man who had come to believe that an independent Northern Ireland was the only political way forward. He was a member of the Salvation Army in Portadown, and his father, an RUC officer, had been murdered in 1979 by the republican Irish National Liberation Army

(INLA). The UULF was short-lived, but it would be the organisation out of which something much darker and more sinister would emerge.

Thatcher's treachery in signing the Anglo-Irish Agreement, which gave the Irish government a formal involvement in the affairs of Northern Ireland for the first time since partition, was the greatest challenge to unionism since the Home Rule crisis. Once again, it was a British prime minister selling them out.

In the aftermath, Paisley and Molyneaux came together to oppose the agreement, drawing 250,000 people to a protest rally in front of Belfast's City Hall. Between the parading crisis for Portadown Orangemen in July and the huge City Hall rally, the UULF had morphed into a new entity: the 'Ulster Clubs'. The rally in front of City Hall, as well as the name of the new grouping, was a hat tip to the network established by Edward Carson seventy years earlier. Carson had helped create the state of Northern Ireland, but arguably his greater legacy was to instil a grim state of mind within unionism – namely that, when confronted by constitutional crisis, threatening armed conflict was the only way to gain London's attention and prevent sell-out.

Alan Wright, who became the leader of the Ulster Clubs, didn't believe Molyneaux and Paisley could bring down the agreement. If the agreement could not be brought down through political means, Wright believed they would have to find other means to do so. According to historian Ian S. Wood, Wright believed that the Ulster Clubs could help to make Northern Ireland ungovernable, a situation that would ultimately scupper the agreement. As a result, Wright 'welcomed the presence within them of the UDA members'. Wood says Wright was at one point asked if the paramilitaries might take over the Ulster Clubs. He responded with a clear malevolent intent, which would later play out with devastating consequences for Catholic civilians in general, and the village of Loughinisland in particular: 'If the withdrawal of consent and civil disobedience fail to bring down the agreement, then you will see force being met with force.'

Opposition to the 1985 agreement crystallised with a day of action in March 1986. Unionists held mass protests across Northern Ireland.

Wright and the Ulster Clubs wanted to be the spearhead of opposition to the agreement, but Paisley and Molyneaux wouldn't concede their authority. Thatcher stood her ground, despite her inherent distaste for the agreement she had signed.

Some loyalists felt once again that they had been let down by their leadership who, when it came to it, were only interested in constitutional means of opposition. They wanted to take the war to their enemy; not to the British government that had sold them out, or to the IRA, but to the easiest of targets: the nationalist population.

***

Amid the political crisis, the killing continued, with three murders within a ten-minute drive of Loughinisland.

UDR Private Robert Hill had joined the UDR when he was twenty years of age. After having been on duty on the last day of June 1986, he returned home in the early hours of the morning, parking his red Ford Fiesta outside his home at Drumaness, a village north of Loughinisland. He worked for a furniture company and, despite only getting home very late, was up again at 7.30 a.m. to go to his day job. He had just pulled out of the driveway when a bomb exploded, ripping his car apart and killing him instantly.

A neighbour told a news reporter that he ran to the scene, not knowing what had caused the explosion, only to see the car in a ball of flames. The private's personal protection weapon was found 100 metres away in a garden.

The IRA claimed responsibility.

Robert Hill had been a member of the Apprentice Boys in Ballynahinch and the Sons of Ulster Accordion Band. His Labrador dog, Sam, shocked at the explosion, ran through the shattered door of his home and into a nearby lake. He was found and returned to the family several hours later.

The next victim was Terry Mullan, a second-hand car dealer who had separated from his wife and returned home to live with his father,

Tommy, and seventy-six-year-old mother, Kathleen, who had adopted him at birth. Four months after the murder of Robert Hill, they were having breakfast at their farmhouse at Dromore Road on the north-western outskirts of Ballynahinch, five minutes' drive from Drumaness, when a masked loyalist came through the back door. He shot at Terry, who was sitting at the kitchen table. Terry escaped through a door, followed by the gunman, who continued shooting, finally catching up with him in the porch at the front of the house. In the chase, Terry was hit five times, with one of the bullets passing through his arm and killing his mother, Kathleen.

At the inquest into the murders of his wife and son, Tommy Mullan said he had been wakened by the sound of a car engine in the yard. When he went downstairs, Terry had warned him not to go outside because he didn't like the look of the men in the car. Tommy went into a bathroom, where he was when he heard the shots. When he came out he found the bodies of his wife and son.

The leader of the UDA, John McMichael, was reported to have ordered the attack. A caller to the BBC, claiming responsibility on behalf of the Ulster Freedom Fighters (UFF) – a terrorist front for the still legal UDA – claimed Terry Mullan was a 'field officer' for the IRA and had been involved in the targeting of Robert Hill. At the inquest, an RUC officer said the victims were totally innocent and that the killers had acted on the basis of 'rumour and hearsay'.

McMichael and the UDA were adamant – Terry Mullan was a legitimate target – and they hinted that they had proof of his involvement with the IRA. At the time it was dismissed as a typical loyalist attempt to rationalise the murder of yet another innocent Catholic.

Only later would McMichael's claims be seen in a very different context.

***

A year after the signing of the Anglo-Irish Agreement, Ian Paisley – building on the Ulster Clubs network – revealed his latest militia iteration. Unlike the previous attempts by the 'Grand Old Duke of York', as loyalists nicknamed him, to raise a 'Carson's Army', this one would have long-term, violent consequences, albeit never achieving his core aim of ending the agreement.

Senior members of the DUP travelled to a farm outside Omagh in Co. Tyrone to meet with Ulster Club representatives to discuss the establishment of a new paramilitary group. According to journalist Ed Moloney, reporting in *The Sunday Tribune*, the procurement of weapons was discussed at the meeting. On 10 November 1986 the plans hatched in the Omagh farmhouse were actioned when 3,000 men were invited to the Ulster Hall for the big reveal: Paisley and the Ulster Clubs had united to create a new paramilitary group called 'Ulster Resistance'. It was going to smash the Anglo-Irish Agreement and lead the unionist fight-back against the IRA. It would, according to the literature handed out by Nigel Dodds, a DUP official at the time: 'Take direct action as and when required.' It was never spelled out what exactly that meant.

Alan Wright was on the platform, along with the DUP deputy leader, Peter Robinson, and Sammy Wilson, the DUP's press officer at the time. The press was excluded but video emerged of Paisley and Robinson donning red berets in front of a paramilitary colour party.

In the days that followed, unionism split over what exactly the raison d'être was for Ulster Resistance. For Alan Wright, the strategy was clear: once the agreement was gone, Ulster Resistance would destroy militant republicanism, Sinn Féin and the IRA. In contrast, Ulster Unionist leader James Molyneaux distanced himself from Paisley's new army, while acknowledging his community's frustrations. He asked, if the new organisation was going to target the IRA, how exactly were the IRA members going to be identified?

After revealing the new force at the Ulster Hall, Paisley and Robinson went on tour. The first stop was in South Down, for a rally in the seaside town of Kilkeel, where they were filmed proudly walking through the town, which had a large Catholic population. Paisley and the Ulster Resistance leadership were going out of their way to antagonise; to send a threatening message to nationalists.

Paisley was creating an expectation that a fight back was coming, that unionists and loyalists were going to determine their own destiny through either peaceful or violent means. There were those, like James Mitchell back in Glenanne, who may have been inspired by Paisley's oratory but had no need of his encouragement for their murderous actions. But there were also others who were ready to take full advantage of any opportunity that would arise out of this new militia.

***

The conflict had changed in personality since 1968, as the combatants on both sides gained in experience and technological ability, particularly the IRA. In parallel, the British government and the security forces had gone through various strategies in their attempts to end the violence. In 1976 Merlyn Rees, who was the Labour Party Secretary of State for Northern Ireland, promoted the 'Ulsterisation' of the conflict, a term taken from the US State Department's 'Vietnamisation' of the war waged by America in Vietnam and furthered by his successor, Roy Mason. The British government, like the Americans, wanted to withdraw their troops and leave the locals, i.e. the UDR and RUC, on the front line. 'Criminalisation' was another strand to the policy, designed to strip the status of political prisoners from those convicted in Northern Ireland's courts. This would directly lead to the republican prisoners' 'No Wash' protest, which lasted for several years, and ultimately to the hunger strikes of 1981.

The 'Ulsterisation' policy came out of a 1975 document drafted by the heads of the British Army, the RUC and MI5. 'The Way Ahead', as it was called, put the RUC on the front line for the first time, with the support of the British Army. Five years later, in 1980, British Prime Minister Margaret Thatcher, requested a review of the RUC's intelligence capabilities and practices. It was conducted by a senior director and future director general at MI5, Sir Patrick Walker, whose recommendations would frame the future of the RUC's role in the conflict for the next twenty years. The real meat in the document meant that, for the first time, the RUC would lead on security, with the support of the British Army.

The Walker Report was enacted by Sir John Hermon on 1 March 1981. It wasn't until 2001 that the then Ulster Television (UTV) investigative reporter Chris Moore was able to reveal the full impact of Walker's recommendations. Moore, the most talented and tenacious journalist of his generation, had been leaked a copy of the report.

In a UTV *Insight* documentary, 'Policing the Police', he set out its significance with typical clarity and authority: 'Tonight we investigate twenty years of Special Branch primacy in the world of intelligence gathering. The Walker Report ... created a policing culture in which all information and ultimately decision-making power resides within Special Branch,' he reported. 'The Walker Report declares that sufficient time must elapse before someone is charged and a court appearance to allow Special Branch to interview suspects. This is declared necessary to ensure that information provided by the person so recruited is handled in such a way that his value as an agent is not put at risk at an early stage.' Moore further revealed that under Walker's guidelines even an arrest of a terrorist suspect wasn't possible without the approval of Special Branch.

To put it in context, the effect of the Walker Report was that the RUC not only led on security in Northern Ireland, but its Special Branch had primacy over its Criminal Investigations Department (CID). MI5 would have officers inside every Special Branch office in Northern Ireland, reporting back to its chief in Northern Ireland, who, in turn, briefed London.

***

The news reporting of murders by loyalists during the conflict invariably included two lines. The first was that it was a random sectarian killing and the second was that the victim was described by his family as having no association with the IRA or republican paramilitaries and was totally innocent. With the new information that has come from the various investigations and reports, however, it is clear that loyalist killings were far from as random as they initially appeared. Still, it came to be accepted that loyalists randomly selected their victims, many of whom were simply said to be in the wrong place at the wrong time. That was particularly true in the 1970s and 1980s.

In 2011 Sir Desmond de Silva was tasked by Conservative Prime Minister David Cameron with examining the murder of human rights lawyer Pat Finucane, shot dead by the UDA in 1989. De Silva's report was published in 2012 and writing in 2013 for the investigative website *The Detail*, my colleague, Barry McCaffrey, set out what he'd found in the report: 'The official position has always been that [intelligence] leaks to Loyalist paramilitaries were confined to rogue low-level members of the security forces. However, declassified MI5 and FRU documents now reveal that a number of senior police and army officers were providing loyalists with high grade intelligence through the 1980s. Many UDA attacks could be traced back to assistance initially provided by members of the security forces. In 1985, MI5 assessed that 85% of UDA "intelligence" used to target nationalists originated from within the security forces. In 1988, each of the UDA's six "brigade" areas were said to have at least 20 individual RUC sources of intelligence.'

One of the central figures in de Silva's report was Brian Nelson, who thrived under the cloak of misperception that the killings carried out by loyalists were random. Nelson had left school at fifteen without any formal qualifications. He joined the Royal Navy, in or around 1963, before signing up for the army, serving in Germany and Cyprus with the 1st Battalion Black Watch. Since 1970 he had been back on the Shankill, putting his military training to good use for the UDA.

In March 1973 father-of-five Gerry Higgins was walking home along North Queen Street in Belfast when he was bundled into the back of a car by armed loyalists, who took him to a drinking den in Wilton Street, off the Shankill Road. He was frog-marched past customers having a drink and taken to a room at the back of the club and tied to a chair. There Higgins was interrogated and beaten for over an hour by Nelson, who first burned his head with cigarettes, then poured water over his hands before attaching them to electrical terminals on a generator. When Higgins couldn't answer his questions, Nelson attached the terminals to his genitals. Only when Nelson attempted to get his victim back into the car, with the plan of shooting him and dumping his body, did Higgins fight back, raising enough of a ruckus to catch the attention of a passing British Army patrol, which rescued him. Gerry Higgins died from his injuries some weeks later.

While de Silva says nothing about what caused Nelson to leave the military, his army medical records stated that he was mentally unstable. According to Gerard Higgins' daughter, Elaine – who researched and found these medical records – he was only discharged from the army in March 1974, following his conviction for the attack on her father. Nelson served three years in prison; he was released in August 1977. He returned to his life on the Shankill Road and, according to de Silva's report, there is no record of him becoming involved with the UDA again until one day in 1984, when, apparently out of nowhere, he picked up the phone and contacted the British Army, offering his services as a source of intelligence. 'A CF [contact form] relating to his first meeting with a FRU [Force Research Unit] handler describes his motivation for informing against the UDA in the following terms: "... in the early days, the UDA was a necessary organisation but it had grown evil and was behind more of the criminal activities in Protestant areas."'

The very man who had sadistically and brutally tortured a father of five was handpicked to become the British Army's leading agent within the loyalist paramilitaries. Despite his conviction for a sadistic, sectarian assault, the FRU immediately welcomed Nelson to their team of agents and instructed him to rejoin the UDA with the goal of initially becoming the intelligence officer for the West Belfast Brigade and ultimately for the organisation right across the North. De Silva recorded Nelson's true motivation, which was shared by his handlers and their superiors in the British Army's FRU, as primarily being to help the UFF target and kill republicans with information fed to them through Nelson. And with the Walker Report now in place, the FRU and the Special Branch could protect their agents from the repercussions of their actions.

Given the lack of intelligence that governed the UDA's targeting of Catholics and Nelson's access to intelligence through the FRU, it wasn't long before he had risen through the ranks. Between May 1984 and October 1985, he is recorded as having met his handlers on sixty different occasions, providing them with briefings on the UDA in return for over £2,000 in cash payments. But who was controlling whom? The FRU had provided Nelson with a get-out-of-jail card. Did they really think a convicted paramilitary was going to follow their orders, or did they consider that he had calculated he could use them as a protective shield while he fuelled the UDA's killing machine?

One of the finest examples of the corruption of the intelligence services is found in de Silva's report. Nelson told his handlers that the UDA wanted him to get together a hit list of newly elected Sinn Féin councillors, which he had duly done. But was that true, or did Nelson tell his handlers that he was only following orders, when, in fact, he was the one who actually instigated the hit list? Either way, a Sinn Féin candidate in the 1985 council election was duly selected for death.

Harry Fitzsimmons answered his front door just after 7 a.m. on 27 September 1985 and was shot three times by a UDA gunman. Though seriously injured, he survived. According to the contact form – a military 'record' of the communication with their terrorist agent completed by their handlers – Nelson had told his handlers all about the planned assassination. Documents found by de Silva stated that Nelson had been told that the RUC Special Branch were also aware of the plot a month prior to the shooting. Yet no record was ever found of Fitzsimmons being warned of the loyalist plan to kill him.

The month after the UDA attempted to murder Harry Fitzsimmons, Nelson left Belfast to take up a one-year contract as a floor-layer in West Germany. De Silva couldn't find any evidence of him having any contact with the UDA or his handlers during his time there, which is extremely hard to believe. The FRU met Nelson regularly in West Germany, requesting that he return home. By spring 1987 Nelson was back in Belfast, living in a house and driving a taxi, both of which had been secured for him by the British taxpayer via the FRU. And, making his return all the sweeter, he got a promotion: he would now be the UDA's chief intelligence officer for the whole of Northern Ireland. So, he was now across everything the terrorists were planning.

His handlers were clear on their motivation. One officer said that they had pushed Nelson to return because of what he described as the 'deteriorating attitude of certain loyalist elements towards the British government as well as the RUC' – obviously referring to the unionists' protests to the Anglo-Irish Agreement. But one of his colleagues went further, putting it on the record that: 'We carefully developed Nelson's case in conjunction with the RUC SB [Special Branch] with the aim of making him the Chief Intelligence Officer for the UDA. By getting him into that position FRU and SB reasoned that we could persuade the UDA to centralise their targeting through Nelson and to concentrate their targeting [on] known PIRA activists, who by the very nature of their own terrorist positions were far harder targets. In this way, we could get advance warning of planned attacks, could stop the ad hoc targeting of Catholics and could exploit the information more easily.'

Many nationalists, and particularly families of victims, are firmly of the belief today that this statement is reflective of a developing British government policy in the mid-1980s that was designed to help loyalists target republicans. Basically, it was a means to take the war to the IRA so that it would weaken its resolve and sue for peace.

Further developments in the years after the Anglo-Irish Agreement only lend further weight to that idea. Members of the UDR were regularly supplied with montages of men the security forces believed to be involved with the IRA and they were given briefings as to their movements. Given that the security forces recognised that there were members of the UVF and UDA amongst the UDR ranks, no one in authority appeared to be concerned that this intelligence could be used to deadly effect by the paramilitaries.

***

South Down had not been immune to the conflict, far from it. From the UVF's bomb attack in Kilkeel in 1969, right through the 1970s, there had been violence from both sides. In 1974 two soldiers died in a bomb attack at the Ballykinler army base. A seventeen-year-old member of the

IRA, Francis Rice, was abducted and stabbed to death in a laneway in Castlewellan. Three men were convicted, but at the time of writing their convictions are being re-examined. The UVF killed two men in 1975 in Gilford and, the following year, two Protestants died in a bomb attack in the same town. But, in the early 1980s, a pattern emerged in South Down that would continue through the decade and into the 1990s. Namely, that UDR members who were also members of loyalist paramilitary groups began to use the security briefings they were receiving from the RUC to target suspected republicans.

Billy Finlay was an RUC Reserve officer. Married with three children, in 1978 he had been awarded the Queen's Commendation after an incident in the town of Ardglass, when he confronted and persuaded a man armed with a shotgun to put down his weapon. On 6 October 1983 he was on duty in Downpatrick's nationalist Meadowlands Estate with his colleague James Ferguson, who was a gardener at the local hospital and close to retirement. Both men were well known on the estate, which was also home to a number of Protestant families. They called into a sweet shop and when they emerged they took either side of the road as they continued their foot patrol. They had not travelled far when they were shot simultaneously by two IRA gunmen. Locals rushed to the scene when they heard the shots and one woman cradled Billy Finlay's head as he lay dying. 'I held his hand and prayed, but he was beyond comfort,' she told news reporters. Both officers were pronounced dead on arrival at the same hospital where Ferguson tended the gardens. The fact that they were community policemen caused a sense of outrage across the community, with the SDLP condemning the killers as psychopaths.

With RUC montages of IRA suspects now in the hands of their members, loyalist paramilitaries believed they knew the republicans responsible for attacks such as that which claimed the lives of Finlay and Ferguson. Even if they were not directly involved, their being deemed suspects by the RUC was enough to make them targets for the UVF.

Fifteen months after the murders in Downpatrick, a television engineer was called to erect an aerial on a house in the Twelve Arches area between Newcastle and Dundrum, fifteen minutes south of Loughinisland. Named after the Slidderyford Bridge built in 1900 across the River Carrigs, it is pure South Down country, with the Mountains of Mourne in the distance and Murlough Bay and the Irish Sea a short walk away. The engineer, John O'Rourke, who made no secret of his republicanism, pulled his van up in the yard in front of the house. He was immediately concerned, as it was clear the property was rundown and abandoned. Despite his misgivings, he was making his way towards the back door when a masked gunman appeared with a shotgun. O'Rourke managed to turn and run a short distance before being blasted in the back and left for dead. However, he managed to stagger to a neighbouring house and was rushed to hospital, ultimately surviving the attempt to kill him.

The two men who had called the engineer to the remote farmhouse were both serving members of the UDR operating on behalf of a newly formed unit of the UVF. For almost ten years, there had been no trace of the terrorist group in South Down. There had been no attacks for which they'd claimed responsibility. But now, with the attack on John O'Rourke, the UVF was re-emerging in the area, its membership made up of violent, sectarian soldiers from the 3rd Battalion of the UDR, where they had been trained in the use of firearms and, critically, had access to the intelligence and montages provided by the RUC Special Branch.

The murders of Terry Mullan and his mother in Ballynahinch later the same year was proof that the UDA too had a presence in the South Down area. UDA Brigadier John McMichael, who lived in Lisburn, Co. Antrim, thirty minutes away, was adamant that they had targeted a republican, which raises suspicion that, at the time, he also had access to the UDR briefings.

For those within the UDR who were also members of the loyalist paramilitaries, this felt like a moment in which the tide was turning. They had access to intelligence briefings and sensitive security documentation; Nelson was back in place as chief intelligence officer. All they needed was modern weaponry to take on the IRA, or kill more innocent Catholics.

At that very moment, Ulster Resistance and British intelligence colluded to help solve that particular problem, in what has since been described as the biggest intelligence failure in UK history. Or, as many victims in Northern Ireland have come to believe, the biggest unlawful arms shipment to loyalist terrorists by the UK government in history.

***

The annual total death toll for the Troubles in the mid-1980s ranged from seventy-seven murders in 1983 to sixty-one in 1986. Loyalist killings had fallen dramatically from the 1970s. In 1983 loyalists had killed nine people; the following year it was seven and in 1985 the figure fell to the lowest since the conflict began: four. Yet it was at that point that the FRU rationalised Brian Nelson going to South Africa in an attempt to import weapons – the very time the loyalist killing rate was receding dramatically.

It is somewhat strange, given his predilection for violence and loyalist paramilitaries, that de Silva finds nothing about Nelson's actions between August 1977 and May 1984, at which time he goes to a phone box and calls the army, offering his services as an agent. But what is more interesting is how Nelson, with apparently no financial support or resources from his FRU handlers, somehow travelled from the Shankill Road to South Africa in 1985 with the sole aim of purchasing weapons for the UDA.

Flying long distance to a country he had never been to before, to meet arms dealers he had never met, would have taken a degree of planning. It certainly doesn't fit into the picture of the UDA at the time, which hadn't developed the sophistication to build an explosive device and was, it is now understood, riven with informers, all of which meant it had a reputation for being the most incompetent of the paramilitary groups operating in Northern Ireland. But somehow, with the help of UDA leader and RUC agent Tommy Lyttle, who purchased his plane ticket, Brian Nelson was able to make contact with arms dealers in South Africa to try to negotiate an arms shipment. Nelson may have been a willing pawn, but there is little doubt that it was the British Army which had orchestrated, planned and supported his trip. However, lack of funds meant agent number 6137, as the FRU and RUC knew him, was ultimately unsuccessful in the audacious attempt to arm the UDA.

De Silva's findings that Nelson travelled without any assistance are scant and frankly unbelievable. The lawyer was able to read contact forms written by Nelson's handlers, who narrated and recorded the episode each step of the way. He clearly cuts the pieces of the jigsaw to fit his preordained conclusion, which seems to be that the FRU was allowing Nelson to travel with the plan that they were going to intercept the arms shipment en route to Northern Ireland.

Nelson was not the only one interested in procuring arms for the loyalist cause. Ulster Resistance had attracted the support of Noel Little, a lanky lieutenant in the UDR and a member of Paisley's Free Presbyterian Church in Armagh. Little had attended the Ulster Hall coming-out parade and, having been appointed a divisional commander in Ulster Resistance, was front and centre at a rally in Portadown, where he was filmed alongside Alan Wright and DUP deputy leader Peter Robinson.

The former BBC *Panorama* reporter John Ware spent significant time in Northern Ireland over the course of the Troubles. During that time, he met and interviewed Brian Nelson and all the paramilitary leaders on both sides. In a statement prepared for a civil case taken by victims of loyalist violence, Ware set out, over the course of 127 pages, an extremely detailed analysis of the South African weapons importation and the *dramatis personae.*

The ever smartly dressed, silver-haired hack explained how Little had come to know UDA Brigadier John McMichael, and how, between them, the plot to ship arms from South Africa emerged sometime in late 1986, following the formation of Ulster Resistance. According to Ware, McMichael had met Douglas Bernhardt, an agent for the South African arms procurement company Armscor, in London earlier that same year. Coincidentally, Bernhardt's Field Arms overseas office in London was staffed by Dick Wright, the uncle of Alan Wright.

Noel Little began talking to Bernhardt, probably having been introduced to him either by Dick Wright through his nephew or by McMichael in late 1986 or early the following year. They held several meetings in

Geneva and Paris. 'At his first meeting with Bernhardt in Geneva, Little explained that loyalists were looking for arms to defend themselves and that his best friend had died in an IRA car bomb attack. Little then asked Bernhardt where he could get weapons. A month later Little and Bernhardt again met in Geneva [and Bernhardt] told Little the weapons would come from Lebanon,' according to the journalist.

Later, Little travelled to Beirut, expecting his visit to end with the weapons being shipped to Northern Ireland. 'The evidence points powerfully to Little having had the dominant logistical role in the [ultimately successful] 1987 weapons shipment,' concludes Ware.

Ulster Resistance succeeded where Nelson had failed.

***

The de Silva report on the South African arms importation is the least detailed account of the operation, with the lawyer devoting a mere two pages of his 829-page review to this, basically concluding that there may be something to see, but it wasn't his remit to investigate. In 2016, when the Police Ombudsman for Northern Ireland, Dr Michael Maguire, published his examination of the Loughinisland massacre, he provided a more detailed exposition – a full forty pages, while Mr Justice Michael Humphreys added to the narrative in a fourteen-page procedural judgment he delivered in autumn 2023, in a case taken by the family of a victim of loyalist collusion.

Maguire reported that Brian Nelson had told police after he was arrested in February 1990 that instructions had come from John McMichael in 1985 to lead an arms importation operation from South Africa. In a 650-page statement, given over two days, Nelson said his handlers told him he had clearance from 'a high level of government – all the way to Maggie [Thatcher]', to participate in the conspiracy. The plan was for an arms dealer to ship the weapons to Europe, where they would be dispatched to Belfast using a bogus company. Nelson said in his statement that while he was in Durban, Charlie Simpson, a loyalist who had been recruited in Northern Ireland after he was charged with arms offences, told him the organisation supplying the weapons was Armscor, the procurement agency for the South African Department of Defence, and, in return, they wanted his help in acquiring the short-range missile technology being developed by the Shorts aerospace factory in a predominantly unionist area of East Belfast. If Nelson could get what they were looking for, Armscor would provide the arms at a reduced price.

Dr Maguire says in his report that he found army intelligence that supported Nelson's statement. 'The intelligence states: "UDA South Africa. A proposed arms deal between the UDA and Armscor South Africa for the procurement of weapons is to take place during the month of June 1985. The plan is for Armscor to ship the weapons from South Africa to a port in either Europe or England using the name of a legitimate firm as cover, or the UDA will open up a business and use this bogus firm as cover.'

Maguire also found evidence that the RUC Special Branch knew how, in the summer of 1984, the UDA – in a joint conspiracy with the UVF – was planning to rob the Northern Bank in Portadown to procure the funds for the purchase of the South African arms.

All of those who have studied the attempts by Nelson and the UDA to procure South African weapons came to the conclusion that his only involvement in the later, successful arms importation was that he was due to be part of the UDA team to pick up their share when they arrived in Northern Ireland, but he cried off on the day.

Ulster Resistance and Noel Little were the main players this time round. The UDA took action on 8 July 1987 to resolve the funding issue that caused the breakdown in the 1985 negotiations, robbing over £325,000 from the very same Northern Bank in Portadown that Nelson and his co-conspirators had considered targeting three years before. Three men were later charged with the robbery, but the money was never recovered.

Following this, the Ulster Clubs, the UVF and the UDA negotiated a joint arms deal through Charlie Simpson, who advised that they'd need £250,000 to make the purchase. By autumn 1987 the RUC knew that the money had been lodged in a Swiss bank account. The payment was set for what was believed to be 'the UDA's biggest ever arms deal', as a judge at the High Court in Belfast in October 2023 described it.

***

In November 1987 the IRA planted a bomb in a building close to the cenotaph in the town of Enniskillen, eighty miles west of Belfast. As members of the public gathered for the annual Remembrance Sunday event, alongside Boy Scouts, Girl Guides and the UDR, the device exploded, bringing down a heavy stone wall from the building. Under the rubble, eleven people died and over sixty were injured.

It was a callous, sectarian attack on a town that had enjoyed strong community relations. In a BBC interview the following morning, Gordon Wilson, the injured father of one of the dead, Marie Wilson (with whom this author attended primary school), said he had prayed for and forgiven the killers.

The world was horrified at the depth of depravity the IRA had stooped to in attacking people remembering the dead of two world wars. On the evening of the attack, Margaret Thatcher spoke to the press outside 10 Downing Street, telling them: 'We'd just got back from the Cenotaph service when, the minute I got in, I was handed a note giving me the news then of this terrible bomb in Enniskillen. It was so appalling. Really, I could scarcely believe it, because every civilised country honours and respects their dead, and every civilised country expects others to honour their dead too. And to take advantage of those people assembling in that way was really a desecration.'

The news reports of the horrific attack, and the emotional reaction by the prime minister, was watched on television at a two-storey house on the main Enniskillen to Kesh road by a very interested party. Ian Hurst was a member of the FRU and lived off the St Angelo military base, from where his unit operated. Hurst says that, for him, Enniskillen changed everything. 'We basically got to do whatever we wanted from that moment. The gloves were off. Thatcher visited us at St Angelo when she came to the Remembrance Day service the week after the bomb,' said Hurst. 'She told us to do whatever was needed to undermine the IRA.'

Ian Hurst didn't know it at the time, but his superiors were at that very moment tracking the arms shipment being prepared for its journey from South Africa to Northern Ireland, destined for the hands of the loyalist paramilitaries. The fact that, despite a multitude of opportunities, they never stepped in to prevent the shipment only supports the theory that the British government had made a strategic decision to arm the loyalists.

On 2 January 1988 a shipping container arrived in Belfast Docks from Liverpool. Ostensibly packed with 24,000 ceramic floor tiles, the weapons in the container had had something of a circuitous journey, having left Beirut, where they had been stored in the warehouse of a Lebanese arms dealer, William Joseph Farouzi, on the *Manchester Trader* on 2 or 3 December, according to the statement by John Ware. In Ellesmere Port, the container with the International Standards Organisation code ELLU 296 499/1 was transferred to a smaller cargo ship, the *Atria*, which crisscrossed the Irish Sea daily. The container was offloaded in Belfast and, according to intelligence documents found later, left Belfast Docks on 5 January. Its destination was the Lough Road home of Glenanne gang leader James Mitchell.

Inside the container were at least 200 VZ-58 rifles (a Czech copy of the Soviet made AK47), rockets, Browning pistols, anti-personnel grenades and ammunition. Michael Maguire found that 'at the time of the importation, the RUC had informants in senior positions of some of the Loyalist paramilitary organisations involved. One of those sources was named in the intelligence as being involved in the importation.'

Maguire went further: 'In a document dated 21st October, 1987, written by an [RUC] Detective Chief Inspector attached to Special Branch, who declined to assist my investigation, it was reported that *"support for the Ulster Resistance (is) likely to be rejuvenated upon procurement of the firearms."* The officer said that *"there was ongoing monitoring by both Special Branch and the Security Service [MI5] and that this would continue,"'* according to Dr Maguire.

Intelligence would have known the *Manchester Trader* was loaded with the weaponry and that it was on its way to Liverpool, where it could have been intercepted. Instead, the cargo was allowed to travel on to Belfast and pass through British customs before James Mitchell's men picked it up and brought it to his farm, where it remained undisturbed for at least three days.

Sir Desmond de Silva said he was 'satisfied' from the discussions between MI5 officials that they were determined to intercept Nelson's shipment in 1985, even if it blew his cover. But Michael Maguire says he could not find any evidence of 'similar discussions' in relation to the 1987 shipment. The police ombudsman also said he found it 'improbable' that the planning undertaken around Nelson's previous efforts had not assisted the successful importation two years later.

The loyalists had now successfully shipped arms from Beirut to Mitchell's farm. Mr Justice Humphreys found that RUC surveillance began at 9 a.m. on 6 January, the day after the shipment had been picked up and transferred to Glenanne, on 'an individual believed to be involved in the arms deal', but he doesn't say if the individual was Mitchell or Noel Little. However, an examination of all the available material on the arms importation builds a clear picture that Special Branch, MI5 and the FRU were all looking in the opposite direction. They didn't want to find the weapons. Not yet. They had been given every chance to intercept them on their journey through the Mediterranean and across the Irish Sea but had failed to do so.

'Whilst there are strongly held suspicions that MI5 and the FRU colluded in allowing the shipment into Northern Ireland (and in the case of Relatives for Justice (RFJ), a conviction that MI5 actually "supplied" them), my own view is that the most likely explanation for the failure to intercept the shipment was a failure by all the intelligence agencies to prioritise the exploitation of the available intelligence, which seems to me to have been considerable. Far from there having been a "lack of prior intelligence" as MI5 has claimed, the evidence suggests there was a vivid intelligence picture lit up like a Christmas tree,' John Ware concludes.

***

Now that they had reached Glenanne, the loyalists had to get the arms into the hands of their members across the North. There was feverish activity in the first week of January 1988 as Ulster Resistance, the UVF and the UDA made plans for the transport and storage of their share of the arms haul.

Ulster Resistance got in first and removed their weapons to a safe place. However, by the time two burgundy Ford Grenada cars specially hired from the rental company Avis by the UDA, and a third car, an Austin Maestro, arrived on Mitchell's farm on Friday 8 January, the RUC had decided to take action.

One of the cars was driven by Davy Payne, a UDA commander from the Shankill Road. Payne was a well-known psychopathic killer who had been involved in numerous sectarian murders. It is widely believed that he drove one of the cars in the 1974 Dublin and Monaghan bomb attacks organised by Robin Jackson and James Mitchell. When he met people, he was known to scream in their face: 'Do you know who I am? I'm Davy Payne. They say I killed Paddy Wilson.' Wilson was a founder of the SDLP, who was stabbed thirty times and had his throat cut by the UDA in a savage 1973 murder that also cost the life of his Protestant friend Irene Andrews. Payne was never convicted of the murders.

Having loaded the large boots of the vehicles with the UDA's share of the South African weapons, Payne led the two Ford Grenadas, driven by James McCullough and Thomas Aiken, out onto the Mowhan Road, turning right towards Portadown. The cars were jammed full of weapons, weighing them down on their axles, with the rear mud guards trailing along the road. Typical incompetency and poor planning by the UDA meant the bloated vehicles were immediately suspicious even to a casual observer and yet Payne was so confident that he had nothing to fear from the security forces that he took the UDA team on a route that would pass the RUC's largest and best-known barracks in Mid Ulster, located on the Mahon Road.

Around noon, as Payne drove straight into a check-point mounted by police on the Mahon Road, it must have dawned on him that he, McCullough and Aiken were to be the sacrificial lambs of the operation, as the RUC attempted to shut the door after the horse ridden all the way from South Africa by their intelligence colleagues had bolted.

Inside the cars, police found a total of sixty-one VZ-58 rifles; thirty Belgian-manufactured Browning 9mm pistols; 150 anti-personnel Soviet RGD-5 grenades, Chinese-made ammunition, magazines and pouches. The RUC had recovered the UDA's share of the shipment. What Payne, who was sentenced to nineteen years in the Maze Prison for his role in the transportation of the weapons, hadn't known was that the cars were bugged (or, as Judge Humphreys described it, 'police had access to a technical surveillance device') and he had been watched from the moment he set out on his journey. (However, somewhat conveniently, the RUC had lost sight of the UDA cars as they approached Mitchell's farm from the town of Tandragee, twenty minutes to the north-east, and only picked them up again as they closed in on the Mahon Road on their return journey to Belfast.)

Ulster Resistance already had their weaponry safe in the thatch. Surprisingly, none of the intelligence agencies could ever come up with any idea as to where their share of the shipment ended up. The UVF, according to Mr Justice Humphreys' examination of intelligence documents, had picked up their share in a lorry that encountered a 'difficulty' on its journey to Belfast but still got the arms back there.

According to John Ware, the RUC didn't have to look far to find the Ulster Resistance connection. 'Noel Little was arrested after the RUC found that David Payne had written a telephone number for Little on the back of his hand. The number was for Little at his place of work, the South Eastern Library Board in Armagh. Little resisted RUC attempts to turn him into an informer by appealing to his born-again Christianity ... [He] said nothing and was released after a few days.'

Three weeks later RUC detectives from the Tennent Street station off the Shankill Road led a raid on a house at Flush Road in the north of the city, on the western slopes of Cave Hill, and recovered thirty-eight VZ-58 rifles, fifteen Browning pistols, one RPG rocket launcher and 100 RGD-5 hand grenades, along with over 40,000 rounds of ammunition. It was part of the UVF's consignment. The house in which the weapons were found was occupied by Laurence Kincaid, a senior UVF member. Following the publication of the Maguire Report, *Sunday Life* reporter Ciaran Barnes reported that Kincaid was the informer who had given up the Flush Road weapons. Arrests followed the discovery of the weapons but, unsurprisingly, no one was charged.

Dr Michael Maguire found in his 2016 report that the Flush Road recovery was all to do with 'local officers from Tennent Street Police Station and not the intelligence operation associated with the 1987 importation'.

In his statement, John Ware analyses the shipment and its dispersal. 'Since 1988, thirty assault rifles, three RPG rocket launchers, and a number of grenades were recovered in other finds, including some from the Ulster Resistance. There remained in circulation approximately seventy assaults rifles, forty-five Browning pistols, and 250 grenades. In any case, whatever the accurate balance of weapons was, they were eventually shared between the UVF and UDA.'

Ulster Resistance had their entire share, but rather than holding on to it for a doomsday situation – the oft-threatened all-out civil war – they cut a deal with the sectarian killers in the UVF and UDA, sharing the remaining spoils. They would go on to use them in the coming years in at least seventy murders and numerous attempted murders.

Having been at the centre of the previous attempt to import arms from South Africa, what was Nelson's role in the 1987 operation? None of the reports from de Silva, Maguire or the Humphreys judgment provide full elucidation. John Ware has spent thirty-five years examining this very question and believes that Nelson had to have been aware of what the bank robbery was for. If British intelligence was behind the plot to arm the loyalists, was it decided by FRU or MI5 not to use Nelson in the successful importation? If so, why? Was it because they had found a more reliable partner in Noel Little and Ulster Resistance? Had Nelson served his purpose and they wanted to keep him focused on his targeting activities? One thing is for sure: none of the intelligence agencies did anything to prevent Noel Little shipping the weapons into Northern Ireland.

***

All of the British intelligence services failed the people of Northern Ireland during the loyalist arms shipment. However, Operation Flavius, mounted by the SAS, was to be very different. Three IRA members left Belfast just weeks after the South African arms had reached the city's docks area. Dan McCann, Sean Savage and Mairead Farrell travelled to the British territory of Gibraltar on a mission to mount a bomb attack on soldiers stationed there. Before they could carry out the operation, the SAS shot them dead. Their bodies were flown back to Dublin on a specially chartered plane and hearses drove them north to Belfast. Thousands of republicans lined the route amid rising tensions on both sides of the border. On 16 March, as their funerals reached the republican plot in West Belfast's Milltown Cemetery, the first weapons from the South African shipment were used by a loyalist.

Michael Stone, a rogue oddball from East Belfast and UDA member, had attended the funeral Mass. Once in the cemetery, he picked his moment, throwing a Soviet RGD-5 grenade over the heads of the mourners towards Sinn Féin leaders Gerry Adams and Martin McGuinness, the grenade exploding as the third coffin was being lowered into its grave.

According to the RUC at the time of the Mahon Road operation, the UDA had lost its entire South African arsenal, yet Stone clearly had access to weapons from the South African cache. As he attempted to escape from the graveyard, Stone fired from a pistol and threw more grenades, killing three men, including a thirty-year-old IRA volunteer, Caoimhín Mac Brádaigh.

Stone was captured by the pursuing mourners but rescued by the RUC, who had been watching events unfold from a helicopter overhead. He was later sentenced to life imprisonment for the Milltown murders, and for a number of others that he admitted to having committed previously.

Two British soldiers who drove into mourners at the funeral of Caoimhín Mac Brádaigh would be brutally murdered by the IRA. There remain unanswered questions as to why two armed, off-duty soldiers would decide to drive along the route taken by the cortège. The British Army said the two corporals had made a mistake that had cost them their lives. The image of a local priest, Fr Alex Reid, praying over one of their beaten and bloodied bodies is a searing reminder of a most violent and brutal period of the conflict.

The events of these eleven days in March saw so much suffering. However, with loyalists now having access to the imported weapons, much, much worse was to come.

The UDA had lost its share of the weapons on the Mahon Road but in the weeks and months after the arrival of the shipment, it had clearly managed to do deadly deals to get its hands on some of the UVF and Ulster Resistance grenades, guns and ammunition.

In November 1988 the RUC recovered an RPG-7 rocket launcher and five warheads, five assault rifles (one being a Kalashnikov-type rifle rather than a VZ-58), a Browning pistol, ten grenades, thousands of rounds of ammunition and combat equipment – all within a ten-mile radius of James Mitchell's farm.

One long-standing member of the DUP was convicted of possessing Ulster Resistance weapons during this period, along with a former member of the UDR. Defending their role with the red-bereted terrorists, Sammy Wilson said that the DUP had cut ties with Ulster Resistance in 1987. However, in an interview with the *Sunday Tribune* newspaper, he defended 'the right of Unionist people to resist' and said, 'Ulster Resistance are doing no more and no less than Lord Edward Carson'. Almost 100 years after unionists began forming militia against the first Home Rule Bill, the DUP were still invoking Carson's Army to defend their relationship with terrorists.

The impact of the South African weapons is clearly demonstrated by one horrific statistic: it allowed the UVF and UDA to more than treble their capacity to murder. The Belfast-based non-governmental organisation (NGO) Relatives for Justice (RFJ), which represents relatives of those killed by the security forces in Northern Ireland, says that in the three years from 1985 to 1987, loyalists were responsible for thirty-four out of the total of 213 conflict-related deaths. However, from 1988 to 1994, after the arrival of the arms shipment, loyalists were responsible for 224 out of 595 deaths, almost 40 per cent. According to RFJ, of those

224 deaths, nearly half (102) were at the hands of UFF and UVF members armed with weapons imported from South Africa.

Michael Stone was the first terrorist to utilise the new weaponry. But he would not be the last. Far from it. In parallel to the re-arming, loyalists also had the intelligence files from the UDR, and the fruit of the FRU's targeting of republican suspects through Brian Nelson, which he was also sharing with the UVF. The British security services had mixed a potent cocktail that would cause the deaths of dozens of innocent people in the years to follow.

4 | Cross-Pollination

The underbelly of the conflict in Northern Ireland was a dark, ugly place; human life had little or no value. Agents, their handlers, the heads of security and government ministers all plotted and schemed. Their currency was treachery and their lives were devoted to the next play, the next job, the next victim. The 'dirty war' or 'war in the shadows' was subterranean for the vast majority of people living in the North at the time. It was hidden, unknown and out of sight, even though they were the very people impacted by the life-and-death decisions being taken.

Daily life continued as best it could, despite the confines imposed by a conflict that threatened to envelope all semblance of a normal, functioning society. Sport, for example, continued to bring people together. Certainly, by the mid-1980s in South Down, GAA and soccer were providing a welcome distraction from the horror of the Troubles.

In 1985 Loughinisland reached the county final, their first in ten years, but were beaten by St Mary's Burren. At county level, the Down Senior football team were at a low ebb in the mid-1980s. The Mournemen had been the first team to bring the Sam Maguire trophy north of the border post-partition, winning it in 1960, when they beat Kerry with two goals from James McCartan and Paddy Doherty. They won it again the following year, beating Offaly with over 90,000 people watching in Croke Park, a record attendance for a final. They won it for a third time in 1968 with goals from Sean O'Neill and John Murphy. Despite sealing their position as a footballing powerhouse, twenty years later they had not been back to Croke Park.

Pete McGrath hoped to be the one to lift Down out of the doldrums. He taught religion and physical education at St Colman's College on the border in Newry. When he first took on a teaching role, his colleague Ray Morgan managed the school football team. McGrath soon joined the coaching team. St Colman's won the MacRory Cup at provincial level and the Hogan Cup in 1975 and again in 1978. Morgan and McGrath would ultimately win five Hogan Cups (schools' equivalent of an All-Ireland) during their time at the school, bringing through many of the players who would be in the vanguard of the county teams for years to come.

In September 1987 McGrath was manager when the Down Minors won the All-Ireland, with many of the St Colman's team in the side, including the promising James McCartan at corner-forward. The team also included the Kielty brothers, John and Patrick, the latter being one of the team's goalkeepers. With the county Minors bringing home the silverware, expectations in Down began to rise, hoping that, with the talent coming through, McGrath could bring back the Senior team's glory days.

There was similar hope building with Irish soccer south of the border. The fans in the Republic had seen Northern Ireland make their way into successive World Cup finals in 1982 and 1986 and, given that they had a much larger pool of talent to draw from, there was frustration at their side's lack of success. When the manager's job became vacant in 1985, the son of a miner from Northumberland threw his cap into the ring.

Jack Charlton had won the soccer World Cup with England in 1966 but, on paper, he wasn't an obvious candidate for the position of Irish national team manager. Ultimately, though, Charlton got the job. As he drove into the city centre on his first day on the job, in February 1986, he may not have noticed a banner articulating the opinions of some fans: 'Go home Union Jack', it read. Manchester United and Northern Ireland star, George Best, had also been critical of his appointment, but Charlton dismissed him as someone without credibility. He told a press conference in Dublin Airport that he had been following the Irish team and thought they had great players. 'It's a job of great possibilities,' he told the media. 'I can talk, but can I manage? We'll see.' His brusque, Geordie no-nonsense style would soon endear him to Irish fans.

Away from the sports field, the conflict was still raging. The attempted murder of the republican John O'Rourke in a shotgun attack in January 1986 in Dundrum, South Down, by two serving UDR members was almost certainly born out of the intelligence briefings in Ballykinler Barracks, south of Loughinisland. But it would be some years before the true story behind the attack was revealed. In the moment, it was denounced as yet another random sectarian attack carried out by mindless thugs.

With rank-and-file UDR and RUC members living in the community, working a normal nine-to-five by day, but being exposed to the most sensitive of security documentation at night, the normal rule of law across the North was left open to manipulation and exploitation. The security forces instilled a sense of fear into many nationalists who came into contact with them. There was always a sense of there being a bigger picture, that there was another dimension to the conflict, which was not visible to the naked eye.

Many part-time Protestant soldiers may have been targeting their Catholic neighbours, but by the mid-to-late 1980s, the IRA was a motivated machine, which had significant support within its community, evidenced by the growing electoral support for Sinn Féin, its political wing. It was also well armed. After Margaret Thatcher's government had facilitated American aircraft bomber attacks on the Libyan capital, Tripoli, in retaliation for the bombing of a Berlin nightclub visited by US military personnel, Colonel Gaddafi responded by sending at least five shipments of arms and explosives to the IRA, only some of which were discovered on beaches on the west coast of Ireland.

The IRA presented itself as the defender of the nationalist and republican community. As a result, the attack on John O'Rourke by the UVF was an attack on the republican family.

And that called for revenge.

**

The four Watson brothers were well known in the village of Clough, just a few miles south of Loughinisland. Staunch loyalists in a predominantly

Protestant village, they were members of the Orange Order and Apprentice Boys. Charles Watson was the eldest and had served as Worshipful Master of Clough LOL 1043, the Royal Black Institution's 1044 lodge and the Clough No Surrender Apprentice Boys Club. He had joined the UDR before leaving to take up a job in the Prison Service, where he worked at Long Kesh – or Her Majesty's Prison Maze, as it was now renamed – which housed all convicted republican and loyalist paramilitary prisoners.

Charles Watson had a personal protection weapon, a pistol, which had been provided by the police for his safety. However, he was dismissed from the Prison Service and had his weapon withdrawn after he was convicted of attempting to run down RUC officers at the Anglo-Irish Agreement day of protest held by unionists in 1986.

Charles and his younger brother Delbert were both in the UVF. Another former UDR soldier, Ronnie Hawthorne, was very close to the Watson brothers. The UDR men had formed a tight bond, becoming the nucleus of all the UVF actions in the South Down area in the 1980s.

In May 1987 an intelligence operation led to the deaths of eight IRA volunteers when the SAS ambushed them as they were about to attack a police station at Loughgall in Co. Armagh. A civilian would also die in the hail of fire unleased on the East Tyrone IRA unit.

Two weeks after Loughgall, on a warm Friday evening, with the Orange marching season already underway, Charlie Watson attended the weekly practice session for the Clough Orange and Blue accordion band in the village's Orange Hall on The Square. Afterwards, he returned home to his wife and four children at their home on the Downpatrick Road outside the village.

Just before midnight, the IRA arrived at the house. Two masked gunmen broke down Watson's back door and chased the UVF man through the house to the bathroom, where it is believed he had hidden a weapon under the floorboards. Before he could get his hands on it, he was shot dead with a 9mm pistol, as his wife and children cowered in their bedrooms.

A friend who was one of the first at the scene said, 'I found Charlie in the bathroom. The gunman had delivered the coup de grâce.' Another said, 'I was talking to Charlie an hour before he was murdered. I couldn't believe what I was hearing on the news.'

It was over a year since Charlie's brother Delbert was one of those who had attempted to murder John O'Rourke, but the IRA had wreaked its brutal revenge. Among the dozens of death notices in the *News Letter*, one stood out. 'Watson, Charles (murdered by IRA cowards). Very deeply regretted by his good friends Ronnie and Hilary Hawthorne. Missing you always, forgetting you never.' Another was from Hilary's brother, Robin Smyth, who ran a store in Ballynahinch selling flute-band uniforms. He would later move to Australia, worried that his life was in danger from the UVF. Hilary's mother and father, Hugh and Murial Smyth, also paid their respects to the murdered UVF man. 'God bless you Charlie, we will miss you.'

In bright sunshine, thousands of mourners walked behind Watson's coffin as it was carried the short distance to the village's Presbyterian church. Women in brightly coloured dresses and wearing Sunday hats lined the route. Ian Paisley, wearing his Apprentice Boys sash, walked behind the coffin, alongside former UDR man and future DUP leader Jeffrey Donaldson. The attendance by Paisley, who had described Watson as 'a very fine man and a very good friend', confirmed for many that Watson was a member of Ulster Resistance.

The coffin was draped with an Ulster flag and the pall-bearers all wore purple blazers, black trousers and their sashes as his coffin was walked from his home to the church on the Castlewellan Road. In comments that angered local nationalists, the Moderator of the Down Presbytery, the Reverend John Dickenson, told mourners, 'We all know there are members of the Roman Catholic community who know the men who committed this act.' He said republican terrorists appeared to be free to roam around Downpatrick, Castlewellan and Newcastle, adding that there was a need for better security and, if required, the re-introduction of internment. He told mourners, 'We may feel today, who shall be next?' Given that he was officiating at the funeral of a UVF volunteer and his congregation was packed with Watson's fellow terrorists, it seemed the minister hadn't read the room. Or maybe he only meant republicans should be interned without trial.

Watson's murder was a huge blow, not only to his wife and family but to loyalists in the area, and to the UVF. Thirty years later, he was remembered by his successor in the role of Worshipful Master of Clough LOL 1043 as 'a devoted family man, a dedicated and loving husband, father, son and brother'. Brother Phil Colmer said Watson was a leading light, not just in his home village, but throughout Ulster and further afield. 'Charlie would not be found wanting by his country when it came to serving and protecting it from our enemies. Regrettably, the same could not be said about the State when it came to protecting him,' he added.

On a wider canvas, some would argue that the conflict wasn't personal. It was the IRA on one side against the British authorities on the other. The uniform made the target, not the person. But look closely at an area such as South Down and you see that it could be very personal. The Watsons had taken their war to the IRA and paid a heavy price.

Clough is a staunchly loyalist village, with a personality honed from a belief that it was under siege from nationalists on all sides. Union Jack flags marked its territory not just through the marching season, but every month of the year. One of the main loyalist paramilitaries had been taken out, but the UVF had already sworn revenge before they left the graveyard on that early summer afternoon.

***

Jack Charlton's first tournament in charge of the Irish football team was the 1988 European Championships in Germany. A few friendlies had helped him cut his teeth and let the fans get used to the fact that an unapologetic Englishman was in charge. Many years later *The Guardian* newspaper would sum up the challenge in front of Charlton: 'Ever since Oliver Cromwell gave his troops no quarter at the Siege of Drogheda in 1649, and maybe even before that massacre, it has been well-nigh impossible for an Englishman to be a hero in Ireland.'

Ireland had also drawn England in their group, setting up a match full of plots and subplots. Charlton had given John Aldridge, born in England but with a grandmother from Athlone, his chance to play at international level. His Glaswegian Liverpool teammate, Ray Houghton, had a father from Buncrana, Co. Donegal. He too got his chance – and in the first game in Germany, against England, he sealed his lifelong hero status as the man who put the ball in the English net. It was a looping header from outside the box after just six minutes. Ireland held on to win the game; Charlton had engineered a famous one-nil win over England in a game that would mark Ireland's coming of age on the international stage.

They subsequently drew against the Soviet Union when Liverpool midfielder Ronnie Whelan shinned a wonder goal from thirty yards to put them ahead, only to be pegged back late on against the run of play. Paul McGrath almost put the men in green ahead in the final game against Holland, but the Dutch got a winner late on, meaning Charlton's men exited the competition at the group stage.

Regardless, the build-up to Germany and the tournament itself had given football fans a new, exhilarating experience. Fans came home with stories that would be told to grandchildren. Charlton had given them something they'd never had: hope.

Next up was qualification for Italia '90.

***

The BBC and ITV current affairs departments were regularly examining the Irish conflict through their weekly series, *Panorama* and *World in Action*. But the 'shock jock' of the late 1980s was Roger Cook, a much-parodied journalist who had been born in New Zealand and brought up in Australia. A big man with a penchant for doing the things mainstream journalism cowed away from, he had become well known for his door-stepping of 'bad guys' in a weekly show that was, in many ways, ahead of its time.

In March 1987, two months before Charlie Watson's murder, Roger Cook had turned his attention to loyalists paramilitaries and, in particular, their extortion rackets in Belfast. The opening words of *The Cook Report* episode titled 'Worse Than the Mafia' left the viewers in little doubt as to what they were going to see: 'Tonight we will show how everyone in Britain is paying for terrorism in Northern Ireland.'

A builder, whose voice and face were disguised, told Cook how the UDA had demanded he pay protection money in order to continue working on a site on the Shankill Road. Despite his profile, Cook set up a sting operation, which two UDA men walked straight into, demanding money with menace. An Omagh man, Eddie Sayers, who was the brigadier of the UDA in Co. Tyrone, was later jailed for ten years.

The programme had lifted the lid on the UDA's dirty secret of extortion and blackmail at a time when the organisation was still legal and Brigadier John McMichael was attempting to present it as having a political brain.

The fallout from the sting would have lethal consequences.

Jack Kielty was a larger-than-life character. During the 1960s he had been a music promoter who brought some of the biggest stars in the music business, including Tom Jones and Roy Orbison, to play in Belfast. He was a member of the GAA and chairman of the Dundrum club, which had been formed in 1934. The club's ground was less than five minutes south of Clough. Kielty was a partner in a joinery company, Kelly, McEvoy & Brown, a role that regularly took him up to Belfast to oversee contracts. It was during one of his trips to the city that the UDA approached him, looking for protection money.

The businessman was in his office in Dundrum on 25 January 1988, just seven months after Charlie Watson's murder, when the dead man's brother Delbert pulled up outside in a blue Vauxhall Cavalier car that had been stolen a week before in one of East Belfast's predominantly Protestant areas, Dee Street off the Lower Newtownards Road, thirty miles north. Earlier the same day, Watson and a Shankill loyalist, Ken Barrett, had been supplied with weapons by a former member of the Royal Marines, William Bell, at a farmhouse between Clough and Dundrum. 'After Charlie Watson's murder a few months before, Delbert Watson was pushing for revenge – any Catholic would do as far as he was concerned,' reported the *Belfast Telegraph*, though there was another motive behind the targeting of Kielty.

After *The Cook Report* episode aired nine months earlier, one of the racketeers who had been identified by the journalist – UDA leader Jim Craig – had threatened to sue for defamation in an attempt to prevent further revelations. Jack Kielty was to be a potential witness for the defence. Craig and the UDA opted not to await the outcome of the legal action and instead sent a murder gang to Dundrum.

Kielty was at his desk upstairs when the two masked gunmen entered his office and shot the GAA chairman six times at close range with a .357 Magnum. This all occurred in front of his secretary, who was later taken to hospital and treated for shock.

The blue Vauxhall was found abandoned ten minutes north of the scene, near Loughinisland, on the Belfast side of Clough – which should have provided police with a very good indication of those involved.

Local parish priest, Fr Michael Blaney, was one of the first at the scene and later spoke of how what he had witnessed reminded him of his own brother's murder some years earlier. In an RTÉ report for the evening news, reporter Michael Fisher interviewed an employee at the firm and a neighbour of the dead man: 'Everybody is just shocked. Jack Kielty was known through Ireland. No matter where you went. If they knew you were [from] Dundrum they'd ask if you knew Jack Kielty,' said the pale-faced neighbour, who was obviously suffering from shock.

Down coach Pete McGrath was teaching his religious education class beside the St Colman's College chapel when Jack Kielty was murdered. 'I remember clearly the morning I heard Jack had been murdered,' McGrath told *Irish News* journalist John Breslin. 'It was James McCartan standing in the corridor, ashen-faced. He said he just heard the Kieltys' father had been shot dead.'

Patrick Kielty, who would later become one of the North's most talented comedians and broadcasters, recalled the moment in a very personal documentary for the BBC. 'I remember going to school and like lots of other kids who were sixteen, putting up your posters for *Comic Relief* [an annual BBC charity fundraising event],' he said. '[I was] called up to the headmaster's office and was thinking, "I didn't ask permission to put these posters up, here we go." The headmaster said, "I think you need to sit down." There was a slow motion [feeling] but very quick exchange. He said, "Your father's been shot." I said, "Is he dead?" and he said, "Yes."'

Many years later Patrick – who would go on to become the presenter of *The Late Late Show* on RTÉ – had a chance encounter with a woman in Belfast, who told him the background to his father's death. 'This woman told me that her husband and my dad had been going to give evidence in the trial against James Craig,' he told the *Daily Mail* newspaper. 'And I didn't know that. Apparently they gave evidence behind a screen but then the trial collapsed and both men were then identifiable. My dad was a brave man, but it was my mum who wanted to protect us. She's the one who raised the family and kept us together. She was forty-six when he died and she never remarried.'

Pete McGrath was a fan of Jack Kielty's, recalling fond memories of the support he gave to his sons and the county Minor team during the run to winning the All-Ireland final just four months before his murder: 'When we beat Kildare in the semi-final Jack came up and said, "These boys have worked so hard, we have to do something for them, maybe get them something special,"' he told Breslin. 'For the players he arranged for every member of the panel to get a gold watch. It was irrespective if we won the final. He was a massive loss to his family but also to Down GAA.'

Dundrum GAC ground is now named Páirc Seán Ó Caoilte in honour of their former chairman.

The murder of the popular businessman began a chain of events that would have repercussions almost thirty years later. In his report on the Loughinisland massacre, Dr Michael Maguire revealed in candid and stark detail the loyalist familial connections and policing failures from the time of the GAA chairman's killing, and the repercussions for the people of South Down and beyond. 'The police investigation into the murder was successful in identifying personalities and associations, including those within a small, embryonic loyalist paramilitary unit operating mainly in the Newcastle Sub-Division of the RUC's G Division. It also identified their developing relationship with elements of the UVF in Belfast.'

Here is the key point from Maguire: 'Police did not, however, fully exploit this information by maintaining an interest in the gang, as a result of which it re-emerged a number of years later as a fully functional UVF unit, embarking on a campaign of murder that would ultimately escalate to the Loughinisland atrocity.'

***

During the making of *No Stone Unturned*, we were helped and supported by many sources. One of them was a former detective based in the South Down area during the late 1980s. The RUC investigation into the Kielty murder was run out of its base at Newcastle. Within days of the shooting, the senior investigating officer (SIO), identified only by Maguire as 'Police Officer 3', was appointed as the lead detective in charge of the case. A legal source in South Down with an understanding of the murder and its aftermath described Police Officer 3 as waging 'a one-man war' on loyalist paramilitaries in the area.

The SIO got a breakthrough on the Kielty case when, according to Maguire, he 'received a report from a member of the public concerning one of the individuals involved'. The individual was Delbert Watson, the driver of the getaway car, who was arrested on 20 May, five months after the Kielty murder, and taken to Gough Barracks in Armagh city for questioning.

At the time, loyalists who were arrested had a reputation for cracking easily under interrogation. (What wasn't appreciated at the time was that only a very small minority of the terrorists weren't already state agents and therefore immune to the force of the law.) Within hours of his arrest, Delbert – who had the nickname 'Del Boy' and, like his brother Charlie, had worked as a prison service officer – was unburdening himself to the RUC detectives, admitting his role in the murder of Jack Kielty. He 'admitted having been the driver of the Vauxhall Cavalier and explained that Mr Kielty had been identified to him by an associate, who was from Dundrum and also a loyalist paramilitary,' continued Maguire. The loyalist from Dundrum was a man called Alan Taylor, who would later become a significant figure in the UVF, along with Ronnie Hawthorne.

Delbert, who had a tattoo of a shield on his left forearm with the word 'Ulster' underneath, gave police a full picture of the aftermath of the killing. He had collected two members of the UDA – one of them Ken Barrett – from a 'safe house' in Clough. After they had committed the murder, he drove them back to Clough, stopping only at the bottom of a laneway leading to the farmhouse owned by members of his family, where he dropped off the weapons the killers had used. He left the two UDA murderers back to the house in Clough and drove the Vauxhall Cavalier to the pre-organised spot close to Loughinisland. Once there, he abandoned the stolen car and fled the scene with Alan Taylor, who, Watson said, had been the person who had targeted Kielty in the first place.

Due to the statements made by 'Del Boy' Watson, Ken Barrett and a second UDA man were both arrested. However, they were soon released without charge, due to police purportedly believing that a prosecution wouldn't stand up in court based solely on Watson's evidence. Barrett would murder Pat Finucane a year later.

Delbert Watson admitted to detectives that he was a member of the UVF and had been sworn into the paramilitary organisation by his friend Ronnie Hawthorne, who was known by the nickname 'Twizzle'. He went further. He said that his sister-in-law, Doreen Watson, Charlie's widow, had welcomed killers into her home before and after the shooting. RUC detectives therefore ordered that Doreen be arrested. According to a source close to the investigation, once she was in Gough Barracks, Delbert made further admissions in a bid to protect her from prosecution.

Knowing that Doreen had made a full confession to her role in the Kielty murder, Delbert decided to get his full 'career' in the UVF off his chest. He confessed that he had conspired with Ronnie Hawthorne and another unnamed member of the UVF to murder John O'Rourke, the republican left for dead in the January 1986 Dundrum shotgun attack, telling detectives that Hawthorne had driven the getaway car. He said that, armed with a shotgun, they had waited at the deserted house for their intended victim to arrive. He was late, however, and they were about to drive off when he eventually turned up. Watson blasted him in the back with the shotgun, but O'Rourke escaped over fields. He managed to get to a nearby farmhouse, where his wounds were treated by a Protestant woman whose two brothers had been murdered by the IRA.

During his time in Gough holding centre, one of three RUC bases in the North where terrorist suspects were interrogated during the Troubles, Watson also revealed that they had attempted to kill another man, Paul McKibben, on the anniversary of the IRA murder of a relative. Hawthorne was his accomplice in the failed attack on the owner of the Renault dealership in Clough.

Delbert and Doreen Watson were both charged with Jack Kielty's murder, along with David Leslie Curlett, a twenty-two-year-old from Dundrum who had known the victim and who had also made a full confession of his supporting role. Alan Taylor was also arrested by police but, according to Maguire, was 'released due to insignificant evidence'. Ronnie 'Twizzle' Hawthorne was later arrested and questioned about the murder of Kielty, but, just like Taylor, he was released without charge.

Based on Delbert Watson's statements, Paul Gavin Peacock from Bailiesmills outside Lisburn was charged with possession of a shotgun. William Bell, who was thirty at the time and from Kilkeel, was charged on the basis of his admissions under questioning. The sixth person charged in relation to the Kielty murder was William Bell's sister, Jackie Bell. The twenty-three-year-old was accused of withholding information.

In his confession, William Bell painted a full picture of loyalist paramilitary activity in the South Down area and of those involved. He also revealed where the UVF's arms and ammunition were stored: in the roofspace at Clough Orange Hall. Bell claimed that he had been in a car with Delbert Watson the previous year and they had stopped at the hall, at which point Watson had gone inside and come out with an Armalite rifle.

The detective decided to take immediate action, but he was careful not to alert the three Special Branch officers based in Newcastle RUC base. He was concerned that they may decide to compromise the operation before he could retrieve whatever was in the rafters. 'He didn't trust Special Branch and they didn't trust him because he was a Catholic,' said the source.

On Friday 19 May – the day after Bell's interview – the detective made his move before Special Branch could do anything to thwart him. Several steel-coloured RUC Land Rovers, supported by British soldiers, poured into the village, surrounding the Orange Hall. All the windows in the hall had been blocked up and outside there were posters celebrating 'South Down 1st Battalion UVF', along with images from the Home Rule Crisis, the signing of the Ulster Covenant and the 36th Ulster Division during the First World War. The dark windowless building had been the centre of activity for unionism in Clough for over 100 years, but it had never before borne witness to the type of raid that the UVF had brought down on it.

Just after 4 p.m., a local member of the Orange Order opened the front door to allow the police search team into the hall. Following Bell's testimony on where the search should concentrate, an RUC constable discovered a loose floorboard at the bottom of the stairs. He pulled it up and could see a black bin bag in the cavity. According to RUC statements at the time, the policeman found an Armalite rifle, a pistol, a revolver, a homemade machine gun, two rifle magazines, a radio, assorted ammunition, black gloves and a balaclava. Another officer, searching a cupboard under a sink in the kitchen, found a photograph album of terrorist suspects. In an upstairs room, maps and battery packs were discovered. Bell had led the police directly to a treasure trove of weapons and evidence.

Police brought the arms find back to Gough Barracks where 'Del Boy' Watson and the others continued to be questioned about the murder of Jack Kielty. The scene in the interview room was recounted by a detective in a statement that was part of the Department of Public Prosecution's case against him. Watson admitted that he had owned a Beretta pistol that had been provided to him by the security forces as a personal protection weapon. 'Watson went on to say that his brother Charlie had been shot dead the previous year and he believed that Charlie had been set up by the police,' the detective recorded.

'Watson was asked was he now aware that we had information that pointed out to us that he planned the murder of Jack Kielty and the planning for it had taken place in the kitchen of his sister-in-law's house, Doreen Watson.' The detectives told Delbert they knew he was a leader of a UVF cell in the Dundrum/Newcastle area. Repeating what Bell had already told them, the detective also asked Watson 'what he had to say about an allegation that he produced an Armalite rifle from Clough Orange Hall'.

The detectives then brought the weapons found in Clough Orange Hall into the interview room. 'Aye okay,' said Del Boy. 'I hid them there, I will probably be expelled from the Orange now,' he responded, showing little appreciation of the fact that he was making admissions that would ensure he served life in the very prison in which he used to work.

Next, Watson was shown the documents of suspects and maps that had originated in Ballykinler and admitted that they were 'ours'. Shown the Armalite rifle, he said, 'Aye that's the Armalite from the Orange Hall'; when the pistol was produced, he said, 'Yes that's the Walther, I had one like it in the prison', and with the revolver, he said, 'Yes, okay, that's ours.'

The detectives' statement from the scene inside the utilitarian interview room paints a picture of a man resigned to his destiny: 'Shown a pair of black gloves in a see-through evidence bag, Watson responds, "Can't be sure, will you take them out?" Watson was told that no we couldn't, they had to be sealed up; stated, "Well it's too hard to tell, but if they were with the weapons then they are ours." Shown the multicoloured jumper found with the weapons he said, "Hey boys, I don't think that was with our stuff but I don't know."'

Watson signed a statement accepting responsibility for the weapons on 22 May 1988 – the anniversary of his brother Charlie's murder. 'I hid these weapons in the hall. They weren't in a special hide or anything, just concealed as best I could. I was given these weapons by a third party I don't want to name.'

But Watson still wasn't finished. Agreeing to be taken from the barracks back to Clough, he led police to three separate UVF weapon hides where they found a sawn-off shotgun, a revolver and hundreds of rounds of ammunition.

Due to Bell and Watson's statements, Ronnie 'Twizzle' Hawthorne was arrested for the second time in six months, on Tuesday, 22 July 1988, at his home in Clough, only 100 yards from the village's Orange Hall. He was taken by detectives to Gough Barracks, just as when he had been previously arrested for the murder of Jack Kielty. The arresting officer told him that he had been arrested 'under Section 12 of the Prevention of Terrorism Act 1984 as I suspected him of being involved in the commission, preparation and instigation of acts of violence'.

His fingerprints were taken and were found to match those on the Orange Hall montages that had originally been given to the UDR, of which he was a member at the time. For the first time, Hawthorne faced a terrorism charge that he 'on a date unknown between the 30th day of August, 1983 and the 20th day of May 1988, in the County Court Division of South Down, without lawful authority for reasonable excuse had in your possession documents, namely an album of photographs with names and addresses, containing information which was of such a nature as was likely to be useful to terrorists in planning or carrying out an act of violence'.

The charge sheet, produced by the RUC as it instigated the prosecution against the UVF man, cited the complainant as its most senior officer in the area, Divisional Commander Alwyn Harris. Hawthorne's first court appearance, the day after his arrest, was recorded in the local newspaper, the *Down Recorder*, under the headline 'Clough Man in Court'. The short report read: 'A Clough man has appeared at a special court charged with collecting information likely to be of use to terrorists. A specially convened sitting of Down Magistrates Court last Wednesday heard that the charge against Ronald Hawthorne, of Main Street, referred to the collection of photographs and documents for an unlawful use. Hawthorne was remanded in custody to appear in court in Belfast on August 12th.'

Despite the evidence of his fingerprints on the montage, the charges against Hawthorne were dropped at some point. There is no record of when or why, and, despite the granular detail included in the sixteen-page report by Dr Michael Maguire, he doesn't record or reflect on this pivotal moment in terms of the UVF in South Down and its potential impact on innocent lives that were lost due to the fact that Hawthorne remained a free man, having completed the only spell in prison that he would ever experience in his terrorist career.

The detective in charge of the investigation was a very determined individual, who would be described as 'one good apple in a rotten orchard'. In a report he authored in the same year that he charged Hawthorne, Watson and the others, he described Hawthorne as a 'main organiser, planner and probably responsible for others now made amenable. It is suspected that [Hawthorne] is still an active loyalist terrorist.'

The detective was so concerned that Hawthorne was still a serving soldier that he made representations to the UDR to have him removed from the organisation. According to the Maguire Report, the Newcastle policeman cited Hawthorne's 'use of material originating from the regiment to assist his terrorist activity'. The detective even came across Hawthorne attending a security force intelligence briefing at Newcastle Police Station. He remonstrated with those in charge, who reluctantly removed Hawthorne. After his very damning report, the UDR moved slowly, only discharging him 'many months later'.

On Friday, 3 March 1989, Delbert Watson, William Bell and David Leslie Curlett were found guilty of the murder of Jack Kielty by Lord Justice O'Donnell. He sentenced them to life imprisonment. Coincidentally, as journalist Deric Henderson reported, Michael Stone had been convicted at the same Crumlin Road court building on the same day for his gun and grenade attack on Milltown Cemetery in March 1988. Under the headline in the *News Letter*, 'Thirty years for six times killer', Henderson wrote that Stone had also admitted to killing a Tyrone breadserver and a Lisburn workman.

Doreen Watson was acquitted of murder but found guilty of manslaughter and given a recorded sentence, which meant she walked free due to the time she had served on remand before the trial. The *News Letter* reported the judge saying that the thirty-three-year-old mother of four, whose husband Charles was murdered by the IRA eight months earlier, had been 'cruelly used' by Watson and Bell playing on her emotions.

Jackie Bell received concurrent two-year suspended sentences on three charges of withholding information.

'The judge rejected claims by former UDR man Watson and [William] Bell, an ex-Royal Marine, that they had only made statements of admission to get their sister-in-law and sister respectively freed,' said the paper, going on to report the judge's directed comments to the convicted terrorists: 'How you, Watson, and Bell and Curlett, when you have suffered from the killing of other people, can inflict the same sort of pain and suffering on another innocent man and his family is completely beyond my comprehension.'

For one of the RUC officers involved in the case, the convictions brought some satisfaction. 'South Down was a terrible place in the 1980s,' he told the author, adding, 'The IRA was killing a member of the security forces roughly every three to four months. A uniformed unit had to be brought in solely to patrol the area to try to prevent attacks.'

The actions of one police officer had single-handedly dismantled the emerging UVF–UFF terror gang in South Down. Hawthorne was still at large, of course, but one Watson brother was dead and the other in prison along with Bell and Curlett. Hawthorne's sectarian bloodlust was undiminished, however, and would return with a vengeance.

***

Five months before Delbert and Doreen Watson and their co-accused were convicted, Ulster Resistance leader Noel Little walked into one of the most luxurious hotels in Paris: the George V. Having successfully negotiated one shipment of arms for loyalists, Little wanted to go again.

He was at the hotel to meet his contact, Douglas Bernhardt. According to court documents, Bernhardt explained the context to the November 1988 meeting: 'the loyalists wanted a bigger quantity than before, worth approximately £500,000. In fact, he confided in me that they had to meet the threat imposed by the IRA and the incapacity of the English to sort out the security problems. On the subject of armaments he talked to me about assault rifles of the AK47 type, of 9mm pistols, of APG7 machine guns and mortars.'

Little had been questioned by the RUC about the first tranche of South African weapons but emerged with an undiminished determination to equip the terrorists even further. He offered to sell the UDA more weapons from the Ulster Resistance stockpile but ultimately believed that another shipment to replace the guns that had been lost was the best way forward for the various paramilitary groupings.

Bernhardt had told Little prior to this meeting that he had to involve the South African embassy in Paris, who wanted the loyalist to bring them the technology and blueprints for the new Javelin missiles being produced out of the Short Brothers factory in East Belfast. South Africa had invaded its neighbour Angola in 1975, to prevent communists aligned to the Soviet Union coming to power. Occurring at the height of the Cold War, the Soviet Union, America and Cuba were involved on both sides in a form of proxy war. Cuba sent thousands of troops to support the Angolans, for example, and as the war continued into the 1980s, even supplied MiG-17 fighter jets, which outclassed the aging South African Air Force. The Shorts-produced Javelin missile system, it was felt, would help recalibrate the conflict in South Africa's favour.

Little had, in fact, already secured these for the South Africans. In April 1988 a briefcase was stolen from the car of a Shorts employee. Inside were eleven Ministry of Defence documents, three of which were blueprints of the Javelin missile system and were viewed as highly sensitive by the police investigating the theft. Six months later, in October 1988, loyalists walked out of Shorts with a Training Aiming Unit for the Javelin under their arms. A third theft, in April 1989, this time of a training model for a Blowpipe missile system, occurred at the Territorial Army (TA) base in Newtownards. Little flew to Geneva, handed the stolen documents over to the South Africans, and was paid £50,000 into his Swiss bank account for his efforts. British intelligence, MI5, the RUC and the FRU were all aware of what Little was up to, but they had decided not to intervene.

However, the French authorities picked up on what was going on and launched their own operation. Another court document set out their knowledge ahead of the George V meeting: 'In the course of diligent enquiry into this area, we learn that a certain [Noel] Little would be involved in the theft of a British missile and would have a clandestine meeting with regard to the theft at George V Hotel. We contacted the British authorities that there had been a recent theft of a training model of the guiding system of the land-air missile Javelin from the premises of the manufacturers: the Shorts Factories in Belfast.'

It is simply beyond belief, since Little had been arrested previous to this and placed under surveillance – his car had even been bugged while he was on a trip to Geneva – that British intelligence was not aware of what the Ulster Resistance leader was doing. But it was French police who broke up the conspiracy, storming into the five-star hotel and arresting Little, along with Bernhardt and two other Northern Irish men, Samuel Quinn and James King. The men had parts of the training model stolen from the TA base in Newtownards and sections of a Javelin missile in their possession when they were arrested. Unbelievably, Quinn, who was in the TA and a missile instructor, had brought his thirteen-year-old son along for the ride. A South African diplomat played the diplomatic card and was given immunity.

The three men spent thirty months in a Paris prison before being found guilty of arms trafficking. They were ultimately handed down suspended sentences. Noel Little and the others returned to Northern Ireland without fanfare and continued life without ever coming to the attention of police again.

The efforts of Little and Ulster Resistance would continue to wreak havoc. Another loyalist attack in South Down on a late summer Friday night in August 1989, the first in the area since the Kielty murder – and two years after Little's weapons had arrived at Belfast docks – would cause the security forces' secret cross-pollination with loyalist paramilitaries to be formally scrutinised by the authorities for the first time since the conflict began.

***

Loughlin Maginn, who worked as a delivery driver, was at home watching television when a loyalist gunman opened fire through the living-room window of his two-storey home at Lizzise Avenue, Rathfriland in South Down. Despite being injured by the first volley of shots, he managed to escape the hail of bullets and go up the stairs. Seeing this, the gunman put a section of carpet over the broken front window and climbed through the shattered glass to pursue him. He ultimately murdered the twenty-eight-year-old father of four in front of his wife and children.

Claiming responsibility for his death, the UFF, a cover name for the still-legal UDA, said the victim was a member of the IRA. In a statement condemning the murder, the nationalist SDLP MP for Newry and Armagh, Seamus Mallon, echoed the growing conviction of nationalists: 'I believe there is direct collusion between some members of the security services and loyalist paramilitary groups.'

Two weeks after Loughlin Maginn's murder, Chris Moore, the journalist who would later reveal the existence of the Walker Report, received a late night phone call at his home north of Belfast from the UDA/UFF. They wanted him to meet them in a car park in Ballynahinch, claiming they had some documents to show him.

The *Washington Post* reporter Glenn Frankel documented the disturbing events that followed: 'Members of the Ulster Freedom Fighters showed reporter Chris Moore of the BBC copies of confidential documents and a videotape appearing to come from government security files that alleged that Maginn was a member of the IRA's South Down Brigade. In a BBC broadcast, Moore said he had been blindfolded by a group of four hooded and armed men and taken to a location south of Belfast, the capital of Northern Ireland. He said he was shown documents containing names and addresses of suspected IRA activists and a video of a number of photographs on a wall, accompanied by commentary identifying each person as an IRA member. Maginn's was among those listed, and the notation "heavily traced as IRA suspect" appeared next to his name. Moore said he was told by his escorts that they had obtained the material from sympathetic members of the security forces. He said a photocopy of a "confidential" government stamp on one of the documents supported their authenticity.'

The loyalists were attempting to vindicate their killing but, in doing so, were only evidencing the fact they had little political nous, while also confirming the fears and beliefs of the nationalist community – namely, that the RUC and UDR were working hand-in-hand with the loyalists who were waging war on them.

In the days that followed, security force montages were sent to a number of men in the South Down area with a note that stated: 'We got Maginn. You are next (UFF).'

In response to the pressure to explain how the loyalists had access to the documents, the RUC called in an outside officer to investigate, a response that would be used in many difficult situations for police in Northern Ireland right up to 2018 and my own arrest.

In this instance, it was Sir John Stevens. An imposing figure, standing over six feet three inches tall in his usual attire of a dark, pin-striped suit, at the time he was the deputy chief constable of Cambridgeshire Constabulary, although he would later be given the biggest policing job in the UK: the head of Scotland Yard. He agreed to lead the investigation into the leaking of the montages and came to Belfast in the aftermath of Chris Moore's revelations to meet with the RUC chief constable, Sir Hugh Annesley, and to start his inquiry. Many years later, Sir Desmond de Silva would also examine the events that led up Maginn's murder. He found that some aspects of the case hadn't been explored by Stevens.

Nine months before the attack, the UDA had 'broken into' the Ballykinler UDR base. De Silva said that Brian Nelson had told his handlers of the UDA's plan to break into the base in order to access intelligence on known republicans held by the regiment. De Silva's report, which was denounced as a whitewash by the Finucane family, found that records held by the FRU, the RUC and MI5 made it clear the RUC was aware of the UDA's plan to break into Ballykinler but decided to do nothing to prevent it. 'An [MI5] internal note recorded the following discussion with [RUC Special Branch]: "[The UDA] was planning to break into a UDR camp on 2nd December to photograph some intelligence reports … We agreed that this was … odd … a view endorsed by the Deputy Head of Special Branch when I spoke to him subsequently. Deputy Head Special

Branch advised that "since the UDA already had lots of this stuff anyway" and that they would find nothing of value there was little to be gained by trying to prevent the activity.'

If nothing else, the deputy head of Special Branch was at least being frank. He knew that the relationship between the UDA and the UDR, and indeed the RUC, was such that there was no need for a break-in. The UDA had access to as much intelligence as it wanted from the security forces.

The police have never explained how the loyalists got through the suffocating security at the base and entered the inner sanctum where intelligence was stored. On top of the montages, they found a video of a UDR briefing featuring a number of individuals, including Loughlin Maginn. Given that video cameras in 1989 were the size of a small carry-on suitcase, that the officer making the briefing failed to realise he was being recorded is beyond belief.

De Silva failed to comment on this particularly stark point. However, he did reveal that Nelson told his handlers just four days following the break-in that he had viewed the tape. Nelson also said that Maginn's killers were offered 'refuge' in the local barracks. Going further, de Silva says that Nelson encouraged attacks against those who featured on the tape and warned of repercussions if they failed to do so: '[Nelson] suggested that if no attacks resulted on any of those mentioned on the video tape the UDR personnel who supplied it would not supply any more.'

A document found in the Ministry of Defence in London recognised the impact of the tape: 'The video was filmed in a UDR briefing room. This video led to the murder of Loughlin McGinn [sic]. [Nelson] also goes on to say that a hit had already been planned in the Castlewellan area. It was also explained that if the hit team could not escape, they would be given refuge in the barracks by certain members of the UDR. This is potential dynamite. Should it become public knowledge the Security Forces, particularly the ... regiment's credibility would be severely damaged,' wrote an author who failed to recognise the damage caused by the fact that UDR men were murdering innocents at will.

A contact form suggested that the RUC Special Branch had also leaked information on the Rathfriland man. De Silva concluded that, despite all the information police had, no attempt was made to prevent the break-in or save Loughlin Maginn's life.

The UDA really didn't have much of a presence in South Down, despite the fact that they had supplied the killer Ken Barrett for the murder of Jack Kielty, and had also taken the life of Terry Mullan, his mother Kathleen and, more recently, Loughlin Maginn. Instead, the dominant paramilitary force in the area was the UVF unit based in the village of Clough and now led by Ronnie Hawthorne, who had formed strong links with paramilitaries in East Belfast.

All the paramilitaries, especially Ulster Resistance, were full of people who would pay their dues but had no stomach for violence of any sort. The UDA and UVF, however, needed men who were prepared to kill. A Special Branch officer who was interviewed for *No Stone Unturned* said, 'A lot of the people who were involved in the murders at that time probably thought they were carrying out For God and Ulster, which was the UVF badge. So they saw themselves carrying out acts on behalf of Ulster. Some of the country people had different views than the town people, but their view would have been very, very simple, you know, [that] all Catholics are targets.'

Asked about the ratio of paramilitary members to killers, he said: 'If I sat down and thought about it and went over numbers ... How many people actually pulled the triggers? Yeah, could have been twenty-five.'

Despite all their resources, intelligence and technical capability, the security forces couldn't prevent them from killing. Or was the British government actually *allowing*, indeed *encouraging* them to kill?

***

While the Stevens inquiry got underway, the IRA was already targeting its next victim, ready to exploit the under-car booby-trap bomb technology that had been developed with deadly effect. The device could be packed into a package no bigger than a lunchbox. A tilt switch with mercury inside ensured that, when the car moved, the mercury would complete the circuit and the device would explode. A large magnet to attach it to the underbody of the vehicle was all that was required, usually done during the hours of darkness. Senior RUC and UDR officers were constantly warning soldiers and police officers to get down on their knees and check their cars before leaving their homes in the morning. Some did it assiduously, others chose not to – so as not to draw attention to the fact that they were a member of the security forces.

Private Robert Hill died in 1986 from such a device. Three years later, and two months after the murder of Loughlin Maginn, the IRA was tracking the most senior officer in Co. Down.

Alwyn Harris was born and grew up in Upperlands, Co. Derry, and after leaving Rainey School he studied at Coleraine Technical College before joining the RUC and entering its training centre in Enniskillen. He quickly rose through the ranks, becoming sergeant and, later, an inspector, before finally rising to the position of superintendent and sub-divisional commander, based at the Newcastle police base.

His name had been on Delbert Watson's and Ronnie Hawthorne's charge sheets, along with every other criminal and terrorist charged since he arrived in South Down three years earlier. Recently, though, he had developed a heart condition and was on long-term sick leave.

On an autumnal Sunday morning in October 1989, Superintendent Harris and his wife, Anne, were leaving their home in Lisburn to attend a church service when the bomb planted under his driver's seat exploded, killing him. His wife was treated for superficial injuries and shock. The couple had two grown-up children, Bryan and Drew. The latter would follow his father into policing, becoming a significant figure in the RUC and PSNI, and later becoming commissioner of An Garda Síochána.

On the day of Alwyn Harris's funeral, the *News Letter* published a report on his murder. At the bottom of the page there were two headlines that reflected John Stevens' work, as he pursued his inquiry into collusion: 'UDR raids anger MPs' and 'Four soldiers in court on ammunition charges'. The newspaper also reported that over the weekend of the RUC man's murder, Stevens had arrested twenty-eight members of the UDR.

'The Reverend Ian Paisley has called for the removal of Deputy Chief Constable John Stevens from the security leaks inquiry,' was the opening paragraph. 'Mr Stevens should pack his bags and take off home and they should send some respectful officer to the Province who is not prepared to simply placate Dublin,' it quoted Paisley as saying.

The establishment wasn't liking the Stevens Inquiry and began closing ranks. Stevens was aware that there was a very serious briefing operation underway in the English media designed to undermine him and his investigation. In his first weeks in Belfast, he had also been getting pushback from Special Branch.

It was the end of a decade that had seen new horrors in a conflict that never ceased to descend to fresh levels of depravity and despair. Ten men had died on hunger strike and eleven innocents were murdered at a Remembrance Day Service. Republicans embraced electoral politics, arms shipments arrived from Libya and South Africa. The SAS had all but wiped out the IRA in East Tyrone, although republicans remained a potent force who still appeared to retain an ability to kill at will. Loyalists had murdered four people in 1985; by 1988 that figure had risen to twenty-three. The old leaderships had been swept away or were in jail. In Mid Ulster, Robin Jackson would be replaced by 'King Rat', Billy Wright. On the Shankill Road, the young Turk was Johnny Adair, who was now in control of the viciously sectarian and drugged-up C Company.

And in South Down, the UVF, led by Ronnie Hawthorne, had cemented a relationship with the same murderous friends in East Belfast who had supplied Delbert Watson's Vauxhall Cavalier getaway car for the murder of Jack Kielty. That bond, the ready availability of South African weapons and Hawthorne's insatiable hunger to avenge the death of Charlie Watson was going unchecked by the security forces.

With peace still a long way off, the 1990s only promised more innocent victims.

5 | The Slow Waltz

For very different reasons, two Englishmen were very much the centre of attention on the island of Ireland as the new decade began.

Following the success at the European Championships, Jack Charlton had gone one step further and qualified the Republic of Ireland for the World Cup finals, to be held in Italy during the summer of 1990. Fans across the island were making plans to be there, whatever it took: cars were sold, bank loans were up and credit cards were maxed out. The gruff Englishman had indeed found the key to realising the team's possibilities while at the same time igniting an inherent passion for the game.

This success overlapped with a new confidence that was manifesting throughout the Republic. Young people were staying home rather than following family overseas, particularly to the US, as better-paid jobs and career opportunities began to materialise. The Catholic Church was still dominant, but scandals were on the horizon that would bring an end to its grip on all corners of Irish society. The first six months of the new decade would see Ireland begin a six-month presidency of the European Union, which brought political leaders in gleaming black cars to Dublin Castle for a special European Council meeting where, following the fall of the Berlin Wall, a historic common approach to the unification of Germany was agreed. The Taoiseach, Charles Haughey, was in power for the second time and enjoying the moment, while in London, Margaret Thatcher was losing her grip on her party due to a split on European policy. According to the economist and journalist David McWilliams, 1990, for the Republic of Ireland, 'can be seen as a bridge between the economic darkness of the 1980s and the renaissance light of the 1990s'.

But in the North, the conflict was entering its fourth decade, its people apparently resigned to the everyday cycle of violence and political stalemate. The Englishman at the centre of attention here had a very different role to play than Charlton.

When John Stevens, who would later be knighted, boarded a Sunday evening British Airways flight at Heathrow bound for Belfast in the first days of the New Year, he was surprised to find two well-known London-based security journalists making the same trip. When he asked why, they told him they were going to cover the raids on UDA leaders *he* had planned for the following Monday morning. The deputy chief constable of Cambridgeshire Constabulary was on his way to Belfast to oversee the arrest of Brian Nelson. He knew immediately there had been a malicious and extremely damaging leak. But the discovery was only the start of his troubles.

Later that evening, at his hotel, he received a telephone call that alerted him that the offices used by his inquiry team at the Seapark Complex outside Carrickfergus on the north shore of Belfast Lough were ablaze. His team, preparing for what was supposed to be an arrest operation the following morning, had left the offices late in the evening. Some of them returned unexpectedly around 11 p.m. to discover the fire, by which stage most of their headquarters had been destroyed. Heat-sensitive intruder alarms installed at the inquiry headquarters had failed to work and telephone lines had been cut. There was no water in the sprinkler system.

Stevens said later that, despite an RUC investigation finding it had been an accident, he believed the fire was a deliberate act of sabotage, probably by the British Army's FRU, designed to curtail and disrupt his investigation. He later admitted to the BBC reporter John Ware, for a *Panorama* programme, that he'd had a vague warning of a threat to his inquiry. 'We were given some notification that something might happen and that's the reason we had another duplicate office in Cambridgeshire, where we had statements which made sure that, when the fire took place in the headquarters, we could continue with the inquiry.'

As Stevens dealt with the fire, Nelson took the intelligence files from the house where he kept them on the Glencairn Estate and left Northern Ireland for England. It was believed he was ferried out by his army handlers. But twenty-four hours later, on the morning of 12 January, officers from Stevens' team caught up with Nelson, arresting him. The head of intelligence for the UDA and British Army agent was charged with a total of thirty-five offences, including two counts of murder and a further thirteen charges of collecting information for use by terrorists.

Nelson, whose fingerprints had been found on security montages and documents examined by the Stevens team, immediately admitted his role as an agent and took the self-serving decision to tell the Stevens team his version of events. Over two months, while he was being held in Crumlin Road Gaol awaiting trial, Nelson provided the Stevens team with a 650-page statement, now generally known as the 'Nelson Diaries'.

He started with the facts: 'I, Brian Nelson, wish to make a statement. I want someone to write down what I say. I am Brian Nelson, aged 42 years. I am the Senior Intelligence Officer for the whole of Ulster employed in the UDA and also Military Intelligence.'

The English policemen had managed to charge Nelson despite the obstructions of the British government, MI5, RUC and FRU. Stevens had consistently been told there was no military intelligence unit operating in Northern Ireland. However, the Nelson Diaries proved these assertions to be lies; the statement laid out the role his handlers had played and the knowledge and detail they had of murder after murder, including the UDA's killing of Pat Finucane in February 1989, as well as of the video that had been filmed at the South Down UDR base that led to the death of Loughlin Maginn.

In his report, Sir Desmond de Silva sets out the background to the Nelson arrest and the obstacles Stevens overcame before charging him. In September 1989, four months ahead of the arrest operation, the Stevens team had gone to the British Army's headquarters in Lisburn for a meeting. At it, they asked a senior officer a simple question: do you run agents? According to a note of the meeting: 'His reply was to the effect that the role of the army in Northern Ireland was primarily to assist and support the Royal Ulster Constabulary and that therefore the army did not itself use informants.' The same officer said in a statement a month later that he was under orders not to cover any 'secret intelligence matters' with Stevens. The officer who had given him those orders later told Stevens that he himself 'was under instructions based upon Special Branch advice that no reference should be made to any of the army's covert intelligence gathering agencie [sic]'. De Silva found the army's denials 'a conscious obstruction of a criminal investigation'.

But that was not the only way in which the army was aiding Nelson. He had a house, set up for him by the FRU on the Shankill Road, in which he could keep and maintain all his intelligence documents. After the Stevens team's first meeting with the army officers in Lisburn, the FRU went to the house and seized 'Nelson's intelligence dump'. However, John Stevens did not become aware of the intelligence dump until after Nelson's arrest, when the FRU finally handed it over. In it, Stevens discovered 'a significant quantity of leaked security force information, including the montage photographs relating to Loughlin Maginn'.

Stevens now knew that Nelson was getting material from both the army and the RUC.

***

While Nelson was unburdening himself, the IRA in South Down was working on the Ballydugan Road, which runs from Downpatrick to Clough. Shortly after 7 a.m. on the morning of 9 April 1990, two UDR armoured Land Rovers from the regiment's 3rd Battalion left Ballykinler Barracks with orders to travel to Downpatrick. The IRA had spent the previous day planting a 1,000lb bomb in the culvert that ran alongside the Ballydugan Road, halfway between Ballykinler and their destination, running a command wire to a vantage point in an adjacent field.

As the Land Rovers made their way along their route, an IRA scout alerted the terrorists. They detonated the huge device as the vehicles passed, blowing a fifty-foot-wide and fifteen-foot-deep crater in the road.

Four UDR men – Private John Birch, Lance Corporal John Bradley, Private Michael Adams and Private Steven Smart – died in what was described by one eyewitness as a 'scene of utter devastation'. It was the UDR's biggest loss of life in a single attack for several years. The two members of the IRA in South Down responsible for the bombing escaped on a motorbike that was later found burnt out in Downpatrick. In the aftermath, police arrested a total of sixteen suspects and charged one – a scout – who was sentenced to fifteen years in prison.

Almost a year to the day later, the RUC had intelligence that the IRA was planning to launch a horizontal mortar attack near St Patrick's Avenue in Downpatrick. Officers from the RUC's Divisional Mobile Support Unit and E4A, covert surveillance specialists, were tasked to the area and dug in around what they believed would be the firing point.

Accounts differ as to what happened next but, shortly after 10 p.m., the leader of the IRA in South Down, Colum Marks, was shot and seriously wounded. Despite his wounds, Marks was conscious and able to speak to the police officers before he was taken to hospital. He died there in the early hours of the following morning, 11 April. The IRA released a statement, saying he had been on active service.

The death of Marks has been a consistent source of controversy in the area. The police officer claimed that he only opened fire as the IRA man was running towards him. However, the Marks family said forensic evidence suggested that he had been shot three or four times in the back and could not have posed a threat. The IRA commander was not carrying a weapon at the time, although a 'ready to fire' Mark 12 mortar device and a radio transceiver were found at the scene. A second man was arrested, while a third managed to escape.

For the RUC and security forces, the death of Colum Marks was seen as the removal of a major player in the South Down area. In 2017 Jim Shannon, a former TA soldier who had been discharged in 1989 due to his association with loyalist extremists and is now DUP MP for Strangford, claimed that Marks had personally detonated the bomb that killed the four UDA soldiers on the Ballydugan Road. Shannon said, 'it was no surprise that when he was shot the activity of the IRA in South Down stopped immediately. That is obviously an indication that he was the person not only pulling the strings and dictating, but taking part in action that was completely unacceptable.'

In May 2023 the Public Prosecution Service announced that new forensic evidence introduced by the IRA man's family, which supposedly challenged the state's version of events, was inconclusive. As a result, the officer would not be prosecuted for shooting Colum Marks.

***

The summer of 1990 was all about the World Cup and the exploits of Jack Charlton's team. In Italy a 5–4 penalty win in their second-round game against Romania made national heroes of goalkeeper Packie Bonner, who made a critical save, and David O'Leary, who held his nerve while the nation held its breath to score the winning spot kick and send the team to Rome, where they would play the hosts in the quarter-finals.

Ireland was in no man's land as far as its history of playing in international tournaments was concerned. Fans in every town and village whipped themselves into a frenzy. Before Charlton, they were barely winning matches; now they were in the last eight of the World Cup.

It seemed as if the island, North and South, came to a halt on that warm summer evening as the two teams lined out at the Olympic Stadium, the Italians typically tanned and handsome against Charlton's pasty-faced journeymen. Bonner, the hero just days before, threw a left-handed punch at a shot from AC Milan's Roberto Donadoni, only for the ball to fall directly into the path of Italy's surprise star at the tournament, the diminutive Salvatore Schillaci. The striker scooped the ball home with his sweet right boot. That was to be the deciding score.

Ireland had gone further than anyone dared to believe possible beforehand and came home to an open-top bus parade through Dublin, the streets lined with 500,000 fans, according to some estimates. Reporting on the homecoming, the *Irish Press* said it was 'like the Ayatollah's funeral. Jack Charlton saying: "If I live to be a hundred, I don't think I'll forget what I've just seen out there."'

In the world of Down Gaelic football in April 1991, the same month as the Colum Marks shooting, the footballer Ross Carr was facing a difficult decision. Having secured All-Ireland Minor success in 1987, two years later Pete McGrath had been promoted and was now managing the Senior football team. But there was no real expectation of what was to come.

'I wouldn't go so far as to say that things were building,' said Carr, the Clonduff footballer born with an educated left foot, which he wielded to devastating effect. During the winter of 1990–91, he had been among several players who opted not to play in the National League. This depleted squad was likely a central reason for Down's subsequent relegation from League One, prompting County Secretary Brian McAvoy to tell the County Convention in January 1991 that 'too many Down players lack pride in wearing the red and black and fail to give the necessary and total commitment which is needed to win championships'.

Despite having serious reservations, the half-forward was coaxed back to training that April. 'I remember rejoining the panel and, I have to say, at that stage as a player I would never have thought we were going to have a Championship campaign with the goal of winning an All-Ireland,' he told GAA.ie later.

In the first game of the Ulster Championship, Down beat Armagh in Newry before meeting Derry in the semi-final. They were seven points up after ten minutes into the second half, but then had Greg Blaney sent off. Joe Brolly then put Derry in front by a point but in the last kick of the game, the number 10 kicked a free from fifty yards out to cries of 'Over the bar, Ross Carr' from the Down fans. They won the replay, with Carr scoring nine points. 'It was really funny, things just began to gather momentum,' recalls Carr. 'From a player's point of view we were thinking then [that] we were just one step away from an Ulster title, [but] we still wouldn't have been thinking about All-Irelands.'

They became Ulster champions by beating Donegal in the final at Clones. Now the panel, having started the season at such a low ebb, began to believe they were good enough to go all the way. In the All-Ireland semi-final against Kerry, a twenty-one-year-old who had started out in the Loughinisland Under-10 team, Peter Withnell, proved to be 'the wrecking ball forward Down had been crying out for', scoring two goals and a point in a game that Down won easily, 2–9 to 0–8.

'We grew up hero-worshipping those Kerry lads,' said Carr, 'I think everybody did. You would have grown up watching that Kerry glory years video on repeat. Yes, we were confident of beating Kerry, but it wasn't because of the history of Down beating Kerry, it was because we were playing well and we felt if we hit form, especially in Croke Park, we'd be hard to stop.'

Neil Loughran, writing in *The Irish News*, recalled it as a defining moment. 'If some of those Kingdom stars were already seeing the light go out on their careers, they were plunged into near darkness that day.'

Down were in their first All-Ireland final for twenty-three years.

***

Since the Jack Kielty murder, with the conviction of Delbert Watson and the rest of the loyalist gang, there had been no further gun attacks in South Down. It was a welcome, albeit temporary, respite for the nationalist community in the area.

After Little's arrest and the arms shipment, Ian Paisley was now denying he had anything to do with Ulster Resistance. Unionists who had taken to the streets in protest at the Anglo-Irish Agreement had given up and were learning to live with the Dublin government having a say in the affairs of the North. Thatcher had appointed Peter Brooke as Northern Ireland Secretary of State in 1989, and he would be her last man in Belfast before she was deposed by her party in November 1990. Brooke, a personable and engaged individual compared to his predecessors, attempted to initiate political talks between the constitutional parties. At the time, SDLP leader John Hume had little faith in the intentions of unionists or the British. In any case, he was already involved in discussions with Sinn Féin President Gerry Adams in a process that would become known as 'Hume–Adams', which would be the genesis of the peace process to come.

The conflict was entering its final, deadliest phase. The IRA was bombing London, firing mortars at 10 Downing Street in February 1991, for example, and targeting high-profile economic targets. In Mid Ulster, 'King Rat' Billy Wright – now believed to have been a British agent just like Jackson and Mitchell – was killing with impunity. His UVF unit shot dead four men – including three IRA volunteers – in an attack at a pub in Cappagh in East Tyrone a month after the IRA attempted to bomb Downing Street.

Later in 1991, while the Down Gaelic footballers were preparing for another visit to Croke Park, for the All-Ireland final, loyalists made their way south too, planting a series of incendiary devices in shops in Sligo, Drogheda and other towns in the Republic. Ian Paisley's daughter and DUP councillor Rhonda Paisley said the bomb attacks were 'perfectly reasonable given the betrayal' of the people of Northern Ireland by the British government.

An article in the *Derry Journal* responded to her comments by stating: 'over the last ten days, following the UFF incendiary blitz across the Border, the Unionist halo of self-righteous allegiance to absolute rejection of force as a political weapon has been exposed as a sham. The old Carsonite dictum about using force if it became necessary in the interests of unionism, has been shown to be still very much a part of the unionist psyche. Rhonda Paisley led the chorus to what unionism perceives as betrayal by the British, interference by the Dublin government and IRA aggression against Protestants. She revealed her ambivalence about the use of force as the UFF tried to justify their murderous plans.'

Before the bomb blitz in the Republic, the Combined Loyalist Military Command, made up of the leaders of the UVF, the UDA and a smaller terror group, the Red Hand Commando, had spent a period of weeks between April and July 1991 on ceasefire, to allow Secretary of State Brooke to try and get political negotiations up on their feet. When the talks failed, they returned to violence.

Over the summer, it was announced that the UDR was to be merged with the Royal Irish Rangers, a light infantry regiment which only served outside Northern Ireland, to create the new Royal Irish

Regiment. This caused anger amongst unionists, who viewed the move as getting rid of the UDR because of nationalist complaints that it was in collusion with the loyalist paramilitaries – which, it turned out, was exactly what Margaret Thatcher was doing. It was, as far as unionists were concerned, yet another betrayal by the British government. Nationalists took little notice, seeing the merger as a cynical manoeuvre by a London government wanting to avoid responsibility for putting intelligence into the hands of loyalists who had caused the death of dozens of Catholics.

***

Getting your hands on All-Ireland final tickets dominates life for GAA fans from two of Ireland's thirty-two counties each and every summer. It becomes an obsession, with every club in the county at the centre of the distribution network.

Adrian Rogan was from Loughinisland. He was known to everyone as 'Frosty', although even his wife, Clare, couldn't now recall where or why he had picked up the nickname. Frosty was Down football to his backbone and the couple followed the team wherever they played. On Sunday 15 September, he headed south for what promised to be one of the greatest days in the history of his county. The last time Down were in a final – in fact, the last time an Ulster team had gone the whole way – was in 1968, a few weeks prior to the Troubles breaking out on the streets of Derry. This game wasn't going to be a bookend; after all, there was little sign of an end to the violence. But it was a moment.

The world was changing, its socio-political tectonic plates shifting. The Berlin Wall had come down and brought the Iron Curtain with it. Germany was going to be united. Mandela, now free, was going to become president of South Africa. Surely a way could be found to end the conflict in the North?

'The [Down] players were adults and they had been living through the environment in the North with the Troubles and the different atrocities and tragedies going on. I'm not saying you become immune to it, but it becomes just the fabric of life,' Pete McGrath told RTÉ. 'People talk about the difficulties GAA teams had in the North and yes, there was harassment going to training and you were hitting army roadblocks, but that was factored in as just being the way life was at that moment. Footballers are generally durable and can adapt to what's going on around them. We did that, as other teams did also,' the manager added.

It had taken Meath, their opponents in the final, three replays to finally put Dublin down in the Leinster Championship. That didn't mean they would be any easier to overcome. It would be the opposite, if anything.

The Rogans joined an estimated 40,000 Down fans who had been lucky enough to get their hands on priceless tickets and headed south, enjoying the end of summer sunshine. There they turned the famous Hill 16 end of Croke Park into an emotional mass of red and black.

Down ran riot in the first twenty minutes. But Meath weren't going to lie down, and they mounted a comeback that caused the Rogans and the Down fans some nervous moments in the stands, and meant that Down's lead had shrunk to four points at half-time.

Down's lightning start to the second half enabled them to regain control of the game, however. They went on a blitzkrieg, building an eleven-point lead at one stage. Meath had their chances to score too, and did once again begin to narrow Down's lead. In the end, though, Down held on for a two-point win, 1–16 to 1–14, bringing Sam Maguire back north for the first time in twenty-three years.

At the final whistle, the green turf of the Croke Park pitch was swathed in red and black as the fans poured onto the pitch to see Captain Paddy O'Rourke presented with the trophy by GAA President Peter Quinn. It was a defining moment in the history of the county, the Ulster counties and the GAA.

Four weeks after the victory, loyalism in South Down gave its reaction, firebombing the GAA-owned McKenna Hall in the village of Kircubbin on the Ards Peninsula. They doubled down by announcing that, as far as they were concerned, from now on, all members of the GAA were 'legitimate targets'.

The Down victory had hit a raw nerve in unionism. Nationalists weren't allowed to be flag-waving winners and to celebrate a historic sporting victory. The UFF simply wouldn't have it. Loyalists had murdered GAA members in the past, but now they claimed that they were going to go out of their way to target them.

Writing in the *Irish Independent*, its Northern Editor, John Devine, reported that 'the UFF declaration yesterday that the GAA is to be a "legitimate target" for its murder squads was described as "tantamount to a declaration of war" on the whole minority population'. Devine said the threat might even force the British government to finally declare the UDA (which used the UFF as a cover name for its sectarian attacks and murders) an illegal organisation.

The following day, Conor Macauley reported that the UFF had refined its threat: 'individual members of the association who support the IRA will still face attack'. The reporter also wrote how the GAA said it always 'unequivocally condemned' murder and did not support the IRA. GAA President Peter Quinn said the threat was ludicrous, as were the UFF's claims in their statement that the GAA provided funds to the republican paramilitaries.

There was little doubt at the time that the loyalists were reacting to Down winning the All-Ireland and the scenes of celebration that they had witnessed, not only by the red and black fans, but across the North. This was confirmed by Unionist MP John Taylor, who told RTÉ Radio: 'I rather suspect that the flying of those Irish tricolours, which was a political act, has led to the silly response by the UFF.'

Peter Quinn defended the ban on members of the security forces playing for GAA teams. He said the ban was socially motivated, rather than political, and would remain in place while the security forces were deemed unacceptable by the vast majority of nationalists.

Writing in *Fortnight* magazine, Maurice Hayes, a highly respected son of Killough, Co. Down, assessed the wider symbolism of the victory in an article that wonderfully captured the cultural, political and sporting significance: 'The Down team found themselves as standard-bearers for a variety of groups; for GAA clubs in Down and their players and supporters, for the Catholic/nationalist tradition, for the followers of most sports in the county, for the people of Down, for the province of Ulster, and for the "wee north". In an organisation which stresses its all-Ireland commitment, it was ironic to see the emphasis put on bringing the cup across the border. All these groups got good value for their money,' he wrote. 'One Dublin sports journalist depicted the Down followers creeping out from behind barbed wire and under the muzzles of guns to breathe the pure air of freedom. What was almost as noticeable as the match itself and more epic in length and in crowd scenes was the progress of the Sam Maguire cup through the county. One thought of Jack's Army of Ireland soccer supporters and the success of Derry City FC in providing flagships of pride, joy, good humour and togetherness.'

***

The main thrust of UVF attacks in 1991 and into 1992 was coming out of Mid Ulster, led by the notorious killer Billy Wright, who had complete control of the paramilitary organisation in East Tyrone and North Armagh and was lauded by loyalists throughout the North for his brazen yet brutal campaign. Wright had no trust in the UVF's Belfast leadership; he saw them as woolly liberals who had abandoned their socially conservative history.

In November 1991 Desmond Rogers offered his colleague Fergus Magee a lift home from the Hyster forklift factory in Craigavon. On the journey they encountered what they must have thought was a UDR checkpoint on the Carbet Road. Resorting to a tactic that Robin Jackson had used in the murder of the Miami Showband musicians almost two decades earlier, a gunman dressed in army fatigues walked along the stopped cars and, when he came to Desmond Rogers' vehicle, he opened fire, killing both the driver and Magee. The weapon used was a VZ-58 rifle from the 1988 South African shipment. A third man, John Lavery, a Protestant, tried to reverse his car away from the scene. Pursued by the killer, he too was shot dead. The UVF later apologised for killing Lavery.

A twenty-four-year-old loyalist from Portadown, Vicky Ahtty, was later convicted of the killings, along with a number of other UVF murders in the area.

Meanwhile, the IRA were on a bombing campaign in England, where they planted incendiary devices in shops and attacked railway lines. Back in Belfast, they exploded a 500lb bomb at the High Court in the city centre.

The Christmas trees in homes across the North were still up when Wright's gang began the New Year where they had left off, killing two Catholics at a butcher's shop in Moy, Co. Tyrone. Soon after, the East Tyrone Brigade of the IRA murdered eight Protestant workers who had been employed at a security base, when they detonated a landmine at Teebane crossroads between Cookstown and Omagh as the workers' bus passed by.

The start of 1992 also saw Brian Nelson appear in court for his trial. The obvious risk to his military handlers and MI5 was that the full extent of his role and the involvement of the intelligence services would be exposed to the world. But on day one of the trial, Nelson pleaded guilty to five charges of conspiracy to murder and fourteen separate charges of possessing information useful to terrorists. A plea deal had been approved by the lead prosecutor in the case, Brian Kerr – who would later become Lord Chief Justice in Northern Ireland – and was done in the dark corners of the courthouse, ensuring that Nelson's handlers in the British Army, along with the RUC and MI5, were not called to give uncomfortable evidence that would only have confirmed what nationalists already knew. It wasn't the first, or indeed the last, time that the British government would go to such lengths to ensure the deep truths behind collusion were not aired in public.

On the morning of the last Wednesday in January, however, Colonel Gordon Kerr, the commanding officer of the FRU in Northern Ireland, did step into the witness box to give mitigating evidence in support of his agent. He told the court that in order to re-recruit Nelson, he had 'first had to consult with the security service [MI5], but, having done that and gained permission to go ahead ... we then initiated the procedures and brought him back from Germany. From then on he was paid a retainer or a salary.' Kerr said Nelson's identity had been known to the RUC and two senior members of MI5.

Kerr, thrown softballs by Nelson's QC, Desmond Boal – who had been one of the founding fathers of the DUP – claimed that Nelson had advised his handlers of 730 threats to 217 people. 'Nelson was a prolific provider of life-saving intelligence,' Colonel Kerr said. 'The statistics ... are witness to that. I firmly believe that the purpose of running agents is not only to prevent terrorist killings, but also to bring about the arrest of terrorists. There were several occasions when targets for assassination were brought to our notice by Brian Nelson,' he continued, with a breathtaking disregard for the court, facts and truth-telling. No one had been arrested on Nelson's intelligence.

In reality, the trial wasn't a trial at all. Nelson and the British authorities had done a deal. Nelson would get ten years, but he would immediately be shipped out a back door to England where he would soon be released and live his life out in a witness protection programme. The UK government was protecting its warped narrative, knowing it was undermining the judicial process, with the collusion of the RUC and the Department of Public Prosecutions. It was a farce.

John Stevens had to simply take his points, as they say in GAA, with the fact that Nelson was off the streets and was no longer going to target Catholics for murder. The inquiries into collusion by the English policeman and his team would continue for another decade, but the BBC and John Ware would claim in a *Panorama* documentary broadcast in June 2002 that Nelson had been involved in ten murders, all with the knowledge of his handlers.

***

Despite John Stevens' inquiry and the prosecution of Nelson, loyalists still had access to the intelligence documents the former soldier had armed them with, and, after Nelson's conviction, the UDA and UVF went on to commit at least two dozen murders and attempted murders.

They also still had those South Africa-sourced weapons. Two weeks after Nelson pleaded guilty, five men were shot dead in a South Belfast bookmakers with weapons that had come from the South African shipment. The UFF said it shot the Catholics, one of them a fifteen-year-old boy.

In South Down, since the Jack Kielty murder and the conviction of Delbert Watson and his brother Charlie's widow, Doreen, and the others, the rest of the loyalist gang appeared to have gone to ground. But while Ronnie Hawthorne was out of the UDR, he was still seething with sectarian intent and, having connected with members of East Belfast UVF, he did eventually find willing conspirators. On 6 November 1992 loyalists from Clough re-emerged from their apparent hibernation. While they were dark, they had become a fully formed UVF unit, which had little or no relationship with the UFF.

Their first target was a well-known republican, Peter McCarthy, co-owner of a 300-year-old public house called the Thierafurth Inn at Kilcoo, a rural village with a population of less than 1,500, twenty minutes south-west of Clough. Ballymacarrett Recreation Centre in East Belfast is a forty-mile journey away and not somewhere from which you would expect Clough loyalists to launch an attack in South Down. But as an Austin Montego car pulled into the car park at the leisure centre that night, the occupants were met by two men who ordered them out of the vehicle and demanded the car keys. The hijacked vehicle was driven out onto the Newtownards Road and off into the darkness. It was found the following morning at Donard Demesne, at the entrance to Tollymore Forest Park, less than ten minutes from the Thierafurth Inn.

In his report into the Loughinisland massacre in 2016, Dr Michael Maguire, using cyphers so as not to identify them, said he found intelligence that a leading member of the UVF in East Belfast, Gorman McMullan, had directed the theft of the car and its supply to Ronnie Hawthorne, Alan Taylor and Trevor Watson for their attempt to murder Peter McCarthy. However, the attack was ultimately called off and the car abandoned because the terrorists were concerned about security forces being in the area.

Less than two weeks later, on 19 November, an almost identical operation was put in place. This time a Ford Orion was stolen from a house in East Belfast around 6 p.m. by two armed members of McMullan's gang. It was a Thursday evening – darts night at the Thierafurth Inn – and the pub was full of regulars.

Shortly after 9 p.m., two masked gunmen came through the front door. One shouted 'everybody down, nobody move' and then they opened fire with a pump-action shotgun and a 9mm pistol. A local man, who was registered blind, was shot in the shoulder. Two others were also hit, one in the chest and the other in the hip. One gunman pointed his pistol towards four men who were sitting at the bar and shot former schoolteacher Peter McCormack in the back as he tried to take cover. He fell behind the bar and died in a pool of blood. He was forty-two years old and had been living at home with his parents.

The killers then fled in the Ford Orion, which was found burnt out the following morning at another entrance to Tollymore Forest Park.

The UVF, as was custom at the time, called the newsroom of Downtown Radio and, after giving a code word, admitted it was behind the killing: 'The UVF claim responsibility for the attack on the Thierafurth Inn. The IRA commander in South Down was in the pub at the time and he was our intended victim. A more detailed statement will be made in the future.'

Chris Hagan, a South Down native writing for the *News Letter*, painted a detailed picture of the murder and its aftermath: 'The tiny County Down community of Kilcoo began coming to terms with the horror of its first taste of the Troubles yesterday following the UVF gun attack on the village bar which left one dead and three injured. People said that the slaughter could have been even worse and that Protestants could have been killed if the gunmen had struck 20 minutes later on Thursday night. A witness said that teams were due to arrive to take part in an annual charity darts match involving Protestants and Roman Catholics from nearby Dundrum and Newcastle. Barman John McEvoy was behind the bar when the gunmen walked in. He saw a gunman on a security monitor but thought the gun belonged to a police patrol. "One of the gunmen ordered the customers to lie down and not to move. I made my escape as the gunman fired at me," he said.'

A local priest, Fr Charles Denvir, told the paper that some customers thought they had seen three masked gunmen at the door, not two, but, in any case, 'it was all over in a matter of seconds. One or two were in the pool room and didn't see anything but heard the shots. It was a horrible sight. I've never experienced anything like this.'

Over 1,000 mourners attended Peter McCormack's funeral, lining the road from the family farm to St Malachy's church, where they heard the Bishop of Down and Connor urge the grieving community to stretch out the hand of friendship to those of a different religion who want to rid the country of 'all the hatred, of all the injustices and of all enmity'. He told mourners there was a common grief between the McCormack family and the family of a Royal Irish Regiment soldier, Ian Warnock, who had been killed by the IRA just four hours before the attack on the Kilcoo bar. 'Who on Thursday morning knew the names Peter McCormack or Ian Warnock – only their family, friends and neighbours. Now their names are in all the newspapers, on the radio news and on the television screens. Now their families share a common grief, their neighbours are shocked, but by tomorrow their names will have gone from the headlines and the two families will be left to grieve alone, to shed their silent tears. And what of the murderers? At present they will probably shed no tears, their hearts hardened but some day sooner or later remorse will fill their hearts. Human nature can never live with the crimes they have committed. One day, in the secret of their own hearts, tears will flow and they will indeed be bitter tears.'

In his 2016 report, Dr Maguire reported that at 5.15 p.m. on the evening of Peter McCormack's murder, Ronnie Hawthorne and Alan Taylor were in a car (the Ford Orion) that had been stopped at a checkpoint in Ballynahinch – presumably set up by the RUC – along with Gorman McMullan. For the ombudsman to find such intelligence suggests that the officer who stopped the car was aware of the danger the three posed.

The SIO who took charge of the investigation into Peter McCormack's murder was Detective Albert Carroll. He told Maguire's investigators that the Thierafurth Inn was frequented by 'bad people' and queried why the schoolteacher had been in the pub on the night of his murder. According to Maguire's report, 'he was not alone in his view of the pub, which was regarded by some police as being associated with republican paramilitaries. This commentary by a senior police officer charged with the investigation is considered to be poor practice and suggests a lack of objectivity,' he added, with serious understatement.

But Albert Carroll had at least spotted the link between the two cars hijacked in East Belfast and abandoned on the edges of Tollymore Forest Park, ordering a forensic examination of the Austin Montego. Nothing was found.

Maguire says that in mid-1993 RUC Special Branch received an intelligence report that Gorman McMullan had 'summoned' Ronnie Hawthorne, Alan Taylor and Trevor Watson to a building in Dee Street in the staunchly loyalist Lower Newtownards Road, which was, and remains, a UVF stronghold. There, McMullan handed over the keys to the Orion car and provided them with boiler suits – the garment of choice for loyalist gunmen at the time due mainly to the fact it could be easily removed and destroyed, which got rid of any forensic evidence of use to police. The shotgun and the handgun had been picked up at a 'location outside Newcastle en route to the murder'. Maguire didn't provide any further detail on where the weapons were being held or by whom. The source had told police that Thursday was chosen specifically because it was darts night, when the pub would be busy.

Like so many intelligence reports at the time, it was marked: 'no downward dissemination/Slow Waltz'. Or, in other words, the RUC Special Branch was ensuring (a) that no one actually investigating the murder, i.e. Albert Carroll, was given sight of the intelligence and (b) that a decision had been taken not to do anything urgent with the intelligence at all, thus ensuring that their source, or agent, was protected above all else, but particularly from any risk of imprisonment.

Maguire said in his report: 'The Special Branch Officers responsible for obtaining this information ... told my investigators that their routine procedure was to forward such intelligence to their Special Branch

Headquarters, where decisions were made as to whether it should be disseminated to CID. On occasions they also informally briefed detectives investigating the crime to which the intelligence related but could not recall if this was done in respect of the information concerning Messrs McCarthy and McCormack. [Albert Carroll] states that he did not receive such intelligence and my investigation has seen no evidence that it was shared with him.'

***

The new UVF gang had tasted its first blood. They had killed a completely innocent, decent man who was doing nothing other than having a pint in his local pub with his friends and neighbours. But as far as the paramilitaries cared, they now had a new team with a proven ability to murder. Many paramilitaries swear an oath but do little more than pay their monthly subs. Ronnie Hawthorne and Alan Taylor were now tried and tested killers. They were now assets for the UVF, ones the organisation decided to use to lethal effect again almost immediately.

Five days before Christmas 1992, Martin Lavery, his wife, Teresa, and three of their four children were at home on the Crumlin Road in North Belfast. It was a Sunday evening, dinner was over and the house was full of festive excitement. One of the Catholic man's daughters was cheerily chatting on the telephone to a friend while her twelve-year-old brother helped his mother wrap presents in the living room, where Martin was playing around with their youngest, Danielle. A maintenance worker with the Housing Executive, he had suffered for years from crippling back pain and only gained some relief and comfort from lying on the hard floor.

Earlier on the same evening, another family in the loyalist Ottawa Street area, minutes away in the Woodvale area of the Shankill Road, were also preparing for Christmas when three men – two of them wearing balaclavas – forced their way through their front door. The man who had opted not to wear a mask grabbed the keys to the family's Ford Escort car and left. Fifteen minutes later, having pulled out the landline telephone, the two men in balaclavas ran out of the house and into the Ford Escort. They headed out onto Heather Street and turned left onto Cambrai Street before taking a final left turn in the direction of the Crumlin Road.

The scene in the Lavery family home was one being replicated the world over that Sunday before Christmas Day – that is, until Ronnie Hawthorne and Alan Taylor burst through their back door. They were the men in the masks. Now armed with a Browning 9mm pistol, they tore through the kitchen and into the living room.

Years later, Danielle Lavery said in an interview that she could still remember the feeling of the whoosh of the bullets passing through her tiny fingers and into her father's chest. Two minutes earlier she had been telling him he should go to bed; now Hawthorne and Taylor were standing over him pumping bullets into him.

Teresa desperately reached for anything she could find to defend her husband, her hands falling on a flowerpot, which she aimed at one of the loyalists. He turned the pistol and shot at her, the bullet missing and hitting the wall behind.

Within seconds of the smashing of the back door, the thuds of the pistol and the killers' hasty departure, there were now only the shocked screams of young children who had just witnessed the murder of their father.

Hawthorne and Taylor ran to the blue Escort, which sped off down the Crumlin Road, turning back onto Cambrai Street before they abandoned it on the Woodvale Road. The three UVF terrorists then ran down Rathlin Street onto Disraeli Street and into a loyalist drinking den, the Liverpool Club, where they stripped off their boiler suits, balaclavas and the surgical gloves that paramilitaries were now using to protect their hands from the gun residue left behind after firing a weapon.

Martin Lavery's brother Danny, a Sinn Féin councillor, says the family were told by someone listening in to the police radio of what happened at the club. 'The family were sent word that it was on the police radio that the gunmen were followed by the RUC to a club in Disraeli Street. Whoever that cop was, radioed in and asked for back-up to go in and recover evidence and he was told by his seniors to pull away from it. That was a missed opportunity to catch the gunmen and get the weapon – who ordered that and why?'

According to the report by Dr Michael Maguire, there were no arrests at the club, although police did enter it at some point later and managed to recover part of one of the killers' surgical gloves, which was sent for forensic examination. However, Maguire said the scientists were unable to find a trace of any fingerprints. Furthermore, when police did enter the club, they had apparently seen Trevor Watson with Gorman McMullan inside. Special Branch intelligence indicated that Taylor and Hawthorne were the shooters. Yet, despite the circumstantial evidence and intelligence the RUC failed to arrest any of the gang.

There's an ironic phrase that's bandied about in Belfast: 'There's only one thing worse than getting arrested, and that's not getting arrested.' In other words, the lack of arrests points to a 'slow waltz' strategy being taken by Special Branch, who had an agent they wanted to protect. That was the priority, rather than seeing them brought before a court and sent to prison for life. This was the true outworking of the Walker Report in all its vile glory. The prioritisation of intelligence over evidence; 'big picture building' over conviction.

The murder of Martin Lavery is, unfortunately, another case study in how the primacy of intelligence corrupted the conflict. 'There was no real investigation into Martin's murder. The sledgehammer they brought with them along with bullet casings weren't even removed from the scene. It was only after the press reported on it that they [RUC] even came back for them, I've no idea if they kept that evidence,' Danny Lavery said in an interview with *The Irish News*.

The UVF would later claim responsibility for the killing and again tried to rationalise its actions to its unionist support base by alleging that Martin Lavery was an active member of the IRA. This was denied by his family and, later, by the RUC.

The loyalists weren't finished with the Lavery family, and a year later they would take the life of Martin's nephew Sean Lavery, whose father Bobby was also a Sinn Féin councillor.

Teresa Lavery said that Danielle lived with constant nightmares following her father's death. 'She dreamt that there was this man with an evil face coming into the bedroom to take her away. She wants to know where I am all the time and why I am depressed. And she wants to know how long has she to wait to go to heaven to see her daddy and will he be able to play with her the way he used to,' the grieving mum told a BBC documentary the year after her husband was murdered.

While Hawthorne and Taylor were killing Martin Lavery, Gorman McMullan – their accomplice when they murdered Peter McCormack – waited for their return at the bar in the Liverpool Club with Trevor Watson. Four men from outside the Shankill Road, where strangers were treated with paranoid suspicion that could lead to a violent attack should they say the wrong thing to the wrong person, no matter their religion, were using an illegal loyalist shebeen as their base for murder. This was confirmation that they were trusted and had been elevated by the UVF leadership.

What was also striking about the murder of Martin Lavery was the Shankill Road UVF shipping in a gang from outside their area to do their killing for them. Since Gusty Spence and his gang began murdering Catholics in 1966, the Shankill had produced more loyalist killers per square inch than any other area in the North. It was highly unusual for Gorman McMullan, originally from the Shankill but now living across the city in East Belfast – never mind Hawthorne, Taylor and Watson – to be called in to do the Shankill UVF's dirty work. Dr Maguire was unable to explain how the relationships had been formed or why the South Down gang were called on by the Shankill Road UVF.

It was also unusual for the four to be involved in murder outside their own area barely a month after they had shot and killed Peter McCormack. Usually paramilitaries on both sides lay low after an attack, to keep out of the way so as not to raise any unnecessary suspicion. What is clear is that, as they partied on the Shankill with their new friends, the RUC missed an opportunity to stop them before they would kill again.

In any case, the RUC detectives investigating Martin Lavery's murder never arrested any of the four-man gang. Dr Maguire was unable to explain how the relationships had been formed or why the South Down gang were called on by the Shankill Road UVF.

Special Branch had supremacy over their CID colleagues, and it would be the intelligence division that would be the first to crack the gang, although, as the people of Loughinisland were to learn much later, that would do nothing to prevent more innocent deaths at their hands in South Down and beyond.

6 | A Night in November

The Martin Lavery murder, and the role of the Hawthorne, Taylor and Watson gang, may have provided an early indication of the shift in the balance of power between the urban and rural leadership within the UVF at the time.

Just as he had in 1992, Billy Wright welcomed the New Year with the death of more innocent Catholics in his Mid Ulster area. Patrick Shields, living in a home attached to the family shop on the crossroads of a hamlet called Lisnagleer close to Dungannon in Co. Tyrone, was planning on spending the night attending the wake of a neighbour and so had gone to bed for a nap early on the evening of Sunday 3 January. When Wright's gang burst in through the family shop, they shot Patrick as he slept. Then they went back downstairs and, in front of his wife and twelve-year-old daughter, shot his sons Dabheoc and Diarmuid. Dabheoc would survive, but twenty-year-old Diarmuid died. Their mother and sister managed to blockade themselves into an adjoining room. Tragically, Diarmuid's heartbroken girlfriend, Julie Statham, took her own life a few weeks later.

At the funeral of Patrick and Diarmuid Shields, the local parish priest, Monsignor Liam McEntegart, said Patrick's only crime was that he was a Catholic and a lover of Gaelic football. 'Let us leave the purveyors of this foul deed to their consciences,' he told mourners. A thirty-one-year-old man, Laurence Maguire, later confessed to the murders, along with three others, and was jailed for life. Maguire said he had shot Diarmuid and his brother, while another UVF member of the gang had murdered Patrick.

More killings followed. Later in 1993, brothers Gerard and Rory Cairns were murdered in their home in Bleary by the same UVF gang. Wright was in an all-out assault on Catholic families in East Tyrone and North Armagh, whether they had connections to the republican movement or not. 'The message we were sending out to the IRA was quite clear: if we can't get you, then we will get your nearest and dearest,' Wright was reported as saying. 'We hit them where it hurt them most, their own families. In the early 1990s the IRA in east Tyrone began to hurt. They were now experiencing the same pain as they had inflicted on the Protestant community for years and they didn't like a taste of their own medicine.'

There is considerable speculation that Billy Wright was an agent working for MI5 or the Special Branch. In a BBC documentary broadcast in 2019, Laurence Maguire – who had driven the getaway car when sixty-three-year-old Charles Fox and his wife, Teresa, were murdered at their home in Moy, as well as killing Diarmuid Shields – told reporter Mandy McAuley that his directions came from Wright, who told him the intelligence that helped him select his targets came from the RUC.

Where they were getting the arms to carry out their murders is not subject to any speculation. That is because it is an established fact that the murders of the Cairns brothers, the Foxes and the Shields were all committed with weapons shipped in by Noel Little, Ulster Resistance and the loyalist paramilitaries – the VZ-58 assault rifles.

The decision to, at the very least, allow the 1988 arms shipment through – or indeed to support loyalists' attempts to rearm – was now coming at a considerable cost of innocent lives.

***

During 1993 the UDA issued a statement, albeit one that only confirmed what the nationalist community in the North already knew was happening. The loyalist group said that it was now planning to target anyone it considered part of the 'pan-nationalist front'. In reporting the story, *The Times* said it believed this meant that members of the GAA, the SDLP, Sinn Féin, the Irish government and the IRA were the UDA's intended targets.

Ever since John Hume announced that he had met Sinn Féin President Gerry Adams for the first time in 1988, unionist politicians had been using the 'pan-nationalist front' phrase. Writing in the *News Letter*, political editor Mervyn Pauley reported a senior Ulster Unionist MP as saying that talks between the two leaders made clear that Hume was seeking 'a united nationalist-Republican front in support of the Anglo-Éire Agreement', meaning the Anglo-Irish accord signed by Thatcher and FitzGerald in 1985. It was a very basic misreading of the Hume–Adams initiative, given that the IRA and Sinn Féin had themselves denounced the Anglo-Irish Agreement.

Despite John Stevens' inquiries and the conviction of double agent Brian Nelson, loyalist paramilitaries still had access to significant intelligence and weaponry. The Shankill Road UVF may have faced challenges that necessitated calling on Ronnie Hawthorne and Alan Taylor to do their killing for them, but in South Down and Mid Ulster the loyalist witches' brew created by British intelligence, the army and the RUC meant nationalists were suffering a wicked fate.

The 9mm Browning pistol that Hawthorne and Taylor had used to murder Martin Lavery at Christmas 1992 was brought out of hiding again two months later and this time it was for a target in South Down.

James Rice was what would be described in the media as a well-known and prominent republican. In 1981 his brother had been convicted of the attempted murder of an RUC officer, following an incident where a police patrol had been lured to a house in Castlewellan where the IRA was waiting. One officer suffered a wound to his neck when he was shot as he approached the house. Rice's brother was given a fifteen-year jail term for his part in the attack.

James lived in Castlewellan and was well known to the UDR, who regularly stopped and questioned him at checkpoints. In 1990 the UVF had tried to kill him at his home. Three weeks before Christmas, they had broken into his house and made their way to his bedroom, where he was asleep. He had been hit in the leg and wrist before the pistol jammed, which saved his life.

Just eight weeks later, in February 1993, they again tried to kill Rice. He was in his car on the Boucher Road in Belfast, a busy commercial route lined with large DIY stores and car showrooms, when he was approached by a masked gunman who opened fire with a Browning pistol, hitting him in the right leg and right hand. The UVF gunman made off in a Fiat Uno car, which had been hijacked in North Belfast the night before.

Six spent cartridges and the bullet heads found in James Rice's car confirmed that it was the same gun that had been used to murder Martin Lavery. The fact that Rice came from South Down and had been targeted before confirms that, regardless of whoever carried out the attack, the threat against his life emanated from local loyalists. Hawthorne and Taylor had gone to Belfast to murder Martin Lavery – had they made the same journey with the support of Shankill Road UVF to kill James Rice? Dr Michael Maguire failed to find evidence to make the connection, although his investigation confirmed that it was the same gun used in both attacks.

There was no doubt about the next UVF attack in South Down, one which would have repercussions for Ronnie Hawthorne and the gang.

Four months after the second attempt on James Rice, the loyalists' next victim was one of his neighbours in Castlewellan. John Henry Smyth had acted as an agent for Sinn Féin council candidate Sean Fitzpatrick in the elections held just three weeks earlier – a decision that may have brought him to the attention of the Clough-based UVF. He was asleep in bed with his wife just after 11.30 p.m. on Monday 7 June, when masked gunmen attempted to break down the front door to his home at Burrenwood Park in the town. The killers couldn't get through the fortified door but refused to leave without attempting to murder their target. They blasted four shots through the bedroom window where Smyth and his wife were sleeping. The couple's two children, aged seven and nine, were in a separate room. Miraculously none of them were injured. The gunmen escaped in a blue Volvo 440 car that had, yet again, been stolen in East Belfast the night before. After the attack, the vehicle was dumped beside a holiday caravan park at Corrigs Avenue, on the outskirts of Newcastle, less than ten minutes away from the Smyth home.

The *Down Recorder*, established in 1836, is one of the main newspapers in the county and would be particularly focused on the unionist community. Two days after the attack, it carried a report that was extremely revealing, although the paper likely would not have realised its significance at the time. 'Police believe the gunmen who attacked the Sinn Féin worker's house in Castlewellan on Monday night were from the same gang which attacked a Kilcoo pub last year,' read the first paragraph. The final sentence said, 'Police believe the attack bears a number of similarities with the attack on the Thierafurth Inn last year when local farmer, Mr Peter McCormack, was murdered by UFF [*sic*] terrorists and three other men [were] injured.'

At the time, it was usual for RUC press officers to brief local newspaper editors on terrorism in their area, even if it was just the version the police wanted the press to hear. They tended to provide whatever background the CID and Special Branch allowed them to put into the public domain. What the *Down Recorder* story confirms is that the RUC was not only aware of the existence of the UVF South Down unit and its links to Gorman McMullan in East Belfast but was prepared to tell a newspaper these critical details about the gang's actions.

Dr Michael Maguire read the Special Branch and CID files on the attempted murder: 'This attack was subsequently linked, by intelligence, to the UVF unit believed to have been responsible for the attack at Loughinisland. [Trevor Watson] was arrested on 10th November, 1993 as police suspected he may have been the driver of the Volvo. Police Officer 5, a Special Branch officer based at Newcastle police station, told my investigators that he understood that CID had established that an unidentified witness had recognised [Watson] at the crime scene.'

One of the most senior detectives in the area at the time was Albert Carroll. Despite the fact that the *Down Recorder* had been briefed on the connection between the attempted murder of John Smyth and the killing of Martin Lavery, Carroll told the police ombudsman's team of investigators that 'he had no idea who was responsible for the incident [the attempt on Smyth's life] and was not aware that [Trevor Watson] might have been the driver of the car or that he had been arrested in connection with the offence.' This was despite the fact that Carroll was the SIO in the case.

Dr Maguire further revealed that, in 1993, police received intelligence that Ronnie Hawthorne, Alan Taylor and Trevor Watson had been responsible for the attack. However, none of the men were ever arrested or interviewed. 'In the context that the detectives investigating the attempted murder of Mr Smyth generated the grounds for the arrest of K [Watson] through their own inquiries; I have found no evidence that the intelligence held by Special Branch concerning the involvement of Persons A, M & K [Hawthorne, Taylor and Watson] was disseminated to the investigating officers,' he wrote.

In other words, Special Branch had allowed a local newspaper to be tipped off that they knew who was involved, but didn't tell their own colleagues, those trying to put the killers being bars. Though it could also be the case, of course, that Albert Carroll had simply forgotten the details by the time he met with the ombudsman's team in 2015.

***

In July 2016 Martin Lavery's widow, Teresa, two of their children, Patrick and Danny, and his brother Danny walked through Belfast city centre on their way to a meeting at the offices of their solicitor, Niall Murphy. They had already filed a complaint with PONI about the RUC's handling of the investigation into the murder, believing there was evidence of collusion between the killers and security forces. The meeting was with the two PONI investigators who were leading the inquiry. The family hoped to receive an update and to push for further action in the case.

'The Lavery family have asked for this meeting to formally request that their case be referred for individual investigation and report,' Murphy wrote in his note of the meeting. One of the investigators explained, 'Your complaint has been fully accepted for the purposes of investigation, however the only issue is the systemic backlog and delay in the capacity of the office to do our work. We don't know where it sits in the priority matrix.' The other added, 'You should, or Niall should, write a strong letter to the Ombudsman setting out why you feel that the case should be investigated sooner rather than later, stressing why you feel it is imperative that the case be promoted further up the priority list.' Teresa Lavery responded that these delays and the lack of any answers were 'very difficult to come to terms with after these years'.

The investigators laid out their understanding of police actions at the Liverpool Club after the shooting. 'The murder was at 7.35pm and the getaway car was abandoned by the gang at the Woodvale Road, and was recovered by police at 7.51pm. As stated in the report, Police believed the Liverpool Club was frequented by members of the UVF and was easily accessible from the location at which the blue Ford Escort had been abandoned, however it wasn't searched until 8.15pm and the latex glove was recovered from the toilet bowl. I suppose that it is 25 minutes, whether or not that could be held to be "standing back", I don't know,' one of them told the family.

Niall Murphy then got straight to the point. Were any of the UVF men involved in the murder of Martin Lavery state agents? One of the investigators answered: 'The intelligence that I looked at, leads me to believe that one of the persons believed in the intelligence to have murdered Martin ... at the time of Martin's murder, he wasn't [an agent]. He became an informant in 1993. He was never arrested for Martin's murder, despite the intelligence that he had been involved in Martin's murder.'

Danny Lavery asked, 'Did he supply police with much information when he started working for them?'

To which the investigator responded: 'He didn't supply much information about anything ever.'

Following the meeting, Niall Murphy shared his minutes of the meeting with senior officials from the police ombudsman's office. The officials did not dispute the solicitor's written note of the meeting. One of the two PONI investigators was later disciplined and the Lavery family believe he was punished by his superiors for the frank and honest admission that one of the killers in their loved-one's murder was protected from prosecution, which allowed him to go on to commit mass murder.

To recap, what the Lavery family was told was that one of the two UVF men involved in the murder of Martin had become an informer, an agent, in 1993. Then we overlay the findings of Dr Maguire – that following the attempt on John Henry Smyth in June 1993, seven months after the Lavery killing, Trevor Watson was arrested. He was the only one of the gang questioned at that time. Was he the agent?

A detective constable posted to Newcastle in 1990 had realised that there was very little intelligence coverage of loyalists in the area. According to Dr Maguire, who gave him the cypher 'Police Officer 5', he set about 'cultivating sources of intelligence in respect of such activities'. The detective and a colleague soon became aware that Ronnie Hawthorne, Alan Taylor and Trevor Watson 'were leading UVF members in the area with connections to the security forces', according to Maguire. 'In addition, the intelligence identified a relationship between [the three] and [Gorman McMullan], who was a senior member of the UVF with links to East Belfast, but who reported directly to the UVF leadership on the Shankill Road, West Belfast.'

The final sentence confirms the connection that led to the South Down UVF being behind the Martin Lavery murder. Dr Maguire continues, 'Police Officer 5 told my investigators that in 1993 he also obtained information that Persons A, M, K and I had been responsible for the murder of Peter McCormack at the Thierafurth Inn, Kilcoo on 19th November, 1992. Police Officer 5 said that he may have verbally disclosed this information to [Albert Carroll], the SIO responsible for the related murder investigation.'

Police Officer 5, having joined the dots on the attempted murder of Smyth and the Lavery and McCormack killings, consulted with his police superiors on how to best 'manage the risks posed by this UVF unit'. As a result of this focus on the UVF in South Down, the detective developed a 'further intelligence asset'. This was in 1993, the year of Watson's arrest.

The detective was so concerned that he went further and advised Special Branch in Belfast of Gorman McMullan's role. But Special Branch told him that they were 'unsighted' on McMullan, which, according to

Maguire, was untrue. They did in fact 'hold intelligence, albeit limited, in relation to [McMullan] and his suspected terrorist activity'. But they refused to share that information with the detectives investigating the UVF in South Down. 'My investigation identified reliable police intelligence dating from the summer of 1993 that [McMullan] had been hi-jacking cars in East Belfast for use in UVF operations in the South Down area,' Maguire found in his report, repeating that McMullan reported to a twelve-man UVF unit on the Shankill.

We now know that Special Branch knew about Hawthorne, Taylor, Watson and McMullan. The RUC detectives, by the summer of 1993, had also put it all together. The security forces now had the identities and an accurate picture of who was doing what, when and how. And, clearly, one of them was now an RUC agent, as the Lavery family had been told.

Yet, despite having all of this crucial information and an intelligence source within the murder gang, police, following the Walker Report to the letter, took the decision that the killers should be allowed to remain free to kill.

***

The early 1990s had seen a changing of the political guard in Dublin and in Washington DC. A Democrat was back in the White House, following the Reagan and Bush dominance of the 1980s. Arkansas Governor William Jefferson Clinton had been at Oxford in the autumn of 1968 and could vividly recall hearing and reading about the events in Derry on 5 October when the civil rights marchers had been attacked by the RUC. During his campaign to become president, Clinton had pledged to send an envoy to Northern Ireland, although, having actually won the 1992 US presidential election, few believed he would follow through on his pledge. In Dublin, Albert Reynolds had succeeded Charles Haughey as Taoiseach, bringing a very different style of leadership to the role. Often dismissed by the Dublin intelligentsia as a 'culchie' or country bumpkin, his background and his experience in business made him a dealmaker, a man with an ability to make things happen.

Throughout 1993 there was growing speculation as to where the talks between John Hume and Gerry Adams were heading. Secretary of State Peter Brooke, despite all his attempts, had failed to get any meaningful talks process underway. Reynolds was briefed on the Hume–Adams talks and took an intense interest in the North, hoping that he could do something to bring the violence to an end during his time in office. In London, British Prime Minister John Major surprised even many within his own Conservative Party by winning re-election to Downing Street in 1992. Major got on well with Reynolds and in one meeting even admitted to the British government's fatalism regarding the IRA.

'Do you think we can defeat the IRA?' asked Reynolds, according to an official note of a meeting in Downing Street.

'Militarily that would be very difficult. I would not say this in public, of course, but, in private, I would say, possibly no,' responded Major.

In the same meeting, both men spoke of their frustration that the Brooke talks about talks were going nowhere. They needed to come up with a new initiative to break the political logjam, with Reynolds telling Major that he believed the IRA was serious about peace, Sinn Féin having published a document called 'Towards a Lasting Peace in Ireland' just a few days before their meeting.

The statistics backed up Reynolds' firm belief. The IRA death rate had dropped from seventy-one murders in 1987 to a total of thirty-eight in 1993. While remaining ruthless, they were going in the opposite direction to loyalists in terms of their level of violence.

By 1993 loyalists were in fact outkilling the IRA. The UDA's unit led by Johnny Adair on the Lower Shankill Road were vicious killers, known for sledgehammering their way into the homes of their Catholic neighbours in North Belfast, in particular, and killing the first male they encountered.

During the summer of 1993 unionists began to hear from sources in London that something was going on in the background between the British government and the IRA. *The Sunday Times* reported in August that the British government had drawn up a secret peace strategy involving contacts and eventual talks with the IRA. The leader of the dominant UUP, Jim Molyneaux, told Orange Order leaders at that year's 12 July parades that he had been told something similar. The speculation caused unease amongst loyalists, with the low-level paramilitary grouping, the Red Hand Commando, announcing that it would now attack bars or hotels where Irish folk music was played, believing that the traditional tunes were all part of the 'pan-nationalist front'.

Following the attempt on the life of John Henry Smyth, the South Down UVF gang remained quiet, although their UVF colleagues murdered a Catholic man in East Belfast and a prison officer on the same day in September. The IRA exploded a 1,000lb bomb in the centre of Armagh city before calling a seven-day truce to allow a US delegation led by a former Democratic congressman, Bruce Morrison, to visit Dublin and Belfast to meet with Sinn Féin President Gerry Adams, Taoiseach Albert Reynolds and others. The delegation was working behind the scenes with the Clinton administration, encouraging it to become more hands-on in Northern Ireland. The White House had installed Jean Kennedy Smith, a sister of President John F. Kennedy, as ambassador to Ireland, and she was making clear that ending the violence was going to be her number one objective, much to the annoyance of John Major's government, who wanted Kennedy Smith – and indeed Bill Clinton – to keep their noses out of Northern Ireland.

John Hume visited Downing Street that September and told the press afterwards that he didn't give 'two balls of roasted snow' for those who were critical of his continuing talks with Adams. The SDLP leader was very aware of the growing unease within his own party. The Dublin media, in particular the *Irish Independent*, had led an all-out assault on Hume in personal and vicious articles and commentary.

Ian Paisley himself went to see John Major and used his trip to again state that John Hume was the leader of a pan-nationalism, which, for the DUP leader, now included the White House.

Despite all its detractors, the momentum of the peace process was building, slowly but surely, although dark times were still on the horizon.

***

The Shankill Road was the original arterial route between Belfast and Antrim, running from the Glencairn area in the Belfast Hills and down into the centre of the city. Its name is derived from the Irish *Bóthar na Seanchille*, or the road of the old church, which comes from a settlement in 455 AD at the junction of the Shankill Road and Woodvale Road, known as Church of St Patrick and the White Ford. In the autumn of 1993, little had changed there in the past thirty years, the road dotted on each side with small, locally owned shops, their goods spilling out onto the pavements in order to catch the eye of a passer-by.

In the early 1990s the Shankill Road leader of the UDA's C Company was Johnny Adair, who represented the next generation of loyalist paramilitary. Born in the early 1960s and having grown up knowing nothing but conflict, he rose through the ranks in the late 1980s. Brian Nelson was a distant relative. In 2003 *The Guardian* reported that 'Adair's fingerprints have been found on at least a dozen military intelligence dossiers uncovered during investigations by the Stevens Inquiry team into collusion between loyalists and security services.'

Adair and his team were high profile; he was the first loyalist paramilitary celebrity, both revelling in and encouraging the growing notoriety that came with being identified in the Sunday newspapers with every move the UDA made at the time. Bald-headed and with bulging muscles that came from his fondness for steroids, he was an irascible character. His hero was Billy Wright and he wanted to be a Belfast version – a leader taking the war to the IRA. The fact that he appeared to be able to act with impunity only added to nationalists' fear and loathing of the UDA leader.

The IRA had attempted to kill him on a number of occasions. In early autumn 1993 another opportunity to take him out was identified. The UDA's Loyalist Prisoners Association (LPA) was basically an organisation that raised money for UDA prisoners and their families, to help support them financially. Tins would be passed around in loyalist pubs or clubs on a Friday night and no one dared not to drop something in, no matter how broke they were. The group had first-floor offices at 271 Shankill Road. But UDA leaders also used the rooms for their meetings.

On Saturday 23 October, at 1.06 p.m., two IRA bombers, dressed in white fishmonger coats, walked down the Shankill Road towards Frizzell's fish shop, below the LPA meeting rooms. The shop was packed as Thomas Begley set a bomb hidden in a box of fish on a refrigerated counter while his accomplice, Sean Kelly, waited outside the door. The bomb, which had been fitted with an eleven-second timer, exploded prematurely.

The building housing the fish shop and the offices above caved in on itself in a cloud of thick, dark-grey dust, enveloping the men, women and children who had been queuing for the fresh fish the well-known owner John Frizzell, aged sixty-three, sold in his shop, sometimes to the sound of background gospel music. Nine civilians, including Frizzell, his twenty-nine-year-old daughter Sharon and two children were killed along with Begley. Dozens of shoppers of all ages were injured.

By the time news crews arrived at the scene, the anger along the Shankill Road was already palpable. Bystanders were digging at the rubble with their bare hands, removing the dead and injured on makeshift stretchers to a fleet of ambulances that had immediately rushed to the bomb site from the Royal Victoria and Mater Hospitals. It was clearly a republican attack. The bombers had used a stolen Ford Escort – driven by a third man who managed to get away and was never charged – to transfer the device from the nationalist Ardoyne area in North Belfast, only minutes away from the Shankill. The reputed IRA commander in the area was a feared and ruthless terrorist who had also been behind the previous attempts on Johnny Adair's life.

As the morgue filled up with the dead and hospitals dealt with the casualties, the IRA called a Belfast newsroom to admit responsibility. 'The IRA today targeted a regular meeting of UFF activists on the Shankill Road UDA headquarters. Eight hours after the operation not all of our volunteers are accounted for, we can only conclude at this stage that those volunteers are amongst those that were tragically and unintentionally killed by a premature detonation of this device. We regret all innocent deaths and understand the grief felt by those loved ones of all those who died today,' the republican paramilitaries said in a statement.

Within hours, the loyalists had responded, warning of the revenge that was to come. 'As from 18:00hrs tonight that's six o'clock on Saturday on the day of the bomb all brigade and active service units of the UFF across Ulster will be fully mobilised. John Hume, Gerry Adams and the nationalist electorate will pay a heavy, heavy price for today's atrocity, which was signed, sealed and delivered by the cutting edge of the Pan Nationalist Front. And finally, to the perpetrators of this atrocity we say this. There will be no hiding place, time is on our side and to Hume, is this part of your peace process?'

***

Martin Moran was new to taxi driving. He was still in the first flush of fatherhood when he picked up a call to deliver a Chinese meal to Donegall Pass, a loyalist area in South Belfast. His partner, Lorraine, had given birth to their daughter, Amanda, just five weeks earlier, prompting him to work nights to raise cash for his new family. The twenty-two-year-old lived on the nearby Ormeau Road and knew the area well. When he arrived at the address, shortly before midnight and just hours after the Shankill bomb, the UFF were waiting. They shot him three times. He died in hospital forty-eight hours later. The revolver used to murder him had previously been recovered by police and deactivated; however, it had since been put back into the hands of his killers.

The new father was the first of a dozen Catholics who would be killed by loyalists in the following week. On the day of Moran's death, the UVF shot and killed Sean Fox, a seventy-two-year-old Catholic in Glengormley on the outskirts of North Belfast. At the time of his murder, Fox was president of St Enda's GAC.

The following morning workmen were gathering in a council depot at Kennedy Way in West Belfast when a white Citroen pulled into the yard. Two men stepped out of the car, dressed in Belfast City Council-type overalls and fluorescent vests – and balaclavas. They opened fire with rifles, one of which, a VZ-58, had come from the South African shipment, killing fifty-four-year-old Jimmy Cameron and twenty-eight-year-old

Mark Rodgers. Just minutes earlier, the two men had been in a meeting discussing how workers could make a gesture of support for the people of the Shankill Road. Margaret Cameron told a reporter: 'Everybody knew something was going to happen after the Shankill.'

The Shankill bomb had been, ostensibly, an attack on the UDA and UFF. In response, Johnny Adair's associates were responsible for three of the four murders in the three days after the bombing, the killers managing to evade police early in the morning and late at night.

The solicitor for the Rodgers family, Kevin Winters, would later tell a court how there was no evidence 'of any surveillance operation carried out into the individuals who were likely to engage in retaliation for the Shankill bomb'. Just twenty-four hours before the attack on the depot, according to the RUC, the UFF had issued a specific threat against 'Catholic depots' – Kennedy Way was the only depot in the Greater Belfast area that only employed Catholics. The solicitor also revealed that he had seen a redacted document produced by an RUC collator that contained intelligence information about the killers. The document was marked 'no downward dissemination' (NDD), the phrase used by Special Branch to ensure that their intelligence wasn't shared with CID detectives tasked with identifying the killers.

Sixteen loyalists were arrested in connection with the Kennedy Way murders. None were charged. And so the onslaught continued.

The Mid Ulster UVF and Billy Wright didn't need to feed off the outrage at the slaughter of the innocents on the Shankill Road for their act of revenge. Their personal campaign had its own sectarian momentum. They had a particular family in their sights in Bleary, Co. Down.

Five days after the Shankill bomb, Wright's UVF killers travelled to the village, on the day of Róisín Cairns' eleventh birthday, bursting through the back door armed with two VZ-58 rifles. One of the killers put his fingers to his lips to alert the little girl to remain quiet. Her beloved brothers Gerard (22) and Rory (18) were in the living room when the UVF men entered the house dressed in boiler suits and balaclavas. Róisín, at first, believed it was a Halloween prank. That is, until the men opened fire, killing her brothers in front of her.

Laurence Maguire, who admitted to being involved in other UVF attacks in the area, told the BBC that Billy Wright and Robin Jackson had planned the murders a year previously, based on intelligence supplied by the RUC. They wanted to kill Gerard, Rory and a third brother, Liam, simply because they were related to a leading Sinn Féin figure, Sheena Campbell, who had been murdered a year earlier. Liam had been fortunate enough to be at a friend's on the night; otherwise, he too would have been killed.

From that day, the boys' parents, Eamon and Sheila, were convinced there was collusion between the killers and the security forces. Maguire's testimony confirmed this, and he told the BBC's Mandy McAuley: 'The police gave [us the] information they were legitimate targets, and I just didn't see them as anything but legitimate targets.'

Church leaders and politicians in Belfast, London and Dublin all appealed for calm and for an end to the violence. There had been twenty-five years of conflict but, despite the talk of peace, innocents were still dying. A darkness had descended, suffocating all hope. The paramilitaries could still kill when and where they wished, it seemed, and the security forces were unable or unwilling to stop it.

By carrying the coffin of Thomas Begley, the IRA man killed by his own bomb on the Shankill Road, Gerry Adams caused outrage at home and abroad. How could he possibly honour someone who had taken the lives of nine people in such a callous attack? It felt like a pivotal moment for Sinn Féin, the IRA and the growing peace process. Some commentators appeared on television and radio to explain how there were those within the IRA who were opposed to a peace process. The Sinn Féin president did not want to see a split in the republican movement, they argued, and carrying Thomas Begley's coffin sent out a clear message to republicans – he would not walk away from the IRA. For unionists and his detractors in London and Dublin, however, Adams was showing his true colours.

Loyalists had already taken the lives of six Catholics, but they wanted more. Nothing more than a similar number of casualties to those who died in Frizzell's in one 'spectacular' incident would suffice. So it was that, shortly before 10 p.m. on the Saturday following the Shankill attack, two men – one armed with a VZ-58 and the other with a handgun – walked into the Rising Sun Bar in the village of Greysteel, nine miles east of Derry city.

Inside, customers were enjoying a Halloween party. Before they opened fire on those guilty of nothing other than enjoying a night out, the killers shouted, 'Trick or treat, you bastards.' Some of those in the bar initially believed it was a prank.

Nineteen of the sixty customers in the bar were hit when the killer armed with the rifle opened fire, casually reloading before spraying the bar for a second time. The second gunman fired one shot from the pistol before his gun, mercifully, jammed. The pungent fumes of gunfire filled the room. Seven people were dead or dying. An eighth would die a year later from his wounds.

An hour after the attack, the UFF boasted that it was their members who had been involved. It was retaliation for the Shankill bomb and a 'continuation of our threats against the nationalist electorate'.

In one week, twenty-four people had died at the hands of terrorists. The situation was hopeless. Gerry Adams was talking peace, but the IRA's actions drowned out his words. Loyalists had the South African weaponry and a strategy – if you can't kill a republican, kill their mother, father, brother or cousin. And on a Saturday night, a bar full of Catholics – and Protestants – will do.

At the funeral of one of the Greysteel victims, John Hume would break down when a family member told him that they had prayed around the coffin for him the night before. Hume would continue to talk to Adams, but the weight on him, and the families of the innocents dying around him, was unbearable.

***

One month after Greysteel, Jack Charlton and his team boarded a plane in Dublin for the short flight to Belfast. In the midst of all the bloodletting, the Republic of Ireland had to get a result against their northern neighbours in order to ensure qualification for USA 1994. Spain would play Denmark on the same night and the results of the two games would decide who would be joining the Spanish in North America.

Republic of Ireland forward Niall Quinn, born in Dublin, was a hurler and had played in an All-Ireland Minor final before leaving for England and landing a full-time contract at Arsenal Football Club. He remembers preparing for the trip north in November 1993: 'The build-up to it was absolutely tinged with sadness [and] doubt that the game would actually take place. FIFA were saying yes one minute and no the next. Greysteel comes to my mind immediately, always will, you know; the terrible atrocity that happened there. Fans of ours again allegedly, you know, sort of, you know, shot for nothing. Not quite on the eve of the game, but it was a real difficult one for us to get our heads around,' he recalled in an interview for the Fine Point Films documentary *Ceasefire Massacre*. 'You are preparing for the game, you weren't sure the game was going to take place. There were these awful security measures that had to be put in place. And there was frantic toing and froing going on between FIFA, the RUC and our own Garda Síochána to see whether we could actually go over the border.'

Somehow, a football match between the two teams on the island had become a focal point. The Republic represented a cosmopolitan Ireland, at peace with its history and growing in confidence on the world stage, politically, economically – and in sport, too. Northern Ireland was politically stunted and economically stagnant. It was full of hatred and unable to come to terms with its past.

Some wanted the game moved away from Belfast's Windsor Park and played at a neutral venue in Liverpool or Manchester, but football's governing body, FIFA, decided it should go ahead on Northern Ireland's home turf.

'So that was the build-up,' said Niall Quinn. 'It was eerie. And then going to the stadium itself. I mean, we were in our bus. We had armoured cars all around the bus. But I can remember very vividly, and it's something that will stay with me till I die, coming into Windsor Park, a crowd of young, very, very young boys, I would say no older than ten, eleven years of age, all lined up on a little bit of a vantage point, on a little bit of a hill, and all pointing to us with imitation guns and pretending to shoot. And this man, this grotesque man got them then to kneel down and another group stood up behind them and did the same thing. And it was awful. Not a lot of people noticed it on the bus, but I noticed it and I got a knot in my stomach, no doubt about that. These kids, what chance have they got if this was the environment they were being trained into? It was a low, low point at the time generally up there. And we were coming into the middle of all this in a freakish way, you know, trying to get to a World Cup.'

His midfield colleague, Ray Houghton, remembered being told not to sit by the windows in the team bus as it made its way from the airport to the ground in South Belfast. Despite the backdrop and the risk, some Republic supporters managed to get tickets for the match and took their seats, knowing they would risk their lives if they were to show any sign of their loyalty.

When the match got underway, Northern Ireland manager Billy Bingham paraded up and down the touchline, waving his arms to get the fans to raise their voices in hostility. The packed Kop End terrace to his left duly responded with the 'Billy Boys', a chorus which includes the line 'we're up to our necks in Fenian blood, surrender or you'll die'. The match was infected with the heavy mood, becoming an attritional affair, with neither of the teams playing anything close to attractive football.

In the seventieth minute, Northern Ireland took the lead through a Jimmy Quinn volley. The place erupted, led by Bingham, who tore out of the team dugout to lead the celebrations. It was a release for the Northern Ireland fans; finally, something to celebrate, to cheer about. The fact that it was at the cost of the Republic made it even sweeter for the predominantly unionist support.

But three minutes later the game was level again, when Alan McLoughlin scored, much to the delight of the few Republic fans who dared to cheer. 'The safest place to be "that night" was on the pitch itself,' McLoughlin told RTÉ in 2014.

The minutes seemed like hours for Jack Charlton. Even when the final whistle went, the tension remained. The team stood on the pitch, waiting for confirmation of the result between Spain and Denmark. Word eventually came through: Spain had won. As a result, the Republic was going back to the World Cup finals.

'We were in the dressing room and it was a strange situation,' recalled Niall Quinn. 'We had qualified for the World Cup and there was great camaraderie and great spirit. But then we also knew we had been in part of one of the most ugliest political sports nights of all times, you know. It was just dreadful.' He added, 'And the thing that saved it for me, and saved is probably the wrong word, the thing that made it a special night for me wasn't that we qualified, it wasn't that we'd got through it. It was that Alan McDonald, the captain of Northern Ireland and from the Protestant half of Belfast, came into our dressing room and gave a fantastic speech about how we should go and represent this island in America, you know. We are sports people, keep politics out of it, delighted that the game had gone ahead, delighted for you guys, now, go and do it. Prove that on this island that we are great sports people. And everybody gave him a clap and he left the dressing room.'

***

Watching the match in New York was Niall O'Dowd, a native of Co. Tipperary who grew up in Drogheda, Co. Louth. He had left Ireland for America in the late 1970s and settled first in San Francisco before moving east to New York, where he founded the *Irish America Magazine* and later the *Irish Voice* newspaper. 'You were always aware of the fact that the sporting arena was one that reflected the broader Ireland, particularly in Northern Ireland,' he said. 'And that game, there was very nasty circumstances where Ireland finally qualified, you know; it was almost in its own way a significant breakthrough. Because it allowed people to look at this and say: "Do you know what, this is something good; this is going to unite Irish people everywhere, right across the world. And we have a team that we can follow." And do you know what, they are not just all Irish Catholics. There's English guys in there. There's all kinds of different nationalities and people from different backgrounds. This was a sort of a flare for the new Ireland being sent up, you know, saying:

It's not the old Ireland, it's not eleven white guys going out and getting beaten by somebody, it's a different team. All that was factoring in and I think it was embodied in many ways by a guy like Paul McGrath, who was this big, larger-than-life hero to a lot of people. I mean, a Dublin, African guy who just had this great personality and great way of playing. So that was very exciting.'

On top of the day job, O'Dowd had become a transatlantic political go-between, working behind the scenes as part of the attempts to bring peace to Northern Ireland. Using his contacts in the US and in Ireland, he had put together a group of key Irish-Americans who shared the same goal of ending the violence. The IRA had called a ceasefire to allow this group, the so-called Connolly House Group – named after the Sinn Féin headquarters in Belfast – to visit Ireland the month before the Shankill bomb and Greysteel attacks to meet with political leaders on both sides of the border. But, in particular, to deliver a message to Gerry Adams in person: Bill Clinton will be a willing partner in peace but, first, there has to be an IRA ceasefire.

The upsurge in violence since the trip had done nothing to persuade the hawks in the American administration that an end to the Troubles was possible. 'You were at this critical moment in the peace process where things were happening, but also you still had this storm and drag of continued violence and you lived in dread of waking up and many days I did wake up to, you know, the headlines from the BBC or RTÉ or ITV saying, you know, bodies were found, bombs had gone off,' said O'Dowd, interviewed for *Ceasefire Massacre*. 'There was a lot of incidents around Heathrow airport with fake bombs being planted there, which was getting huge coverage here in America. So it was a very fraught and tense time in the sense of, was this all going to work?'

In the weeks after the violence of October 1993, the London and Dublin governments came together with a renewed focus on the North. When *The Observer* in England broke the story that John Major's government had been having secret talks with the IRA, unionists were stunned. Ian Paisley was thrown out of parliament for calling Secretary of State Mayhew a liar, as unionists sought to come to terms with the news.

Albert Reynolds and John Major came together to publish the Downing Street Declaration, designed to foster 'agreement and reconciliation, leading to a new political framework founded on consent and encompassing arrangements with Northern Ireland, for the whole island, and between these islands'.

Ian Paisley reacted in typical fashion, announcing a series of rallies in opposition. However, UUP leader Jim Molyneaux insisted the declaration was not a sell-out, despite what the DUP leader said. Their reactions were a reflection of the mix of hope and fear felt within the unionist community. They wanted peace but had paid a high price in the number of those who had died.

For Reynolds, Adams, Hume and Niall O'Dowd, the Downing Street Declaration meant one thing only for the peace process: it was game on.

7 | The Black North

Listening to a Chicago Cubs baseball game on a radio was one of US-born Bill Flynn's fondest recollections. The fact that he heard the game while visiting Loughinisland was, in part, what made it such a stand-out memory.

His father, who was born in the village, had left Ireland years earlier when he was between eighteen and twenty. It was 'back in the 1880s,' Flynn explained. 'He mined copper. And from there he moved into ship building in Seattle. And when things got slow in Seattle, he moved on to New York where he met Mother and a new life began, and I was part of that new life.'

Bill Flynn was born in 1926, just ten years after the Easter Rising and six years since the establishment of the Northern state, in the New York Borough of Queens. In an interview with the author in 2013, he spoke of the impact his Irish-influenced upbringing had on him: 'The stories of the Troubles in the North of Ireland have been with me since the late twenties, and that's a long learning period, so I was very much aware of the difficulties that Irish people in the North had with the British and with troops and the law. I can remember, during the early days of World War Two, when the British carrier *Hood* was sunk. It was an incredibly sad thing, [but] I know people that cheered that the *Hood* was hit. And it was really terribly sad and it was against the Allies, but the enmity between some Irish, principally from the North, and the British was such that that was [treated as] good news. And I never saw that happen again, but that was very early in the war and there were feelings that were pretty strong,' he recalled, adding: 'You felt a sense of sympathy for an oppressed people, the same feeling oppressed people everywhere elicit.'

Flynn had made his first visit to the village of his father's birth in the 1960s, taking his mother, who hadn't returned to Ireland since she arrived on Ellis Island as a ten-year-old. Many years later, when he spoke to the author, the memory still burned bright of his family and friends gathered around a tombstone radio. 'I was a young fella, and I can remember meeting some of [my father's] brothers and relatives. I remember going [out] one evening to meet a few friends in an underground, I'd call it an underground bar ... a meeting place. It wasn't really a bar, except liquor was served. But it was very dark and the main interest, believe it or not, was a short-wave radio which was on the whole evening with a game out of Chicago, the Chicago Cubs were playing baseball and I never got over why anyone in Ireland would know about the Chicago Cubs. And they loved it.'

Flynn studied for a year to be a priest, but, after thinking better of it, he left to join the US Army Air Corps. Later, he graduated from Fordham University in New York, married his wife, Peggy Collins, and moved into the insurance business, joining Equitable Life Assurance Society. The National Health & Welfare Mutual Life Insurance Association was in difficulties when Flynn was appointed chief executive in 1971. Over the following twenty years, he rebranded it as Mutual of America and made it one of the country's largest financial services firms.

By the time he was in his late sixties, in the early 1990s, he was looking for a new extra-curricular challenge. As a result, his gaze turned to his ancestral homeland. This is what led him to become part of Niall O'Dowd's Connolly House group, which was leading the push for Bill Clinton to become involved in the peace process.

By January 1994 Bill Flynn, who stood tall at six foot three, was at the centre of a diplomatic dispute that threatened what the British liked to call their 'special relationship' with America. And all because he had dared to invite Sinn Féin President Gerry Adams to come to New York and speak at an event. Adams had delivered an IRA ceasefire to coincide with the American delegation's visit in September 1993 – proof for those seeking it that Sinn Féin's push for peace was sincere – and now payback was required. There was pressure on O'Dowd, Flynn and their colleagues to have the US authorities grant Adams a visa to visit New York. He had already been turned down in May 1993. It was time for the Americans' sincerity to be put to the test.

Once Flynn issued the invitation in the opening weeks of 1994, the British government made its position very clear, both publicly and privately. Namely, that giving Adams a visa was rewarding IRA violence. But Albert Reynolds and John Hume were both for it, and between them and O'Dowd's group they managed to persuade Senator Ted Kennedy, a hugely influential Irish-American figure, and, ultimately, President Clinton himself to grant the visa.

Adams travelled to America where he spoke at the National Committee on American Foreign Policy, which had been organised by Flynn. 'Symbolically, it was very important,' Adams told the BBC years later. 'It was important in showing that you could build an alternative ... an alternative to armed struggle. And you could enlist support from powerful people in the USA.'

It was a wake-up moment for the British government, which realised that the White House was now an active participant in the peace process.

Back home, Clinton's decision to grant the Adams visa was ridiculed by unionists and by victims of IRA violence. And the violence did not desist. Ten days after the Sinn Féin leader returned to West Belfast, the UFF launched one of the mortars that had come in on the South African shipment at his party's headquarters in Andersonstown. No one was injured. Days later, the IRA killed an RUC officer and injured two others in the Markets area of the city with one of its homemade mortars.

Throughout all this, the three leaders – Reynolds, Hume and Clinton – were working in the background with Sinn Féin, while John Major's government tried to placate the unionists; however, on the streets of Northern Ireland, the constant cycle of murder, funerals and condemnation continued unabated.

But somewhere between the cracks of violence, a new dynamic was emerging. There was a growing sense of confidence south of the border and among the Irish diaspora. Entrepreneurs such as Flynn and his colleague on Niall O'Dowd's delegation, Chuck Feeney – who was already a billionaire – had made it. Their Irish identity hadn't held them back. They were proud of their heritage and were now in a position to share the spoils of their success. Feeney was a philanthropist and was beginning to give away his fortune; Flynn was determined to help bring peace to the North by using his network and wealth in any way.

Success breeds success, whether in the boardroom, on the stage, or in the sporting arena. That was the message that was beginning to roar out of the twenty-six counties. However, even the most inspired, most optimistic, still struggled to believe that change could also happen in the 'black North'.

**

Two separate loyalist attacks in April and early May spoke directly to the strategy they were continuing to ruthlessly pursue. The UFF murdered thirty-four-year-old mother of two Teresa Clinton at her home on the Lower Ormeau Road in Belfast. Her killers flung a breeze block through her living-room window while she was watching television before opening fire with an automatic weapon, killing her instantly. Her husband, Jim, was a former Sinn Féin election agent. In his report, Desmond de Silva found that the security forces had been aware that Jim Clinton was being targeted by loyalists but had done nothing to prevent the attack. Sinn Féin said that Teresa was the twentieth person to die within five years who had been connected to the party directly or related to a party member.

A month later, on the evening of 8 May, seventy-six-year-old Roseann Mallon was visiting her sister-in-law at her home on the Cullenrammer Road outside Dungannon when the UVF opened fire with another of the VZ-58 rifles, killing her. The loyalists said they had intended to kill the pensioner's nephews, Christopher and Martin Mallon, who were both connected to the republican movement. An inquest was later told that the security forces had two cameras fitted with specialist lenses dug into a field opposite the house, but they were turned off at night to save their batteries. Special Branch had failed to tell their CID colleagues of the cameras' existence or share any of what had been recorded.

The Historical Enquiries Team, set up in by the PSNI in 2006 as a way to set aside Troubles investigations with which the then chief constable, Hugh Orde, didn't want the new modern-day police force to be encumbered, found that the weapon used to murder Roseann Mallon had also been used in the murders of Charles and Theresa Fox at Moy in 1992, as well as in the killing of the three IRA members and a fourth man, Thomas Armstrong, in the UVF attack on Boyle's Bar in Cappagh, East Tyrone in 1991. Billy Wright and Robin Jackson were linked to all the attacks.

'I genuinely believe that we were very successful, and that may sound morbid but they know that we hammered them into the ground and we didn't lose one volunteer,' 'King Rat' told *The Guardian*. 'Indeed, members of the security forces had said that we done what they couldn't do, we put the East Tyrone Brigade of the IRA on the run. It was the East Tyrone Brigade which was carrying on the war in the North, including in Belfast. East Tyrone were decimated, the UVF wiped them out and that's not an idle boast,' he concluded with a statement that was clearly delusional, given that his campaign had been primarily focused on taking the lives of republican families.

Billy Wright and Johnny Adair had little in common. Despite being a sadistic killer, Wright claimed to profess a strong Christian faith, while Adair had been a glue-sniffing skinhead whose charismatic ruthlessness led to his rise in a UDA previously bereft of such dominant characteristics at leadership level. Yet they were similar in their determination to go further than their paramilitary predecessors, and they saw the peace process as a means of placating violent republicanism. Adair had 'Shove Your Doves' painted on a wall in his Lower Shankill housing estate. In the spring of 1994 these two loyalists, above all others, were in a common state of mind – namely, they were in no mood for any peaceniks within their ranks. There were hundreds of loyalists imprisoned in the Maze who would, it was predicted, benefit from any peace agreement if it were to come, but the cost of any such compromise was incomprehensible for the UVF and UFF leaders.

However, if the speculation that Wright, Adair and the vast majority of loyalists were, in fact, active agents was true, then their actions had to be seen as part of a wider British policy, one designed at the desks of MI5 in Whitehall and executed in the homes, workplaces and bars of innocent nationalists. The loyalist surge after the arrival of the South African weapons was, after all, in direct parallel to the Hume–Adams initiative and the growing push for peace by nationalists in Belfast and Dublin in the late 1980s and early 1990s.

As the loyalists' death toll mounted, the question was asked constantly: did Whitehall want a peace process at all? Or were the hawks, or 'securocrats' creating chaos and disorder in the North with the intention of maintaining the conflict until they could militarily defeat the IRA, something John Major had admitted to Albert Reynolds was impossible?

***

Topographically, very little had changed in Loughinisland from the time of Bill Flynn's first visit to when he visited in the 1990s. The village dates back to the seventeenth century, when, according to the records, there were seventeen English and Scots families and seven Catholic families living there by 1659.

When Flynn visited Ireland in the autumn of 1993 with the Connolly House group, he and a close friend made their way to Loughinisland. His friend was Bill Barry, the bodyguard who grabbed the gun from Robert F. Kennedy's assassin in a Los Angeles hotel in June 1968. Barry would blame himself for the senator's death for the rest of his life.

Flynn recalled their visit to Loughinisland fondly: 'Bill Barry is one of the finest former FBI men [and] my bosom buddy. He loved the place. He loves Loughinisland. He's as old as I am, so we have learned to enjoy quiet places. There was a day when we had [a chance] to be in Dublin or Belfast to enjoy ourselves; [but we chose to go to] Loughinisland. It does it all for us. I really grew to love that little place. My first stop – other than the family house – is always the cemetery. There are two cemeteries in Loughinisland, one's the old cemetery and one's the new cemetery. And I have family in both. My grandparents are in the old cemetery. And it's in an area next to old churches … the remnants still standing, and some of the locals told me a story about those churches, how Catholics would go on one day and the others would go on another day. In other words, people got together and respected one another, and you didn't need two churches in a little village, you could have one, provided you were willing to share. I like that.'

While the goal of the Connolly House group was primarily ending IRA violence, they also engaged with loyalists. Flynn became their point man. Niall O'Dowd recalled Flynn's relationship with the paramilitaries: 'He was a John Wayne figure who dominated every room he stepped into [and] his relationship with the loyalists was something to see. On one of our early trips to the North, a loyalist community leader, Jackie Redpath, brought the leadership of the UDA and UVF to see us. To say there was immediate suspicion is an understatement, but Flynn swept it all away,' said the newspaper publisher, adding that Flynn opened up a new dimension to the peace process through his relationships with loyalism.

At the outset of each meeting, Flynn reminded them of his background. 'All throughout I made it clear that I was a son or grandson, if you will, of Loughinisland,' he told the author. He also spoke of the respect he had for the loyalist who had been the first to take up the gun. 'Gusty Spence was really a fine man. How it turned out that he fired the first shot in the armed fight that took place is beyond me. I think myself, though he never said this, we became good friends, he never expressed remorse for firing that first shot, or for his activities, never. Nor did very many express remorse for that. But nevertheless, I could see a man who was full of remorse for what had gone on.'

Years later, the man who played such a pivotal role in gaining the Adams visa would reflect on what he had said in those meetings with the loyalist paramilitaries, and the potential impact they'd had, at a time when those across the table from him were still at war with the nationalist community.

***

There's no evidence that Bill Flynn met Barney Green on any of his visits to Loughinisland, but the two men would have had a lot to talk about, given their shared love of South Down. Barney was fourteen years old when Ireland was partitioned in 1921, five years before Flynn was born. During his short life to that point, he had witnessed the Third Home Rule Bill crisis, the rise of Craig and Carson, the emergence of the UVF, the Great War of 1914–18 and the formation of the Northern state. Still, for the teenage boy from the townland of Teconnaught, outside Loughinisland, the world at war was a long way from his hospital bed in the Abbey Hospital, Whiteabbey, where he spent months, having contracted tuberculosis (TB).

At the time, TB, or 'the disease of the young people', was a serious threat to life. According to research by Professor Greta Jones, Ulster University, 216 persons for every 100,000 of the population died from pulmonary TB in Ireland in 1901, compared with 155 in Scotland and 128 in England and Wales. Barney was a bright and happy child despite his illness. His niece Moira said he became a favourite on the wards of the hospital: 'He got to know all the nurses and he was very jovial; he could have made a bed. He knew how to tuck in the corners,' she remembered.

Later, after recovering, he married his wife, Brigid, and worked in the building trade and farmed pigs at home. Their home became the place to be on a Sunday afternoon, Moira told the author: 'We spent a lot of my time down there and I'd cousins that lived in Downpatrick and they came out on a Sunday and there was always loads of us running about. I can remember we were allowed to play and what not, but if there was a football match on – and in those days it was the radio you were listening to Michael O'Hehir commentating [on RTÉ] – and you had to get away outside or go for a walk, because it was very important. Barney followed the football very seriously.'

Sunday, 29 May 1994 would have been one of those days for Barney Green, and all the other supporters of the Down Senior team. It was a day that would come to define the Mournemen and their opponents, Derry, the reigning All-Ireland Champions.

Frosty and Clare Rogan and their children, nine-year-old Tony and eight-year-old Emma, all made the journey to be in the stands at Derry's Celtic Park for the 'showdown of showdowns' as the Down manager, Pete McGrath, would describe it in the *Belfast Telegraph* as the All-Ireland champions of 1991 and 1993 faced off.

The team trainer, Pat O'Hare, had taken the panel to the brink of their physical abilities. They were in the best shape of their lives. Mickey Linden, already holding one All-Ireland medal, remembered the words of the team captain before they left the changing room. 'Nice guys win nothing,' he told his teammates. 'I've never witnessed a changing room like that before. The hair was standing on the back of my neck and I'm sure the other fellas were the same,' the corner-forward told the BBC. 'We were in the best mental state we could be for that game. When there's a wee bit of hurt in the team, that's when the focus is really there,' he added, recalling the deep open wound of the 'Massacre at the Marshes' the year before, when Derry comprehensively outclassed Down.

The Rogan family went to the final with their friends Willie Rice and his wife, Pat. There were eighteen scores in the first half but little between the two sides. The pace was relentless but when Derry went three points ahead in the second half through a Fergal McCusker goal, the champions looked to be moving up a gear. But almost immediately Down's James McCartan picked the ball up on the forty-metre line and, showing balance, strength and skill, he shook off two tackles to place the ball over the bar with his sublime right boot. The Down fans erupted. 'It was one of the greatest points every seen on a Gaelic football ground to turn the tide,' said Derry's Joe Brolly.

With six minutes to go, Down's Greg Blaney, out on the left, picked out Micky Linden, who laid it off for Ciaran McCabe, who in turn whipped the ball high to the right of the keeper from eight yards out.

'No better man would you want at the end of that pass, Ciaran was a prolific figure,' said Linden later to the BBC.

The final whistle blew and the Rogans, the Rices and the rest of the Down fans behind the goal erupted in a sea of red and black. Down had beaten the All-Ireland champions by one point. 'I think it will always be remembered because of the quality of football that was played and it was probably as sweet a win as we ever had,' said Linden, who had personally run Derry ragged on the day. 'It's definitely the finest game I've ever played in a Down shirt.'

The nationalist community in Down were exultant, but they were about to witness one of their darkest days.

***

Ulster Gaelic football was thriving and the Republic of Ireland football team was preparing for another World Cup, but for loyalists little had changed despite all the efforts to end the violence. Their myopic determination to spread fear throughout the nationalist community remained resolute.

As Jack Charlton's team trained in the heat of Florida ahead of their first game in the World Cup, Maurice O'Kane from Ligoniel in North Belfast was working in the hull of a tanker docked at Queen's Island in Belfast Lough. The fifty-year-old had retired from the shipyard back in 1989 but had returned to work as a welder. Two of his sons were now working in the yards, which made the decision to go back much easier. On 9 June one of his workmates walked past Maurice and asked if he wasn't going to take his tea. 'But he didn't answer,' the docker told a reporter, 'and as he was in a sitting position, I assumed he was working on.' Only later, when his colleagues realised he hadn't moved, did they approach him and discover that he was dead, having been shot in the back of the head.

The UVF later admitted that it had killed the Catholic man in retaliation for an IRA attempt to kill Billy Wright in Portadown five days earlier, an incident where he had got into his car outside his home but immediately noticed something wasn't right and jumped out before the bomb under his seat exploded. Assistant Chief Constable (ACC) of the RUC Ronnie Flanagan described the murder of O'Kane as 'brutal, cowardly and sectarian', but admitted that the RUC had no idea how the loyalists had been able to bring a gun into the shipyard and shoot a welder in broad daylight.

The shipyard was notoriously sectarian, with Catholics having been intimidated and forced to leave their jobs in the past. However, after the killing of Maurice O'Kane, 2,000 of his workmates – most of them Protestants – staged a walk-out. In itself, it was an early indication that members of the unionist community were turning away from the violence and wanted a different future. The Catholic Bishop of Down and Connor, Patrick Walsh, told O'Kane's funeral that his murder had been 'an evil act that would serve no cause'. He said the victim had been a Christian man who had been killed by people facing the wrong way in society.

Despite the encouragement coming from Church leaders, politicians and grassroots unionism, the UVF and the UFF were still addicted to death and destruction.

A week after Maurice O'Kane's murder, leading members of the UVF were chatting in the sunshine on the Shankill Road. One of them was Colin 'Crazy' Craig, who just happened to be a suspected Special Branch agent. After the IRA's failed attempt to kill 'King Rat', Craig had been part of a unit tasked with murdering IRA leader Sean 'Spike' Murray. According to author Aaron Edwards, Craig failed to turn up for the attack, saying his jeep had broken down. Three accomplices were then arrested by the RUC as they prepared for the attack at a safe house. Given the track record of the UVF in Belfast, the idea of them being able to travel into West Belfast and murder a leading IRA man was somewhat far-fetched for an organisation that was more prone to shooting welders as they worked.

Trevor King, the UVF's West Belfast commander, was also present on that sunny day, at a bus stop close to the Co-op store. He had been jailed in 1972 for possessing three rifles and over 1,000 rounds of ammunition.

When he was arraigned for his trial, he told the court: 'As a volunteer with the Ulster Volunteer Force I refuse to recognise the court as it is the instrument of an illegal and undemocratic regime.' The *Belfast Telegraph* reported that King had admitted in police interviews to possessing the weapons. He had served a further sentence in 1976 and, on release, resumed his role with the loyalist paramilitaries, rising through the ranks. According to Sunday newspaper reports, there were growing suspicions that Craig was an informer, although in the history of loyalism there are very few examples of UVF or UFF members being shot for being a 'tout' or agent, certainly compared to the IRA, who ruthlessly and murderously dealt with such treachery.

With King and Craig was another UVF member, Davy Hamilton, who had been King's driver for a period and, therefore, would have been close to the plans being made by the UVF commander.

A two-man INLA hit team was cruising the Shankill Road as the UVF men gathered. Reports differ on how the shooting happened, but when it stopped, Craig was dead and Hamilton and King were both seriously wounded.

Jim Cusack and Henry McDonald wrote in their book *UVF: The Endgame* that 'Hamilton was showing King and Craig some pictures of an album of loyalist murals when a car pulled up beside them. Out of it stepped a gunman who, at point-blank range, shot each of the trio in the head.' Others said the gunman had raked the three from the car or had dropped to his knee, military style, before firing. Hamilton would die twenty-four hours later, and King would be on life support for three weeks before he, reportedly, asked for it to be switched off.

A Protestant minister who was involved in peace talks with loyalists at the time was nearby. The Reverend Roy Magee told BBC reporter Peter Taylor that the scene was one of pandemonium. 'You could see the leadership of the UVF was quite naturally very, very broken and disturbed about the shooting of their colleague [King],' he said.

Reports following the shootings suggested that, as Craig lay on the ground, a senior UVF figure had approached his body and removed an 'RUC panic button' from his pocket. It was also reported in the *Sunday*

Life that his family discovered over £30,000 in his bank accounts. Craig's UVF memorial headstone was later destroyed by his former comrades in seeming confirmation that they believed he was an agent.

The INLA was a vicious breakaway grouping known for some of the worst atrocities of the Troubles. But their ability to single out King and Craig on a busy Shankill Road was out of character for the time. (The INLA killer who shot them, Gino Gallagher, was himself shot dead two years later at a government unemployment benefit office on the Falls Road, as part of an internal INLA feud.)

For those in the North hearing the news, the initial reaction may have been in line with Jesus Christ's words in the Gospel of Matthew: if you 'live by the sword, [you'll] die by the sword'.

However, history dictated that more Catholic lives would be lost in the UVF's lust for revenge.

***

If we take the word of former RUC officers, they say that, by 1994, all the paramilitary organisations, including the IRA, had been 'highly penetrated' by the intelligence agencies, Special Branch, MI5 and the FRU. Their narrative is that the terrorists were aware of the agents within their ranks and were, effectively, looking for a way to end the war.

In the hours after the murder of Colin Craig, with King and Hamilton fighting for their lives, the UVF began planning their response. How the intelligence services were not able to move to prevent the inevitable response, with all the agents and technology available to them at the time, is unfathomable.

As already mentioned, one Special Branch officer admitted to the author that there were only around twenty to twenty-five active loyalist killers at the time spread across the North. Half of them would have been UVF. Why were they not targeted for surveillance in the knowledge that, if there was going to be retaliation, they were the ones going to be involved? Lack of resources is sometimes given as a reason or excuse; however, this was a time when indisputable evidence shows that the

British government was signing a blank cheque to the RUC in its attempts to combat terrorism.

Taxi driver Gerald Brady picked up two men in Antrim who told him to take them to Carrickfergus. Once there, they shot him dead. The twenty-seven-year-old father of two was found by residents in Blackthorn Park slumped behind the wheel of his red Renault car. An RUC patrol arrived only minutes later, apparently unaware of the shooting, according to a report in the *Carrick Times* the following week. His Protestant partner, Michelle, who had given birth to their baby only ten weeks earlier, described the killers as 'the scum of the earth'.

Later that same day, the UVF murdered a thirty-year-old Protestant builder, Cecil Dougherty. His colleague William Corrigan would die in early July from his wounds after their workmen's hut was raked by a gunman near Rathcoole on the northern shore of Belfast Lough.

Under a headline 'New plan for "all Ireland" authority', the *Irish Independent* reported that the latest violence had dominated an intergovernmental conference in Dublin as 'senior Garda and RUC officers reviewed all aspects of security'.

The headline on the story above that one read: 'Boys in Green out to settle an old score' with an opening paragraph that stated: 'Ireland will come to a virtual standstill tonight as the Republic takes on Italy in their long-awaited opening game of [sic] World Cup Finals at The Giants Stadium, New York.'

The date was Saturday, 18 June 1994.

8 | 'Fenian Bastards'

Most residents of Loughinisland, like those across the island, were arranging their Saturday around the match. But not the owner of The Heights Bar, Hugh O'Toole. Along with fifteen of his regulars, the publican – who was approaching his fiftieth birthday – had chosen to leave Loughinisland that morning on a mercy mission to Romania, where they were to help build an orphanage with the £10,000 they had raised from charitable locals. Like so many across Ireland, Hugh had responded to the horrific television images of pain and squalor coming out of the former Soviet bloc country and wanted to play his part in helping ease the suffering of the orphaned children. In the car park south of the main pub, which more resembled a family home, they had gathered early in the summer morning sun to set off for the capital, Bucharest. Wives and children were there to wave them off on the 2,000-mile journey. Among them was Hugh's wife, Frances, and son, Aidan, who would be looking after the bar until his father returned.

As Hugh O'Toole, who had worked as a plasterer and part-time in The Heights Bar before taking it over from his brother Eamon just two years before, left for the airport, the villagers were planning the day ahead. 'I was here [in the bar on] the night that Ireland got through, they beat Northern Ireland, and it was great,' says Clare Rogan. 'It wouldn't really have mattered which team got through, everybody was here just to watch the football and have a bit of craic. And then, as the time went on and the World Cup drew nearer, people were excited and everybody wanted to be Irish. And everybody wanted to support the team,' she recalled.

The Heights Bar was structured with the windowed entrance porch in the middle of a whitewashed two-storey structure, and it sat just above the T-junction at the centre of the village, facing east towards St Macartan's church. A 'T' sign for Tennent's, which was illuminated at night, was hung on the southern side of the building.

Moira Casement wasn't a soccer fan, but on that day she was going to support the team: 'I didn't follow football, but, I mean, even my daughter, well, she knew more about it than me. It was an important occasion that Ireland [had gotten] so far.'

Barney Green, who was now eighty-seven years old and long since recovered from his TB, was married to her aunt, Brigid. He had a nephew, Dan McCreanor, who was fifty-nine and was due to go into hospital in Downpatrick for a hernia operation the following week. Dan wanted to go out to watch the match and so he called Barney and asked if he wanted to go to The Heights with him, an invitation that was readily accepted. 'It might have been the last, well, it was going to be the last occasion that they were out for a while,' explained Moira.

Dan McCreanor's nephew Patrick called to see him before he left for the pub. 'I was talking to him in his yard about farming at about 8.30 p.m. and he was going back into the house to go and get dressed and get washed up to go and meet Barney and take him to the pub for a drink and watch the match together,' he said.

In contrast, Eamon Byrne had no real interest in watching the game. He and his wife, Marie, had four sons under the age of eleven; the youngest, Declan, was only three months old. 'I first met Eamon when I was seventeen,' said Marie. 'We met at a dance at Dunmore dance hall at Edendarriff [west of Loughinisland]. Eamon was from Ballykinler [home to the UDR base], and I am from Drumaness. We married in 1981 and set up home in Drumaness.' The Byrnes' plan that evening was to go out for dinner in nearby Ballynahinch, their first outing since Declan was born.

Eamon's brother-in-law, Patsy O'Hare, who was thirty-five years old, also lived in Drumaness and, like him, had no real interest in the match that night. A single man, he lived at home with his parents and one of his four sisters, Roisin. 'There were many nights I would hear a knock on the back door and it would be Patsy coming back from the local club,' his sister Marie told Barry McCaffrey in an interview for *The Detail*. 'He just wanted to call in for a chat on his way home from the pub and then off he would go up home to Mummy. He was one of the gentlest people in the world.'

Malcolm Jenkinson also had a busy day ahead. He was going to paint the eaves of the home in Loughinisland that he shared with his wife, Ann, and their three children. Their eldest sons, Paul and Mark, were already up and away, working in England. But Paul had asked his friend Colm Smyth to help his dad build a wardrobe for his sister, and, if he could convince him, take him out for a pint on his behalf that night to celebrate Father's Day, which was on Sunday.

'I met Malcolm at a nurses' dance,' explained Ann. 'He was working as a carpet fitter at the time. His father had come up from Caledon in Co. Tyrone to find work in Belfast. When I met Malcolm his family had already lived in Belfast for a good number of years. He had four sisters and two brothers.' Within three weeks of the couple having met, Malcolm had asked Ann to marry him. They married in September 1965 and moved into their first home at Carryduff on the outskirts of East Belfast before, eleven years later, buying a plot of land in Loughinisland, a few miles east of O'Toole's bar, where Malcolm – who was born a Protestant but converted to Catholicism when he married Ann – began building a new family home.

Their daughter, Louise, recalled an idyllic childhood. 'Daddy loved families and children. At Christmas time it used to be a big thing to go to our granda's house in East Belfast,' she told Barry McCaffrey. 'All Daddy's nephews and nieces and cousins would be there. We would all be crammed into Granda's wee house and everyone would be fed and have a great time. I always remember us driving home to Loughinisland one year in the snow and not knowing whether the car would make it. Everything was an adventure. We never witnessed the Troubles. They never came to Loughinisland when we were growing up. They were a lifetime away.'

Colm Smyth had spent a couple of years living in Guernsey before coming back and starting a degree at college in Limerick. In 1994, at the end of his first year, he returned home to Loughinisland and his best friend's father, Malcolm Jenkinson, offered him some work. 'I was very grateful and Malcolm, as usual, paid me too much,' Smyth wrote in his book, *The Loughinisland Massacre: A Survivor's Story*.

Meanwhile, at his home outside New York, Bill Flynn – whose preferred sport was handball – was preparing to go to the game. 'Actually, it started out to be one of the loveliest days. The sun was out,' he said. Niall O'Dowd and Bill Flynn were to be Albert Reynolds' guests at the game; they could enjoy the spectacle and discuss the peace process on the side.

For Niall O'Dowd, the build-up was a very special moment: 'It was unbelievable. It was just the most fabulous time. I don't think it will ever be touched again. The one image I will always remember is going out to Giants Stadium, the day of the game, and seeing these car registrations from everywhere – Alabama, New Mexico, Minnesota, California – all with Irish flags on them. And realising, do you know what, guys, this is a home game for Ireland. This is unbelievable. They had come from all over the country. It was like this mythical 40 million Irish-Americans that everyone thinks of on St Patrick's Day had suddenly coalesced and gathered together out here at Giants Stadium and were going to watch the embodiment of the Irish emigrant experience, which was the Irish soccer team with their many English players, still flying the green of Ireland and representing, not just a country but an idea, which was the Irish worldwide. It was an enormously exciting time,' he recalls, still amazed years later.

The Irish team had flown up to New York from their base near Orlando, Florida, and were keen for the games to begin. In Italy four years earlier, goalkeeper Packie Bonner had kept the team in the tournament with a critical save in a penalty shoot-out. 'There were expectations,' he says. 'Whether we could do well or not was another question in those conditions. And the more success you have the more sort of expectations build up among the fans and among the media and everybody concerned. And I felt it myself, from a pressure point of view. Because we had done so well in Italy, and we had – personally for me too, having saved a penalty. [But] to do it all over again was going to be a big challenge.'

The six men who died in the Loughinisland massacre. Clockwise from top left: Adrian 'Frosty' Rogan, Patsy O'Hare, Eamon Byrne, Malcolm Jenkinson, Dan McCreanor and Barney Green. (Courtesy of the families)

The blood is still visible on the floor of The Heights Bar in a picture taken in the immediate aftermath of the massacre. (© Pacemaker)

Speaking to the press during a visit to Loughinisland the day after the massacre, the British Secretary of State, Sir Patrick Mayhew, promises the killers 'will be caught. The RUC never gives up.' (© Pacemaker)

Mourners walk behind the coffins of eighty-seven-year-old Barney Green and his nephew Dan McCreanor as they are taken to the Holy Family church, Teconnaught. (© PA Images/Alamy Stock Photo)

A VZ-58 assault rifle similar to the one used in the Loughinisland massacre.

The Thierafurth Inn, Kilcoo, on the night of the UVF attack, 19 November 1992.
(© PSNI)

The forty-two-year-old former teacher Peter McCormack, who died in the bar.
(Courtesy of the McCormack family)

June 2016: Police Ombudsman Dr Michael Maguire delivers the findings of collusion in the Loughinisland massacre. (© Pacemaker)

Niall Murphy gives his reaction to the Maguire Report surrounded by the families of those killed and injured. (© PA Images/Alamy Stock Photo)

The premiere of *No Stone Unturned* at the New York Film Festival in October 2017. Alex Gibney is fourth from the right, and to his right are editor Andy Grieve and Niall O'Dowd, who participated in the documentary. (© Paul Zimmerman/Stringer)

The Durham detective Darren Ellis, who led the investigation into the leaked documents on behalf of the PSNI. (© PA Images/Alamy Stock Photo)

Barry McCaffrey and I leave the PSNI station on the day of our arrest flanked by John Finucane (far left) and Niall Murphy (far right). (© PA Images/Alamy Stock Photo)

The Loughinisland families hold a vigil outside The Heights Bar on the evening of our arrest, 31 August 2018. (© PA Images/Alamy Stock Photo)

On the steps of the High Court in Belfast after winning the judicial review. Loughinisland family members joined us, along with members of the NUJ, Patrick Corrigan (Amnesty International), Daniel Holder (CAJ) and David Davis MP. (© PA Images/Alamy Stock Photo)

Outside the Royal Courts of Justice, London, before the May 2024 Investigatory Powers Tribunal hearing. (© Sarah Kavanagh)

For the Liverpool player Ray Houghton, by the time the team approached Giants Stadium they were amazed at what they were seeing. In an interview for *Ceasefire Massacre* he recalled the scenes: 'We were told, you know, prior to going that it was going to be 75 per cent Italian support and 25 per cent Irish. I remember we were travelling along and seeing a lot of Irish fans and thinking: "This is not right, you know. If there's only supposed to be 25 per cent of them, there seems to be an awful lot here already."'

Even the staunchest fan knew the Italians were favourites to win the tournament. Paolo Maldini, Roberto Baggio, Alessandro Costacurta, Roberto Donadoni – they were the rock stars of world soccer, who could make the game look easy; indeed, they played it at a different level to mere mortals. Italy always turned up on the world stage and brought a class and skill to which the rest of the teams could only aspire.

Ireland did have the likes of Paul McGrath, Denis Irwin and Steve Staunton, who had experience of playing at a World Cup and had won major trophies with their club sides. For Roy Keane, however, this was his first experience of a major tournament. He had joined Manchester United from Nottingham Forest the previous year and was already making his mark on the team and his opponents. His vivid memory of the journey to the stadium made it into his autobiography: 'As always with an Irish team, our spirits were high. On the coach on the way to Giants Stadium we played our rebel songs, which told stories about English oppression and how our Irish heroes fought gallantly. And were shot. Or hanged. The English-born members of the party sang as lustily as the rest of us,' he recalled.

Niall Quinn was, unfortunately, going to sit out the competition due to injury but travelled as a pundit. 'I was part of, in a way, within the camp, so the spirit was good and we feared nobody and there will be a belief in that dressing room that doesn't have to be shouted out from the rooftops, but we know it's there, it's solid. And it was just, you know, one of those occasions where you keep your fingers crossed and hope this thing doesn't go bad.'

As the Irish fans streamed into the New Jersey stadium, The Heights

Bar was beginning to fill up – not that it took many people to pack the small bar, which was situated to the right side of the building. There was also a lounge bar to the left, but it was only ever opened on special occasions.

Customers entered through the porch then turned right into a room that was no bigger than a normal family living room. In the far left-hand corner of this room was a set of stairs. The bar counter, with a mirror and optics behind, was in the far right-hand corner with a small portable television hung on the wall behind the bar, meaning that everyone in the pub who was going to watch the match would do so with their backs to the door. The right-hand wall of the bar was split in the middle by a door into a small store, on which Hugh O'Toole had put up a poster of Romanian orphans. There was also a fireplace with a set of antlers over it, below which there were another half-dozen chairs dotted around a couple of knee-high tables, providing a snug in the corner to the right of the entrance door.

It was identical to pubs the length and breadth of the country, the kind of place where locals returning home make their first call; the spot where young people would start their night before going on into town, or return to for the 'late one', the last drink of the night. The pub that growing up you thought was full of old men but came to be your favourite place on earth apart from your own home. Where you felt most comfortable, amongst your own people, your family and friends, the people who knew you before you knew you.

'Protestants, Catholics, unionists, nationalists, it didn't matter; everybody just came together in here,' says Clare Rogan. 'There was a sense of community and belonging and neighbourhood, all friends. It didn't matter what your religious or political beliefs were. This was the place where everybody met and your beliefs and political aspirations were left at the door. Nothing political or religious was ever discussed in here, it wouldn't have been allowed. We respected one another's views and it just didn't matter.'

For Frosty and Clare and their kids, June 1994 was a very special moment in their lives. 'We had just come home that morning from holiday in Spain, our first European holiday, if you like, our first holiday out of Ireland,' says Clare. 'Whenever we were in Spain we met other people, other Irish people from different parts of Ireland. It was the word on everybody's lips, everybody was talking about the World Cup.'

For her husband, it was a dream weekend. Not only was there the World Cup on the Saturday evening, but Down would play Monaghan in the Ulster Senior quarter-final the following day in Armagh. For fans of the Mournemen, Ireland may not beat the Italians, but after beating Derry, they were certain that Down was going the whole way; the Sam Maguire trophy was coming back north. 'He wanted to watch the Ireland match alright, but mainly he went to the pub to get a GAA ticket for the next day. And one of the girls from the O'Toole family who owned the bar had got him a ticket and he was going to collect it.'

Barney Green might have been going to the pub, but his niece, Moira Casement, was going to watch it at home. 'We were sitting glued to it,' she said. 'Barney did follow the Gaelic and World Cup obviously, and that particular night his nephew Dan had taken him up to O'Toole's.'

Aidan O'Toole was twenty-three-years-old. He had worked behind the bar since he was fourteen, first for his uncle and then his father. The evening began much like any other Saturday night, with his younger sister, Elaine, helping out before leaving to spend the evening with friends in Warrenpoint. Aidan then took over bar duties for the rest of the night. 'There was a few people came in after Mass, so they did, and all to watch the match, like, and have a bit of craic … it was good old banter, hoping that Ireland was going to win,' he remembers. 'There was a few away to Romania that morning, so there was only about fifteen in the bar. A nice wee crowd, just a nice crowd, all watching the match.'

Patsy O'Hare had attended evening Mass in Christ the King church in Drumaness, as he did every Saturday. 'Patsy went to Mass and once my daddy [Willie O'Hare] saw him he said he'd go for a pint with him in O'Toole's. Daddy was from Loughinisland and always went back to Mass there. He loved O'Toole's,' said his daughter Marie.

While Willie and Patsy were settling in for the evening in the bar, Marie and her husband, Eamon, were finishing a meal at a restaurant in Ballynahinch. Eamon planned to simply have a 'quiet pint' at the restaurant before heading home. But afterwards, in a spur of the moment decision, he opted to drive south to meet Willie and Patsy in Loughinisland. Marie joined them for a drink, but did not plan to stay for the full game as the couple's four boys – Martin, Paul, Stephen and three-month-old Declan – were being babysat by her mother and sister.

Malcolm Jenkinson changed out of his work clothes after a day working around the house with Colm Smyth. Speaking before her death in 2019, Malcolm's daughter Louise said, 'If Mum and Dad were going to a dance or anywhere special, Dad would always have worn a suit. He was colour-blind and couldn't differentiate between brown and green. I used to have to go up to Mum and Dad's wardrobe on Saturday night to pick out a tie to go with his shirt. Dad would pick the shirt and I would have to pick a tie to go with it. I dropped the boys off at the pub around 8 p.m. and went on to see friends in Strangford.' Smyth had wanted to go to his favourite bar, at Drumaness GAA club, but the compromise to get Malcolm out for a pint was O'Toole's. 'I was a little disappointed that we would be going to O'Toole's, which was quieter than the one in Drumaness,' he admitted in his book. 'There would not be many people there on a Saturday night to watch soccer. We would have to make our own craic.'

***

Inside Giants Stadium was a sea of Irish tricolours and tomato-red faces in the unforgiving afternoon sun, with flags draped over the balconies on the three tiers around the ground known locally as 'The Swamp'.

The match kicked off in eighty-degree heat at 4 p.m. local time, which was 9 p.m. back in Loughinisland. Right from the off, Ireland looked like a team that had come to America with a single-minded determination to avenge their defeat in Rome four years earlier. Within the first eleven seconds, Steve Staunton had already had a pop at goal although it went wide and didn't trouble the Italian keeper, Pagliuca.

High up in the stands, Bill Flynn, his family and Niall O'Dowd were taking their seats alongside the official Irish government delegation. 'The

Taoiseach, Albert Reynolds, had a box, yes, a very important box. And members of my family were invited to join, so we had a large box,' said Flynn.

The stadium rang out to the first chants of 'Ooh, Ahh, Paul McGrath' as the Man United player shepherded Baggio away from the Irish goal, all while showing worrying signs of having a problem with his left arm, which he seemed to be carrying a little awkwardly. Up front, Tommy Coyne was looking lonely but was making the Italian captain and defender, Franco Baresi, look uncomfortable. McGrath once again was forced to step in to prevent Baggio getting a shot away. It was a testy start in the heat.

Then, in the twelfth minute, the match, both in the ground and on television, seemed to move in slow motion as Italian defender Baresi attempted to head a ball that had been pinged into the box away from danger, only putting it onto the chest of the diminutive midfielder, Ray Houghton, to the right of the box. Houghton chested it awkwardly into his path, the ball almost falling behind him and beyond his reach, before releasing a left-footed lob over the Italian keeper, who could only wave at the ball as it soared over his head and into the net behind him.

Houghton had scored! Ireland were one up against the mighty Italians.

Only as Houghton somersaulted in celebration did the world move out of slow motion, the Irish fans erupting in celebration inside the ground and around the world. The heat, the nerves, even the debt the fans had run up just to get here, were all forgotten for that one heavenly moment.

Back in the tiny barroom in The Heights Bar, the RTÉ commentator George Hamilton narrated the build-up to the goal to a hushed audience. 'It's Houghton, it's Houghton with the shot. And it's in!' The rest of his words were drowned out by the noise of the Irish fans inside the stadium – and likely by the noise of those in The Heights – but no one in the bar needed to hear them; they had seen the goal go in with their own eyes.

Patsy O'Hare, his father, Willie, his sister, Marie, and brother-in-law Eamon Byrne weren't there for the football but enjoyed the celebrations nonetheless. Another man, Brian McLeigh, was sitting on a stool at the end of the bar. Barney Green, who was sitting just inside the door with Dan McCreanor, had his pipe in his mouth and his stout and whiskey chaser on the table between them, and he joined in the celebrations as Aidan O'Toole danced behind the bar and Frosty Rogan, Colm Smyth and the others jumped out of their stools in front of him. Through the match, Frosty – sitting to his right – had been keeping the bar entertained with stories from his holiday abroad. 'He told us about the fireworks he'd brought back for Halloween. "Planning ahead," he joked,' Smyth wrote in his book.

In the Giants Stadium, the Italians were having plenty of possession but were doing nothing to trouble Packie Bonner. McGrath wasn't giving Baggio a sniff of the ball and when the Italian did manage to get a shot away it seemed to come back off the face of the centre-half. Ireland were trying to keep cool, despite the fact they were one up and they were melting in the heat. 'Olé, olé, olé' echoed around the ground as Phil Babb and then McGrath cleared the ball from Ireland's lines.

The half-time whistle was greeted with a huge roar in the ground and a rush for the toilet in O'Toole's. The bathroom 'was no more than a few feet away from the bar but it was always better to wait until half-time just in case you missed something in the game,' wrote Colm Smyth. 'Bladder emptied. Another round ordered, cigs strategically placed to the front so as not to get in the way of the drinking arm, perfect.'

Brendan Valentine, known to everyone as 'Brenny', had decided to watch the match at the home he shared with his wife, Anne, and their four children. It was less than a mile away from the pub on the Tannaghmore Road. At half-time, caught up in the excitement, he changed his mind and headed for O'Toole's: 'I wouldn't say I was, you know, a real big football fan, but I was supporting the team. And after the first half I decided to come down to watch the rest of the match. And I probably was only into the bar when the second half was kicking off,' he said in an interview for *Ceasefire Massacre*.

Brenny, who worked for British Telecom, got a spot standing at the bar. Colm Smyth, Malcolm Jenkinson and Frosty Rogan were sitting on stools in front of him. Down the bar, in the snug area, were Patsy O'Hare and his father, Willie, his brother-in-law Eamon Byrne and his sister Marie.

Marie decided to leave before the half-time break ended. 'I remember looking at Daddy's watch as I was about to leave, and it was 10.05 p.m. I remember as I was walking out of the bar it was a lovely night. The sun was shining, it was a beautiful, clear, bright evening.' As she pulled out of the car park at the side of the bar and headed towards home, she passed a red-coloured car coming in the opposite direction. In the pub, the customers settled down for a second half that promised to be nothing less than an exhilarating rollercoaster ride.

At 10.10 p.m., two men dressed in boiler suits, boots and black woollen balaclavas got out of the car that Marie had passed, pulled open the door into the porch at the front of O'Toole's, turned right and opened the door into the bar. The first of the two gunmen was armed with a VZ-58, part of the South African shipment. The second had a Browning pistol and he kept the door open as the killer in front of him dropped to one knee, military style.

With George Hamilton's commentary continuing in the background, he announced his arrival with a shout of 'Fenian bastards' and proceeded to squeeze the trigger of the automatic assault rifle, emptying the full thirty-nine rounds he had loaded into the magazine into the small country bar.

It took the killer little more than three seconds to spray the bullets in an indiscriminate semi-circle from left to right. The first customer hit was eighty-seven-year-old Barney Green, who was sitting less than two feet from the muzzle of the weapon.

Willie O'Hare, who suffered from a heart condition, fell onto the floor as the bullets ripped through their victims' flesh, including his son, Patsy.

The barman, Aidan O'Toole, had his back to the front door when the shooting started but instinct told him to get out of harm's way. 'All I heard was cracks of gunfire. I ran up the bar and into the store and closed the door,' he said.

In his book, Colm Smyth says he first saw flashes in the mirror behind the bar and immediately thought of Frosty Rogan. 'Thinking he'd let off his fireworks, I turned around, expecting to see him in the doorway, laughing at us. But what I saw were boiler suits, blue boiler suits, complemented by balaclavas. "We're being hit," I shouted. I heard Malcolm shout as he turned to throw himself on top of me, attempting to shield me from the bullets that were racing towards us. I fell backwards off my stool and again I glimpsed the men in boiler suits at the door; one of them had a machine gun. I felt two thuds hit my legs, one in my lower left leg, another on my right thigh. I assumed they were bullets, they couldn't be anything else, but I felt no pain. I had nothing to compare this with.'

The gunman wasn't picking out specific targets; every human being in the bar was a target as far as he was concerned. His sectarian motivation was made clear with his 'Fenian bastards' announcement before he opened fire.

Like Colm Smyth, Brenny Valentine first thought it was fireworks. 'It was a very warm night. I'd ordered a pint and I had just taken a drink and set it back down on the bar. I was watching the game and the next thing, bang! I thought somebody threw a squib, I don't know why, but I thought somebody threw a squib in. So I ran. But the only way to escape was up the stairs towards the pool room. I quickly realised it was shooting. When I got up the stairs – and it will always stick with me – the blood seemed to drain from me, and I was standing with a pool cue. And the next thing I heard the squeal of tyres, it was the getaway car. And I could actually feel the blood going back into my body. I thought I heard footsteps. So I got the pool cue and I eased my way down the stairs. It was Willie Rice [that I heard] in the bar and I looked round the corner and he says: "Look at my mate Frosty",' Brenny recalled, still suffering from the after-effects of what he witnessed. Asked what exactly he saw, Brenny responded: 'Ah, I can't, I can't, terrible. I couldn't, I wouldn't even explain it, terrible carnage.'

Colm Smyth was on his back, staring at the ceiling: 'Malcolm, lying on top of me, was completely still. I slid out from underneath him and looked around. Nothing was moving. In front of me were the bodies of three or four men, all in a heap where they fell on top of each other. The smell of blood and bullets was in the air and on me. The boiler-suited men were gone.'

Aidan O'Toole emerged from the storeroom to the horrific scene. 'Just bodies piled on top of each other. I knew then that there was at least five or six dead at that stage. The way they were lying; they were piled on top of each other, so they were, at the door. I thought wee Brian McLeigh was dead too,' he recalled, surveying the room again in his mind's eye.

'I looked at Malcolm as he lay on the floor beside me,' wrote Colm Smyth. 'There were no moans, no breathing, just silence. I tried to open his mouth in the hope that this would help him breathe more easily, but it was impossible. I took him in my arms and blessed us both and said the Our Father as best I could.'

These were the immediate actions and thoughts of two young men standing on the edge of their adult lives, both aged twenty-three and full of dreams and aspirations, struggling to comprehend the carnage that had been caused by one man in a few short seconds of pure, blinding hatred.

The room was now filled with smoke, blood and the moans of the injured. Aidan O'Toole had the presence of mind to rush to the phone behind the bar and call 999, watched by Colm Smyth, who was still on the floor in a pool of blood.

Brenny Valentine was in a state of shock and wasn't aware that he had been shot. 'By this time my foot started to get numb, I thought my ankle was broke when I'd run [up the stairs]. I went outside. And there was a guy, Kevin Gordon, came along, and he thought I was drunk. And I can remember him opening the door [of his car], the passenger door, and taking his cigarettes and lighter and throwing them up onto the dash and he says: "Jump in." I says, "Kevin, there's six dead in here."'

Kevin Gordon did think Brenny Valentine was drunk. 'I stopped and he said: "Kevin, Kevin, help us, they've shot us. There's six dead in there." I abandoned my car outside the door, I came in and the bodies were lying,' he told the BBC. When Gordon entered the bar, George Hamilton was telling viewers that Ireland were still 1–0 up and holding on against the Italians.

'I could see the television above the bar and the match was still playing,' says Colm Smyth. '"Turn it off!" I shouted. I couldn't understand why the referee hadn't stopped the match when the shooting started.' He added, 'It was a relief to see Kevin Gordon, to know we were not alone. He had a quick look around and moved to help Frosty Rogan who had been hit in the stomach and was in a bad way. Wee Brian McLeigh was also in a lot of trouble. He was lying just around the corner of the bar counter. I could only see the bottom of his legs, which seemed to be at odd angles, blood was flowing. The panicked voices from those helping him told me he was in real danger.'

**

The ambulances arrived within minutes of Aidan O'Toole's call and paramedics began to treat the injured. Word soon spread that something had happened in the bar. Clare Rogan's intentions had been to join her husband in the bar, but first she needed to drop her children off with her sister for the night. En route, she came upon a military checkpoint. 'There was a queue of traffic as far back as I could see,' she now recalls. 'I can remember the soldier who spoke to me had a strong Belfast accent.'

When she got back to Loughinisland, Frosty's father, Mick, offered to drop her down to O'Toole's. As they approached the bar, she saw a man she knew to be Jim Toman, who lived directly opposite the bar, in his garden. He was waving them down, but Clare, not suspecting anything was wrong, sounded the horn and waved back. But, as she arrived at the bar, Frosty's friend Joe Rice met her at the door. 'He said: "Don't go in there, there's been a shooting." And for some reason I thought, there was a few boys around here would have went out and shot rabbits or whatever, and I thought, somebody's been in there with a gun and it's went off accidentally. He said, "No, no, don't go in, it's terrible, we need a clergyman."

'So I did go in. And what greeted me will haunt me till the day I die. It was just carnage. It was something that I had never, ever thought that I would witness. We had been to see a hypnotist when we were on holiday. And he had hypnotised people and they all lay on top of one another. And that's what it reminded me of, just, you know, there was bodies lying everywhere, the smell, the smoke was lingering, broken glass. I couldn't see it, I had to walk away, I had to run out, I couldn't, I just couldn't believe it. It was absolute carnage, people were crying, men were staggering. It was something that I just … I don't think about it a lot, I try not to, because it would really drive me insane.'

Frosty Rogan had been hit five times on his left side and once in each leg. 'People kept telling me he was okay. I was outside [the bar] and, my brother he came out and he said, "He's all right, he's going to be all right." And then after about ten minutes he came out and he said, "No, he's gone." You know, because I had this vision, sure he'll be okay. He might be in a wheelchair, he might be disabled, but he just said, "No, he's gone." And that was it,' said Clare.

Cortisol and adrenaline were still coursing through Aidan O'Toole's veins when Clare Rogan arrived at the bar. He still hadn't realised there was a bullet lodged in his kidney. 'I met Clare Rogan at the door; she kind of squeezed my side, I felt the pain then, but I thought it was only a wee nick, like. I was all hyped up on adrenaline. I suppose I was just more concerned about the rest of the people than I was for myself,' said the barman.

When Marie Byrne arrived home early, her sister suggested that they go back down to the bar and pick the men up after the match. But then there was a call to the house from an aunt, saying there was news of an accident at the bar. An uncle then arrived and advised them not to go to the bar, but, even at that stage, Marie thought it was nothing serious or sinister. 'I thought Patsy had only hurt his leg or something minor like that. My uncle said he'd take me over to the hospital. It wasn't until we were in the car that it came on the radio that there had been a shooting,' she said.

After she had left her father and Colm Smyth off at the pub, Malcolm Jenkinson's daughter Louise drove on to meet friends in Strangford. 'I remember being in a bar later that night and a newsflash coming on the television. It said that a bar called McMullan's had been attacked in Co.

Down and there were people dead. But within ten minutes the radio news started to say that the attack had been on a bar in Loughinisland. No one knew what to do or who was dead or injured. Nothing like this had ever happened in Loughinisland. My friends took me straight to Downpatrick Hospital to see if Daddy was one of the injured.'

Ann Jenkinson, Malcolm's wife, was on night shift as a nurse at the Royal Victoria Hospital in Belfast. She got a call at work from a friend, who broke the news of the shooting. She immediately left and made the thirty-mile journey to Downpatrick on her own, not knowing if her husband was dead or alive.

As with the others, it was a phone call that alerted Moira Casement to the unfolding horror: 'It was my aunt Brigid on the phone. And she said her brother-in-law in Ardglass had heard on the radio that there was an incident in Loughinisland. So my husband was in Loughinisland GAA club playing cards, and we didn't have a second car. So I kept talking on the phone to my aunt and my daughter ran out onto the road and ran down to her house. At that stage we didn't know much: was it fatalities or was it injuries? And then the parish priest and another fella arrived up and we knew then, we knew that Barney definitely was dead. There was no in-between at that stage,' she said.

Dan McCreanor's nephew Patrick was at home with his family, celebrating Ireland's win over Italy, when the phone call came to confirm his uncle had died. 'Dad answered the phone and he just couldn't take the news in and I remember my mum, my sister and I going to comfort my dad, you know, with hearing the devastating news. It was just unbelievable, unbelievable. We just couldn't take it in. To be on such a high and then to be on such a low, you know, [we] just, just couldn't, couldn't take it in, you know. Just lives wrecked; changed forever; absolutely changed forever.'

The first RUC officers on the scene had tended to the injured before ambulances took the men to Downe Hospital. 'One officer came over to me, took a look at my wounds and used a bandage from his surgical pack to tie up my right thigh,' Colm Smyth recalled. 'He said I would be okay and moved on to the others. That was it. I did not want the police officer to walk away. The shock was setting in. Another police officer helped me up onto a chair. He said I'd several gunshot wounds and I'd lost a lot of blood. There were dead bodies at my feet, blood spreading over the floor, frantic screams. One by one, the living were taken away. The dead were left where they fell. I couldn't walk so they used the chair I sat on and carried me to the ambulance. On the other side was wee Brian McLeigh, still being worked on by the paramedics. They were fighting to keep him alive. I held on to the handrail in the ambulance as it rolled from side to side as we sped along the country roads,' recalled the college student.

Brenny Valentine still thought he had only broken his ankle in his bid to escape the killers' bullets: 'The RUC had arrived and the policeman came over and he says: "Have you been injured?" And I says, no, I'm not, I think I've gone over on my ankle. And then it come to the stage where I couldn't put my foot on the ground. I was more or less skipping on one leg and somebody came over again and says, look, you have been injured. And there was a fella that just lives over the road, James McClements, and the policeman said to him: "Take that man's shoe off." And he took my shoe off, and my sock, and the blood hit the road. The bullet had went up the centre of my foot, right up the middle up to somewhere here [pointing to his thigh]. The next thing then I was put in an ambulance,' he said in an interview.

Giants Stadium was a metaphorical million miles away from the scene in The Heights Bar. There the fans were oblivious to the fact that their fellow fans were dead or dying while they watched the final minutes click down. But Niall O'Dowd, sitting alongside Taoiseach Albert Reynolds and other members of the Irish government and advisers, began to pick up that something was very wrong. 'I remember people just started to whisper about this, that something had happened in Northern Ireland … I was thinking: What is this? Where is this coming from? It was all very jumbled. But then I remember speaking to somebody from the Taoiseach's office and he told me it was in Co. Down. I had never heard of Loughinisland. And he said it was particularly horrific,' said O'Dowd.

A few seats away, Bill Flynn heard Loughinisland mentioned for the first time. 'I couldn't believe what had happened, and that it happened in a town, Loughinisland, from which my father came, stunned me even more. Loughinisland is known for the lovely people who live there. There's no industry other than farming. It's a town of old churches, historic churches, one small lake. And, as I say, numbers of lovely people of both Catholic and Protestant background, and never an argument between them. How, into this peaceful spot, can men with guns and fast cars [enter] and try to ruin this section of the world, how do you explain that?'

As the RUC sealed off the area and put up the white tape that the people of Northern Ireland had become so used to over the previous twenty-five years, country people began to do what country people do in such situations: comfort each other. Lights stayed on all night in the homes and cottages in the greater Loughinisland area as they began to gather in the homes of the dead and the injured.

Moira Casement had gone to be with Barney Green's widow but returned home in the early hours: 'People were coming into the house. It was a still summer's night and one of the things I do remember was my husband deciding to cut the grass. He went out and cut the grass. It seems strange now, but people were coming and going, and I don't think anybody slept in the whole country; it impacted on a lot of people. We talk about it being our JFK moment, everybody can tell you exactly where they were or where they heard it or who they heard it from. The Troubles hadn't really impacted on us out here in the country, and it was just, it was incredible that our wee community had been shattered.

'But when my husband was outside, three RUC men were standing guard on the road; this was near morning. And there was a neighbour came down, rolled down the window of the car and he says: "You need look no further than those ... there." He said that. The man, God rest him, he's gone now, but that was his immediate reaction: "You need look no further than them there." The police, yes. We didn't know at that time, we were naive. We didn't realise.'

PART II

PART II

9 | The Aftermath

No one in Loughinisland slept on the night of the attack, nor would they for many nights to come. The village could only be described as convulsed with anguish, having no ability to contextualise the enormity of what had been visited upon them. Not one of the families that lived within a five-mile radius of O'Toole's bar was untouched.

The effect of the attack that had claimed the lives of six men and left a further five in hospital sent reverberations across the North and beyond. Other places had suffered similar atrocities at the hands of loyalists in the previous few years – the Lower Ormeau Road, Greysteel – but it was the unique mix of both place and timing that made this attack all the more abominable, coming on a night when the island as a whole had celebrated success at the World Cup, where an Englishman with so many English-born players had taken on and beaten the Italians.

Prior to the massacre, the speculation that ceasefires were coming, maybe just weeks away, had been growing. There had been a real, palpable sense that the darkest days of violence were over. That the 1990s offered the chance for the North to have normality. That's all. Normality. It wasn't much to ask, really; however, from the moment dawn broke on the morning of 19 June 1994, it once again seemed beyond the reach, indeed the capability, of the population of Northern Ireland. From that moment onwards the name of Loughinisland would be forever associated with the word 'massacre'. The blood of the victims had seeped into the very ground of the village and would remain there forever.

The RUC records that still exist detail how they received two calls from The Heights Bar: the first at 10.20 p.m. from Aidan O'Toole, which was picked up by a station duty officer manning the front desk in Newcastle police station, ten miles south, and a second call eight minutes later. The second caller provided key information – the colour and type of car used by the killers. It was a red Triumph Acclaim. The caller also outlined how the gang had pulled up in front of the bar and while the two gunmen were inside, the driver had turned it around so that, in their getaway, they could drive thirty yards and take an immediate left up the Loughinisland Road, passing the lake, towards the village of Annacloy. He was unable to provide the number plate, but his information was critical and gave detectives a very early lead on the trail of the killers.

By 10.25 p.m. – just fifteen minutes after the shooting – the RUC had already given a name to the murder investigation. Operation Aristocrat was up and running.

A neighbour told the first police to arrive on the scene that he had also seen 'a red-coloured car which I think was either a Triumph Acclaim or a Honda Accord. It was a four-door saloon with a boot.' Another witness who had seen the car speed past her house provided significant details: '[I] saw a red car with three men in it. I saw it swerving around the corner from the direction of the pub and along the Loughinisland Road. There were two men in the front seats and one in the back ... All three were smiling. The one in the front passenger seat had a white T-shirt on. He had ginger hair, quite short. The one in the back had a black top on and he had short hair. I think he was clean shaven. I couldn't see the driver,' she told the RUC officers.

The security forces set up checkpoints on all the main routes leading out of and into Loughinisland, but the killers were long gone by the time the police and army began to wave down cars with their red torches.

Members of the media soon began to descend on the scene. Downtown Radio, based on an industrial estate outside Newtownards in North Down, had a well-deserved reputation for attracting talented broadcast journalists. The editor at the time, Ken Johnston, was right out of central casting: a chain smoker with a beautiful turn of phrase usually including several expletives per sentence. When the first reports came in of the attack, he went straight to the scene, arriving well before the rest of the press pack, and was therefore first to break the news of the massacre.

By the time Johnston arrived in Loughinisland, the UVF had called the station to admit responsibility. The first call, using the recognised code word for the UVF, was less than thirty minutes after the attack, at 10.40 p.m. The caller said that as long as the INLA continued to attack loyalists, nationalists would 'pay the price'. A second call was made to the same newsroom after midnight. Having shot six innocent men in the back, the loyalists displayed contempt for their memory by saying first that there was a republican meeting in the pub, and then, in the second call, that it had been a republican function. Johnston reported only that they had admitted they were behind the attack, recognising the lack of any credibility in the loyalist statements.

The five injured men had already been taken to the Downe Hospital in Downpatrick, which was put on a mass casualty alert. Aidan O'Toole, Brenny Valentine, Andy Milligan, Brian McLeigh and Colm Smyth were all treated in the emergency room in separate cubicles. 'When we got to the hospital it was in chaos,' Colm Smyth, who had been shot four times in the legs and backside, recorded in his book. 'I was placed on a trolley and given an aluminium blanket to keep me warm. There seemed to be dozens of people in Accident and Emergency. I lay on the trolley … as the doctors and nurses frantically dealt with those more seriously injured.

'I was scared and started to feel a lot of pain as the initial shock wore off. The trembling in my hands spread throughout my body and the room felt suddenly colder. Then my trolley started moving and a nurse told me I was being taken down to the X-ray room. The bullets had missed my bones. I looked down at my legs and saw the bullet wounds and the empty space where my thigh muscle was supposed to be. Ping, ping, ping was the sound the bullet made as it fell out of … my leg onto the tiled floor of the hospital ward. It was hard to believe that for the last two hours this bullet had been bouncing around between the hole in my leg and my jeans.'

Colm Smyth didn't know it, but one of those being treated in the same Accident and Emergency unit was the man who had been standing immediately behind him in the bar. Miraculously, given his proximity to the gunman, Brenny Valentine had only been hit once. 'The bullet was lodged in my leg. [At] the hospital they took my shoe off, but they couldn't find the point of entry of the bullet. So they stripped me to try to find it,' he said in an interview for *Ceasefire Massacre*. The doctors came to the conclusion that the bullet had passed through another of the victims before entering Brenny Valentine's foot and settling in his thigh.

Louise Jenkinson's friend drove her to the Downe Hospital, where they awaited the arrival of her mother and news on her father. 'In the beginning a nurse kept on apologising and saying that she couldn't tell me anything, but when Mummy arrived they finally told us [that my father was dead]. Everything was just a blur after that. Nothing seemed real but unfortunately it was all real.' They would later learn that a bullet had severed a cerebral artery in his brain. If it had passed through his head a fraction of an inch in either direction, Malcolm Jenkinson could have survived.

Patsy O'Hare's sister Roisin was at the hospital hoping to find news on her brother and brother-in-law, Eamon Byrne. Her father, Willie, who had survived the attack without injury, and her mother, Anne, were also on their way, hoping for the best. 'When I got to the hospital the paramedics were physically brushing the blood out of the ambulances. That's how bad it was.' Very shortly after, she was told that her brother had died. 'A bullet had hit an artery and as quick as they were giving him blood he was losing it again.' Nurses allowed Roisin into the room to sit with her brother's body. It was still warm.

For a time, Eamon Byrne's wife, Marie, believed her husband had been taken to Daisy Hill Hospital in Newry, or to the Royal Victoria in Belfast, only to later have the news broken to her that, in fact, he was dead and his body was still inside the bar.

Willie O'Hare had suffered a massive heart attack thirteen years before the shooting in 1981. He had slipped as the gunman began firing, which probably saved his life. 'They must have thought he was dead, otherwise they would have shot him as he lay on the floor,' said Roisin. It was a small consolation amid all the loss. 'It broke my mummy's heart to lose her only son, Patsy, and son-in-law, Eamon, who was more like a son to her. Patsy adored Mummy and he was the apple of her eye. All she kept saying that night was: "Not my only boy, not my wee boy."

Still struggling to come to terms with what she'd witnessed in the bar the night before, Clare Rogan now had to break the news to her two children, who only twenty-four hours before had come home tanned and full of stories from their first holiday abroad. It was Sunday 19 June – Father's Day. The children had stayed the night in her sister's home as Clare had hoped to join Frosty for a night's craic in the bar. 'We woke the children up and told them that bad men had come to the bar and shot their daddy. Tony was only coming ten years of age. My sister remembers him tying his laces and saying that he hoped they would rot in hell,' recalled Clare.

Father's Day would never be celebrated in the Rogan home again.

***

By the time Clare had made the journey to Downpatrick to give her children the dreadful news, the world was beginning to learn what had happened at The Heights Bar. Journalists and camera crews were allowed as far as the T-junction that the killers' red Triumph had sped through as they made their getaway. The only exceptions were the one photographer and cameraman that the RUC decided to allow into The Heights to picture and film the inside of the bar, capturing the pools of blood still on the floor and Brenny Valentine's pint still on the bar, along with the half-smoked cigarettes and unfinished whiskeys. Those pictures subsequently went around the world.

Overnight, the RUC forensic experts had recovered from the bar twenty-eight VZ-58 rifle cartridges and twenty-four bullet heads that had missed their targets or passed through the bodies of those who had been killed and injured.

After she'd had the conversation no mother should ever have to have with her children, Clare Rogan had gone to 8 a.m. Mass at St Macartan's. It made sense to be around her neighbours, even if they were all numbed with pain. The parish priest, Canon Bernard Magee, encouraged the friends and neighbours to help the relatives of the victims to bear the burden of bereavement and said that the community would pray for the wives, children, parents and family circles. Bishop of Down and Connor Patrick Walsh cancelled his planned appointments to be at the early morning service. 'People are crying out in their grief for peace. If the people who carried out this atrocity could only look at their own families. For far too long has the storm of violence engulfed our community. This storm broke here in this parish last night.'

One of the reporters sent to the scene was Richard Sullivan from the *News Letter*. He told readers how one parishioner described the attack to him as unbelievable. 'I always thought I was lucky to live in a beautiful village untouched by the Troubles or any kind of violence. Now I live in a village where six people were slaughtered.' Several other parishioners spoke to the reporter to convey their own personal tribute to the victims.

By this point word had also spread to Romania. Not long before the shooting had started, Hugh O'Toole had made it to Bucharest to help others less well off than himself. One of the group of pub regulars on the trip had called home. 'He was told, get Hugh to ring because there has been a terrible shooting,' Hugh's brother, Kieran, said, speaking to reporters at the scene. 'They just came in and sprayed the place,' he told the news reporters. 'Men and women were everywhere, screaming. It was horrible. This is such an isolated place. It's mainly Catholic but there are quite a few Protestants and they are just as devastated.'

As the families' thoughts turned to the funerals ahead, the British Secretary of State, Sir Patrick Mayhew, arrived in the village to visit the scene with his wife, Jean, and senior RUC officers, including ACC Bill Stewart. They paused to view the flowers that had been left outside the bar and spoke to local political representatives before marching down to the gathered press. Mayhew wore his British Army regimental tie in the colours of the Dragoon Guards, in which he had served as a subaltern, as, in his very establishment, aloof manner, he sought to give assurances to the victims and the nationalist community at large. Accompanied by local SDLP MP Eddie McGrady, he walked from the bar to speak to the media, positioned by police at the 'stick' – the T-junction on the southern side of the bar. He promised that the killers would be tracked down. 'This was an inhuman act of savagery and injustice. The moral squalor of those who carried it out is beyond description. These people speak for no one, act for no one but themselves, they bring disgrace upon whatever cause they claim to represent – a cause that rejects them just as the people of Northern Ireland reject them. Let us just picture a future conversation you may have with your daughter who asks you what you did in your so-called war, Daddy? You will say, "I killed a man of 87. He was sitting with his back to me. He was watching the World Cup. I shot him dead, he was 87." She won't think that the record of a hero, will she?'

As the local and national press huddled around in front of him, he continued: 'In time they will be caught. The RUC never gives up. So many behind bars can confirm this. Once convicted, the law will ensure that they too endure long years locked up in prison. I have faith that the Province is going to put behind it the foul madness and sectarian murder perpetrated by so few. On behalf of our whole community, I call on anyone who knows or suspects anything that can help the police catch these criminals, and others like them, to pass that information to the RUC. They can do that safely and in total confidence. No matter how slight it might seem, they must leave it to the police themselves to assess its value,' said the former British attorney general, making promises that would come back to haunt the RUC and the British.

Whether Mayhew realised it or not, at that moment the RUC had already identified the chief suspects responsible for the massacre. Furthermore, a decision had been taken not to arrest them.

With some prescience and without the indisputable evidence that would only emerge much later, Sinn Féin's Martin McGuinness described the Secretary of State's appearance in Loughinisland as 'completely nauseating, given the fact that it was Patrick Mayhew, as British Attorney General, [who] sanctioned the deal that allowed Brian Nelson to avoid standing trial for the murder of five nationalists in Belfast'. The Derry republican leader said he had no doubt that the rifles used to murder the six men had come from the South African shipment and called on the

RUC to release the forensic tests on the spent bullet cases recovered at the scene. 'There is nothing new in the fact that the British government is using loyalist killers as their proxies; the history of British collusion with loyalist death squads stretches back twenty-five years. Incidents such as the Dublin–Monaghan bombings are only the tip of the iceberg.'

Three prominent SDLP politicians were also in Loughinisland in the hours afterwards, and again on the Sunday. They were local MP Eddie McGrady, his assistant Margaret Ritchie, who would later become an MP and party leader, and a local councillor, Patsy Toman, who was at the scene of the attack within minutes and would later become a significant figure in the story of Loughinisland. 'There was utter chaos, people screaming, grown men crying, wives, girlfriends, mothers not knowing when their sons had left home, what bar they were going to or where they were going to watch the match,' he told the press, adding that he had visited the Rogan home. 'The children there were crying. They had lost their father.'

The attack was condemned by politicians from across the political spectrum and Church leaders of all denominations. Local DUP councillor Bill Alexander was reported as having visited the homes of some of those bereaved. He said that the murders were not carried out in the name of Protestants and that his community was for praying for the victims. The Ulster Unionist security spokesman and Fermanagh–South Tyrone MP, Ken Maginnis, raised an interesting point in his response. 'You cannot protect every little hamlet. What the terrorist godfathers have simply said to the gunmen is get out to a little pub outside Belfast, you will be as safe as houses, and take out as many Roman Catholics as you can,' said the former UDR major.

He was right; the security forces did have huge resources to hand, but they couldn't protect every nationalist village. But could they have prevented the killers from carrying out this attack? That was a very different question, one which would only be answered many years later, after the families finally lost faith in the police and pushed to be told the truth.

***

The Pope, Queen Elizabeth and US President Bill Clinton all sent messages of sympathy to the victims' families and condemned the killers. 'I was deeply shocked and saddened by the brutal crime in Loughinisland. Please convey my heartfelt sympathy to the bereaved and injured,' wrote the Queen. The Holy Father urged the people of the North not to lose heart but to 'continue untiringly to work for peace and harmony', saying he was 'always saddened by news of violence in Northern Ireland from whatever source it comes. [I've] been deeply shocked by the latest killings in Loughinisland.'

In America, the Irish football team had picked up on news of the attack while still in Giants Stadium. Jim Gracey, sports editor with the *Sunday Life*, was filing his copy, expecting his story to be front-page news. 'I rang the office [back in Belfast] to speak to the deputy editor at the time, a guy called Jim Flanagan. It was probably fifteen, twenty minutes after the game. And if you can imagine in a press centre below the Giants Stadium, full of Italians and full of Irish, very excitable people. And then you have all these journalists who are, you know, trying to make deadlines. They are quite excitable as well at that sort of time. There is a lot of excitement and tension as well with people. And, you know, emotions are running high anyway. But they are all good emotions. And I remember getting Jim on the phone back in the office. And I said: "This is brilliant, Jim, it's got to be page 1 tomorrow." And he said, "It won't be page 1 tomorrow." I said, "Why not?" And he said, "We have had an atrocity. We don't know yet how many people have been killed. It's in a little village called Loughinisland. And we don't know yet, but we know that there's multiple fatalities. I'm afraid you won't be on page 1 tomorrow." I went: "Jesus", you know.

'I was standing holding the phone and Mark Lawrenson, a former Republic of Ireland and Liverpool player, was doing some work for Irish television. He just happened to be standing beside me in the press room. And I said, "You are not going to believe this. There's been a killing back home." He said, "What kind?" I said, "It's multiple fatalities in a little bar in Co. Down." And he summoned some of the Football Association of Ireland officials who were within the vicinity, and they went into a little huddle. The next thing I know the Republic of Ireland football officials, the guys in the blazers who had been standing celebrating with a beer a moment earlier, they're ashen-faced. And they go further on down to the dressing rooms and they inform the team. And the whole atmosphere just sank, completely.'

Niall Quinn was in the same press room and was told of the atrocity by Mark Lawrenson. 'I was trying to ring home, see how things were going in Ireland. And then there's this sort of awful downer came when we heard about Loughinisland and there was a terrible tragedy and that our own fans wearing the shirts, supporting us through the game, had been sort of attacked and were callously, you know, left to die by laughing assailants. And it knocked lumps out of everything. I remember having a drink that night and it was a sombre drink, despite the fact it should have been a party really for us. It reminded us all, you know, that this country we are representing has its problems.'

Jim Gracey was on the flight with the team back to their base in Orlando. 'I remember getting to the airport and we were in a VIP section of the departure lounge and I could see some of the players in a huddle. The next thing someone then came over and said to us: the team have decided that as a mark of respect there will be no drinking on the plane. There will be no singing on the plane. There will be no celebrating on the plane. People just want to reflect and to pay their respects and to show a bit of dignity in a situation like this, that, you know, something matters more than just football,' he said.

The goalkeeper, Packie Bonner, remembers the team being in a bubble but being affected by the news as it was being relayed to them: 'It was incredible to think that people were in there enjoying themselves, watching us perform, you know, and having that emotion earlier and for that to happen.' Ray Houghton says the players weren't told everything by the Irish football authorities but picked up on the news from the press on their way back to their base in Orlando: 'The plane ride was so sombre and so quiet, which was so unlike us; normally afterwards it would have been a party mode, but it certainly wasn't. It was the quietest plane journey and the quietest we have ever had after a match ever,' he recalled.

Packie Bonner, who was from Burtonport, across the border in Donegal, believes Loughinisland had an impact over the rest of the tournament for the Ireland team and fans: 'It put a cloud on things. For us to be celebrating and for us to be going through a wonderful moment in Ireland, the World Cup and being there for the second time, and for that to happen, all collectively being in a pub watching and enjoying us. Especially when you come from the border and you know people and so on. I don't know if it had a huge effect, but it had definitely an effect,' said the keeper.

In another sporting sphere, the day after the massacre, the match that Frosty Rogan had gone to the bar to get a ticket for ended just as he would have hoped. Pete McGrath described it as 'a game without emotion'. The manager had received a call late on the Saturday night from one of the team selectors, Danny Murphy, to alert him to the attack. The Ulster Championship semi-final against Monaghan was in obvious doubt, but by morning, the decision was taken that it should go ahead. 'You said to yourself, what would be achieved by calling the match off? These people had gone in and murdered GAA people. If the [game] is stopped, it would be an added victory for the people who went in and committed the atrocity. If the game went ahead it would be a sign of public revulsion,' Pete McGrath told Thomas Niblock on *The GAA Social* podcast.

'The grey skies that hung over the Athletic Grounds reflected the sombre mood inside the ground,' reported *The Irish News*. 'At times it was so quiet you could clearly hear players shouting instructions to one another. An Ulster final place was up for grabs but nobody really seemed to care as supporters stood in small groups, trying to process the horror that had taken place less than 24 hours earlier.'

Making his first appearance in the 1994 Ulster Championship was Gary Mason. He knew Frosty Rogan and Malcolm Jenkinson, who had bought hay from his father. Mason went to the bar after he heard about the shooting. 'We didn't know the extent of what had happened, but my brother Damian would have been up to The Heights a couple of times around then. He wasn't a drinker, but he would've socialised there the odd time. We immediately hopped in the car and went up to the bar. We weren't inside but we were that close you could smell the aftermath of the gunfire in the air. It was horrendous; the place was just mayhem,' the footballer and schoolteacher told *The Irish News*.

He added: 'There's a lot of different things going through your head at that time, but it's mostly just the sheer shock of seeing people losing the strength of their legs, collapsing on the ground at hearing that their loved ones had been murdered. Everybody was just ... stunned. It was just so hard to believe something like that could happen somewhere as quiet and as peaceful as Loughinisland.'

Pete McGrath had offered him the chance to sit out the game, but he said he wanted to play. '"I know the people who were killed. I want to play for them." It was a hugely powerful thing,' the manager said in the interview with Thomas Niblock. Afterwards, having scored six points, Mason went to Frosty's wake. 'I was probably fairly anxious going up because I didn't really know had I made the right decision or not by playing the match. I didn't know how the family felt about it. But when I arrived at the door Clare Rogan, Adrian's wife, greeted me with open arms; she told me Adrian would've wanted me to play. That was a massive relief to hear that.'

As the Down team prepared for an Ulster final, and the Irish team got ready for their next match against Mexico, in Loughinisland the families prepared for the funerals to come, while the injured began their long road to recovery. 'Even when you are lying in the hospital, you know, you are getting stories coming in: such a one's dead,' explained Brenny Valentine.

The funerals were held over the course of ninety minutes on one day, the Tuesday following the massacre. Dark clouds and incessant heavy rain drenched the thousands of mourners who walked the county lanes behind six coffins. Alongside a front-page picture that captured her wrapping her arms around her heartbroken children, Marie Byrne, the *News Letter* reported, clung 'to her sons as she carries the weight of a double tragedy – the joint funeral of her husband, Eamon, and her brother, Patsy O'Hare'.

The Requiem Mass took place in the Holy Family church in the neighbouring hamlet of Teconnaught and was quickly followed by a second, for Barney Green and his nephew, Dan McCreanor. Canon Bernard Magee, speaking in St Macartan's church in Loughinisland during the Mass for Malcolm Jenkinson, told mourners of his widow's forgiveness: 'The love in the Jenkinson house was very evident and the grief very intense. Eventually we said the Rosary and at the end, Malcolm's wife, Ann, said: "Would you please say a prayer for those who killed him?"'

The priest, who himself was carrying a bullet in his brain since 1974 after he was shot and miraculously survived a loyalist sectarian attack at St Colmcille's church in East Belfast, long before he had moved to the Loughinisland parish, said that he had witnessed many, many murders during his time in Belfast but had never seen such 'carnage' as that in the O'Toole's bar. He said that watching a football match was a very innocent way of spending a few hours. 'Friends among friends, happy and content. This was in stark contrast to the evil in the hearts of those who came that night with hatred and murder in their hearts,' he told a packed church, with many more mourners standing outside in the rain.

As her father was being lowered into his grave in the adjoining cemetery, eight-year-old Emma Rogan could be heard crying: 'I want my daddy. I want my daddy back.' Emma and her nine-year-old brother, Tony, carried red roses that they placed on his coffin. Eamon Byrne and Patsy O'Hare were buried side-by-side alongside their friend Frosty.

In Downe Hospital, Brenny Valentine's wound was healing but he was overwhelmed, desperately struggling to come to terms with the enormity of what had been visited upon his community and him personally. 'I was in the hospital when the funerals were on. I was able to see them on the television: terrible, terrible. And the big factor was [that] you were living, and these craters [sic] were dead, and you were going to have to go out and go to them people's houses and shake their hand and say sorry, you know. Innocent, you know, wee childer [sic] never seen their fathers again.'

10 | To Annihilate Truth

With his thick scouse accent, Jimmy Binns was well aware that he couldn't deny he was from Liverpool but, for some, it was his religion that was the real problem. He had joined the British Army when he was just seventeen years old and served as a mechanic soldier, completing two tours of duty in Northern Ireland in the late 1970s. He left the army in 1981 and three weeks later joined the RUC. He was stationed first in Magherafelt, South Derry, before joining the Mobile Support Unit, which he found 'was very much like being back in the army, basically'.

After receiving republican death threats, he was moved to Donegall Pass, a loyalist enclave on the southern edge of Belfast city centre. 'It was the busiest station in Northern Ireland and you did ordinary police work with the background of terrorism going on,' he recalled in an interview for *No Stone Unturned*. In 1991 he became a detective and, following a stint in Dungannon, Co. Tyrone, he was transferred to Downpatrick.

He always felt like an outsider in the RUC. 'I can see it in their faces. The minute I start talking it's like: "Why are you making that noise?" I was told I was the token Taig, because I'm Catholic as well. [I served] with some out and out bigots. But also some very brave, honest people who outnumbered the bigots.'

When he began work as a CID detective, Binns saw a very different side to policing in Northern Ireland than in his native Merseyside. 'Let's say on a murder inquiry, you never got the impression that Special Branch told you anything. All they would do is confirm something that you have told them. When I was in the [Mobile Support Unit] … you were aware that touts [informers or agents] were being protected. You would be searching a number of houses to protect a tout and you'd have to put up with that. We felt abused, we felt the public were abused and the tout [had a] higher [value] than anybody else,' he told the producers.

Jimmy Binns began to believe that even his own RUC colleagues were being sacrificed for the 'bigger picture' of Special Branch intelligence-gathering. 'The way I reconciled it with myself, you know, was a bit like Coventry. [On one night during the Second World War, 300 German bombers dropped 500 tons of explosives, killing over 500 civilians. Prime Minister Winston Churchill was believed to have known of the attack in advance, but he did nothing to prevent it in order to protect the fact that Britain had broken Germany's Enigma Code.] If you let Coventry burn, we are going to save five other cities. So, if you let one policeman burn, then we're going to save five others.'

On the night of the Loughinisland massacre, Binns was in his caravan in Portaferry on the Irish Sea coast. 'There were no mobile phones but you had beepers. I contacted the station and was told to come in [the following morning]. It was only then [after he reported for work] I realised what had happened. I wouldn't say the place was in chaos, it was just fragmented. There was no sense of collective vision, if you like.'

This did not bode well for any investigation that Binns' colleagues in Downpatrick would now undertake.

Early on the Sunday morning, on the Listooder Road north-east of Loughinisland, a farmer noticed a gate into his field was ajar. On further examination, he came across the gunmen's red Triumph Acclaim getaway car hidden behind a hedge in his field, the driver's door still open. According to the farmer, it was clear that the UVF gang had experienced a mechanical problem, which caused them to push the vehicle off the road and into the field. When they arrived to take the vehicle away, the police struggled to start the car and had to push it up onto their trailer.

The car just happened to have been abandoned close to the farmhouse belonging to Ronnie Hawthorne's parents, a fact missed by police who never searched the property.

The farmer who had discovered it mused on the car. If it had broken down, would that not have seriously upset their getaway plans? It was normal for one car to get the gang away from the immediate scene, only to be dumped and burned, while they transferred to another vehicle to complete their getaway.

One of the police officers who led the investigation, Albert Carroll, confirmed that the gang did indeed have car troubles. 'I remember the thing being abandoned in the field; the engine had seized up. They couldn't get it to move,' he told a producer on *No Stone Unturned*.

Why had they not destroyed the car, given the risks of forensic evidence being recovered from it? In previous attacks in the area, such as the murder of Peter McCormack at the Thierafurth Inn, when they dumped the car on the edge of the Tollymore Forest Park, they burned it. Why had they taken a different direction this time? These were questions that Albert Carroll and his colleagues were seeking to answer.

'It was that first morning and it was a case of just getting bodies out to do specific tasks,' Jimmy Binns said in his interview. He had a feeling that he was being kept on the periphery of major investigations in Downpatrick. 'I felt I wasn't to be trusted. There was a very strong team in terms of the regional crime squad, and the staff in Downpatrick had been there for numerous years, so you were trying to break into a family,' he said.

When the team leading the investigation ran the number plate on the car through their systems, they were able to track its history to Belfast. It had been through four different owners in eight weeks. Binns was told to go to Belfast and track down where and when the getaway car had been purchased and by whom. He was told to liaise with his colleagues at Tennent Street RUC Station, off the Shankill Road. So he followed orders and drove up to the city, where he discovered that the registered owner of the car had sold it on for £150, but that the vehicle hadn't been re-registered in the new owner's name. 'I spoke to the man who sold the car, I felt he was being open and honest with me,' he recalled, adding that the previous owner still had two of the £20 notes that the buyer – who he named – had given him, which he handed over to the detective. The person who bought it from the registered owner immediately stood out: a Catholic man who had joined the UVF, Terry Fairfield.

But before Binns could track Fairfield down, his Tennent Street colleagues stepped in. 'I was told who I would interview and I was told who I wouldn't be interviewing. Obviously there was an informant and the guy, the cop, I was talking to was obviously looking after [Fairfield]. I wasn't getting to ask awkward questions or scratch below the surface and probe. It felt very choreographed.' Dr Michael Maguire would later describe the investigation of the car's ownership as 'superficial', which resulted in potential evidential opportunities being missed.

Binns returned to Downpatrick without getting to speak to – or having been prevented from speaking to – the man police had established had been in possession of the killers' car: Fairfield. He said he felt 'like being sent out for the shopping by your mother and only coming back with half the stuff. I don't remember feeling uneasy about it, it was the nature of the beast, as it were, and they were happy to accept it. There you go, you know [was the attitude].'

But a link between the killers and Belfast had been established.

After the Thierafurth attack, police had briefed the local newspaper that cars were being stolen in Belfast for use by South Down UVF. A year previously, mid-1993, Special Branch had intelligence that identified Gorman McMullan as the critical linkman who was stealing and supplying the cars used in attacks. Despite everything they already knew about the Triumph Acclaim and the fact that it had been in the hands of one of their informers, the RUC made a public appeal for information about the car, which now appears to have been done to give the false impression they were chasing the killers: 'Were you in Loughinisland or the general area surrounding the village that night or in the recent past? If so, did you see anything suspicious? Look at this photograph of a car found on the Listooder Road, Crossgar, and believed used in the incident. It is a Red Triumph Acclaim car Reg No HJI 807. Did you see it recently but particularly on Friday 17th or Saturday 18th June 1994?'

The RUC was giving the public a sense of action being taken, of leads being followed, of a determination to bring the killers to justice. It was all a charade.

The Maguire Report in 2016 found that there was significant confusion as to who was leading the investigation. One possible candidate was Detective Superintendent David Russell, who gave a statement to the inquests into the murders. He was based in Gough Barracks, Armagh, and was attached to the CID South Region. He had gone to the scene on the night of the attack and had 'supervised the various specialist agencies' in their examinations before returning to Downpatrick Barracks, where he 'supervised the setting up of an investigation and incident room to investigate these murders'. Then there was Albert Carroll, who had been the SIO in the murder of Peter McCormack. He too was involved in the Loughinisland investigation. However, Carroll was due to go on annual leave. 'I had already booked to go on holiday. I was getting ready to leave that evening when the phone call came through … I had discussions with the Senior Investigating Officer [Superintendent Russell] and he was quite happy to let me go, so off I went, and I returned about four or five weeks later,' Detective Carroll told a *No Stone Unturned* producer.

When Dr Michael Maguire reviewed the investigation, some former RUC officers refused to speak with his team, and he didn't have the power the compel them to co-operate. He found that 'the absence of records relating to investigative policy and decision making, coupled with the decision of Police Officer 8 not to assist, hindered my investigation's efforts in establishing the rationale behind a number of key policing decisions and strategies'.

Away from the investigation, the initial shock within the community was settling into a deeper stage of grief. The process of bereavement in rural areas of the North, such as South Down, is a very intimate yet collegiate experience, with families coming together to give each other comfort and support. In the countryside, neighbours and friends sit up overnight in the homes of those who have died. They'll bake cakes, make trays of sandwiches and bring pots of tea for the family who have suffered the loss. Cars will line the country lanes and roads leading to the 'wake house', home of the dead. This is especially true prior to the funeral, but even after, the house can be full of people for days. But, eventually, the crowds thin out and the bereaved begin to pick up the pieces of their lives. There is of course another element when your loved one, neighbour or friend has been cut down in a sectarian massacre. The community was heavy with questions, to which there were no immediate answers.

Moira Casement's neighbour had told her husband as dawn broke on the morning after the massacre to look no further than the RUC. But the Loughinisland families had no choice but to put their full faith in the police force of the day. 'I was brought up to respect the forces of law and order, and we lived our lives, we didn't break the law or at least we went out of our way to try not to break the law,' says Clare Rogan. 'We didn't do anything wrong. I mean, we got letters from, I got a letter from the Queen, a letter from the Pope. This made world news, and I thought they can't let this go. I mean, the eyes of the world are on them. They have to be seen to be doing the right thing here. And these were six innocent men who had absolutely no affiliation with any paramilitaries, any political organisations, nothing. And surely they deserve justice,' she added.

While the victims had all been in the same place at the same time, they didn't all know each other, so in the aftermath their families had no cause to come together to share their experience. Barney Green's niece, Moira Casement, who lived at Teconnaught, recalls that, in the days and weeks after the atrocity, 'we didn't know what was happening, because previous to the massacre, I didn't even know the other people. I only knew of Malcolm because my husband reared turkeys and Malcolm was the last man to come on Christmas Eve to pick up his turkey. And we knew they were all gone, they were all sold once Malcolm came after the pub closed, got his turkey and he always cooked it on Christmas Day. I knew him and I knew Barney and Dan, but I didn't know the people from Loughinisland that were murdered, or the ones that were injured. And I didn't know the survivors and the relatives. Even though we only lived a short distance apart, we didn't know each other.'

While all the families were dealing with the traumatic loss of their loved one, they were looking to the RUC for answers. As Clare Rogan says, 'We were reassured that there would be justice. A policeman visited my home and told me it was like cracking a nut, and he said: "We haven't cracked it, but we've chipped it, we're getting there, just wait, bear with us. We'll sort this out." But time went on and we chose to stay quiet because that was our nature, that was the nature of this community, just get on with your life. So we waited and we waited and we had a few visits from the police and they would say, yes, we're getting there, we're getting there, we're on them. You know, we were drip fed bits of information and we kept thinking: Right, this is it now,' she said, looking back with a sense of bitter disappointment.

***

The sun shone on Clones as Loughinisland's Gary Mason scored five points to help Down overcome Tyrone in the Ulster final on Sunday 17 July. Despite Tyrone going into the game as favourites, Mickey Linden, Ross Carr, with a goal and four points, and Greg Blaney helped Down win in style, beating the Red Hands by six points, 1–17 to 1–11. Tyrone's day would come, but for now the Mournemen had their eyes fixed on winning a fifth All-Ireland title, something they would indeed accomplish later that summer, defeating Dublin 1–12 to 0–13. Pete McGrath knew that beating Derry – the last Down game that Frosty attended – had set them up for another Sam Maguire, their second in four years.

The World Cup finals had ended for Ireland in defeat by Holland in the second round. The Dutch had cracked Jack's 4–5–1 code, winning 2–0. The Italians recovered from their Irish defeat to make the final against Brazil in the Rose Bowl stadium in Pasadena, California on Sunday 17 July, with a lunchtime (in the US) kick-off that suited audiences in Europe. It provided loyalists with another deadly opportunity similar to the Loughinisland massacre.

The Hawthorne Inn at Annaclone, between Rathfriland and Banbridge, lies about twenty miles west of Loughinisland. On the night of the World Cup final it was a clone of the night of the Italy game in The Heights Bar: the target was in South Down, isolated, in a predominantly nationalist area and packed full of Catholics innocently, collectively watching a big sporting occasion. After Loughinisland, the RUC had issued a warning of further attacks as Irish fans watched the football matches in bars and clubs, Deputy Chief Constable Blair Wallace admitting that police (through the informers who were working for them) 'have specific concerns about a number of events where people are likely to gather in numbers'.

Around forty customers were in the Hawthorne Inn, some of them Down supporters celebrating on their way back from Clones, with others there to watch the Brazil and Italy match. Landlord John Loy had been to the Ulster final and had locked the pub's heavy mahogany front doors as the World Cup game went into penalties. There was a hush in the bar as both sides missed their first spot kicks. As the sporting drama unfolded, two bursts of gunfire came through one of the pub's two main windows to the front of the building, sending customers diving for cover. There were concerns the gunmen were going to come into the bar, but as quickly as it started, the shooting was over with the sound of screeching tyres.

'Annaclone was lucky,' read the *Irish Times* report. Seven customers, including a fourteen-year-old boy, were injured, most by flying glass. John Loy told the *News Letter* that he had seen a suspicious car, fitted with Belfast registration plates and four men inside, outside the bar two weeks previously and had called the police, who told him 'more or less, to be careful'. His wife, Valerie, who was pregnant, had been working behind the bar when the gunmen struck. 'There was total silence … I thought they were all dead. It must have been some sort of inspiration that John had to close the doors when he did. It could so easily have been a repeat of Loughinisland,' she told the *Irish Times* reporter Suzanne Breen, who wrote that, fortunately, the gunmen had fired into the left-hand side of the bar while most of the customers were on the right-hand side, watching the football on the television.

One survivor said all he could remember was hearing the shots and people screaming as they dived to the floor. Rosemary Hillen believed her fourteen-year-old son, Martin, was only alive because the pool machine had jammed. 'He wanted to play pool but couldn't get the ten pence into the machine and went and sat down. A bullet hit a radiator where he would have been standing had he been playing.' Rosemary herself had a miraculous escape when a glass she was being handed by her husband was shattered by a bullet.

In a statement, the UFF claimed responsibility and said that two 'locked, heavy mahogany front doors prevented our volunteers from inflicting heavy casualties'. In an interview with the *News Letter*, Hugh O'Toole said that the attack 'brings it all back' and he still didn't know if he would reopen the doors of his pub ever again.

***

There had been no history of the UFF being able to mount such attacks in the South Down area prior to these incidents. Between 18 June and 17 July the RUC had failed to arrest a single suspect for the Loughinisland massacre. However, on the morning after the Hawthorne Inn attack, six men, including Alan Taylor and Gorman McMullan, were arrested and taken to Gough Barracks for questioning.

In a statement to the *Belfast Telegraph* reporter Darwin Templeton, an RUC spokesman said the arrests had been carried out at dawn in several areas throughout Co. Down and Belfast. The RUC told the reporter that they were looking for information about a blue Metro car that had been found burned out at Katesbridge, two miles from the scene of the attempted massacre. The killers had fled in the direction of Clough, abandoning one car as they came to the main road, only to get into another that had been waiting. The Metro had been bought in Belfast, just like the car used in the Loughinisland atrocity.

Eddie McGrady said it was intended to be 'a carbon copy' of the Loughinisland massacre and said the only thing that had saved the men, women and children from being shot was the fortuitous bolting and closing of the door. 'It is obvious that these gun-toting thugs are clearly intent on killing indiscriminately in their continual bloodlust,' he added.

It was the RUC who linked the two attacks, briefing the media on their connection. Darwin Templeton's first paragraph read: 'A number of men were today being questioned about last night's UFF attack on a bar near Banbridge and the Loughinisland pub massacre.' Only those UVF members who had already been identified as being members of the South Down/Belfast gang were arrested. Along with Gorman McMullan and Alan Taylor, the RUC had arrested Ronnie Hawthorne's brother, Trevor, and Trevor Watson. In Belfast they arrested a leading UVF figure on the Shankill Road.

All of them were released without charge. On the day of the police operation against the other members of the gang, Ronnie Hawthorne's home was searched but, crucially, he wasn't arrested on this occasion. Dr Michael Maguire could find no explanation as to why he wasn't detained by police.

Two weeks later, on 2 August, the RUC had yet another breakthrough in the Loughinisland case. Police recorded that two workmen working on the Carsonstown Road, just over eight miles north-east of Loughinisland and two and a half miles from where the getaway car was found, discovered a holdall in a hedge. They immediately thought it was suspicious and called the police. When it was opened, it was a veritable treasure trove for the detectives investigating the massacre. Inside was a magazine for a VZ-58 rifle, a .38 calibre Rossi revolver loaded with five bullets, a .38 calibre Smith & Wesson revolver, also loaded with five bullets, and a 9mm Browning semi-automatic pistol with eleven bullets in a magazine. Police also found a VZ-58 rifle hidden nearby minus its wooden stock. As well as the weapons and ammunition, there were three boiler suits, three balaclavas, three pairs of surgical gloves and a single pair of woollen gloves.

The 18 July arrests may or may not have led to the discovery of the weapons on the Carsonstown Road. Did two workmen really come upon the weapons by pure chance? Or might it have been a similar situation to that which followed the murder of Jack Kielty, when police discovered the montages and weapons in Clough Orange Hall after William Bell and Delbert Watson had been broken during questioning? Might one of those arrested have given up the weapons, just as Delbert Watson had in the earlier case? Martin Lavery's family had been told that one of his killers became an informer in mid-1993, so was, therefore, a state agent at the time of the Loughinisland attack.

Sixty-four days after the Loughinisland massacre, Ronnie Hawthorne was finally arrested at his home in Clough in front of his wife, Hilary, and baby son, and taken to Gough Barracks. Alan Taylor and Trevor Watson were again detained on the same day, 22 August, but not Gorman McMullan. Police already had Hawthorne's fingerprints from his arrest in connection with the Orange Hall weapons find in his village. Now they took a sample of his hair and a buccal swab test, which is basically a smear of the inside of the mouth. Taylor also had hair samples and a buccal swab taken.

But, after forty-eight hours of questioning, the three men were released without charge.

***

On 31 August, nine days after Ronnie Hawthorne's arrest, the IRA declared a ceasefire. The decision by John Hume in the summer of 1987 to enter dialogue with Gerry Adams, much to the dismay of his party and supporters, had paid off. The war was over. In London, Dublin and Washington DC, the decision was welcomed as a new dawn for Northern Ireland. Unionist leader Jim Molyneaux said it was one of the most 'destabilising events since partition'.

Six weeks later, Bill Flynn was in Belfast when the UVF and UFF declared that they too were ending their violence, Gusty Spence offering their victims their 'true and abject remorse' in a statement Flynn helped to write. Hugh O'Toole told *The Irish Times* it had come 'four months too late' for those who had died in his bar. The local SDLP councillor, Patsy Toman, who had been at the scene on the night and whose home had been the target of a bomb attack by loyalists, told the paper: 'Four months ago, the UVF murdered six good people and left this community with a loss which will never be replaced by any apology. For Gusty Spence, the first man to carry out a murder in the present Troubles, to tell us they are sorry sits lightly on the people who have lost husbands, fathers and brothers.'

For the Loughinisland families, the lack of progress in the police investigation was only adding to their grinding grief. During the first days and weeks, the RUC had visited their homes, keeping them up to date with what was going on and filling them with hope that the men who had massacred their loved ones would be caught and jailed, as Sir Patrick Mayhew had so publicly promised. But, like the mourners who eventually drifted away to leave them to pick up their lives, the police stopped calling. 'It just stopped,' remembers Clare Rogan. 'There was no contact. And we chose just to stay quiet and hope that some day somebody would be brought to justice or they would get to the bottom of it. But nothing happened. On reflection, sometimes I kind of feel a bit guilty that we didn't speak up because it seems now that we were almost … [it's like] that's what they wanted us to do, they wanted us to stay quiet and this would go away.'

Moira Casement was having similar thoughts. 'We didn't realise, that there was so much going on further up, that it wasn't just the policemen on the ground, that it was strings were being pulled from further up the ladder. And we didn't know until a long time later how much involvement there was from various agencies and that there was investigative opportunities that were, that should have been exhausted, and were missed at the time. The police never, ever came near us or told us. We didn't know what was happening. We were just trying to rebuild our lives, because nothing was ever, ever going to be the same again. On a personal level, on a family level, we weren't going to just get up and get on with it the next day. I suppose, we got strength from one another.'

Marie Byrne told Barry McCaffrey in an article for *The Detail* that it was the everyday needs of her children that demanded the family try to carry on with a normal life. 'The children had to eat, they had to go to school. We had to be strong for them. It was one day at a time. You couldn't even look towards the next week. But it was hard on the children because they adored their daddy. Martin had terrible nightmares. He used to wake up standing straight up in the bed. That went on for two years. It was hard for Martin because people were telling him he had to be the man of the house now. He was only 11 years of age, little more than a child. He felt an awful lot of pressure on his shoulders. He had to receive counselling. The rest of the boys just clung to us.'

With the pressure of caring for four young boys, Marie Byrne put her faith in the police to bring the killers to justice. 'The police told us they would catch the people who did this and put them behind bars for a long time and we trusted them, why wouldn't we? We are quiet country people. We didn't know any better.'

The RUC had called to speak with Marie at her home in Drumaness in the aftermath of the shooting, asking for pictures of the family.

'At the time, we were promised they would return them within weeks but we're still waiting. We have no photograph of us all together. All those cherished memories of the good times taken away,' she said. The RUC lost the family pictures and never explained or apologised.

A month or more after the Loughinisland attack, Jimmy Binns was in a bar in the coastal town of Killough, south-east of Loughinisland, in the early hours of the morning when two detective colleagues came in for a drink. Jimmy was with a crowd of friends and invited them to join his company. At the time, RUC officers were known for their hard drinking, it was the way in which many drowned out the white noise of the conflict.

Very quickly, as the rest of the customers began to leave for home, one of the two detectives got into an intense conversation with the Scouser about Loughinisland and made a truly explosive revelation: 'He told me that [police knew] the car had broken down the Saturday night [on the way to Loughinisland] and the tout had contacted his handler and had told him, "The car's broken down, they're not going ahead." But the job did go ahead. And at that it was just like, I mean, [I realised that] they could have stopped it,' the detective told the author in an interview.

Taken aback by his story, I pushed for clarity: 'So Loughinisland, in which six people died, you were in a bar drinking with two of the detectives who were involved in the investigation into who carried out the attack?'

'Yeah.'

'And they said actually there was a tout, there was an informant, there was an agent working within the [UVF] team that was responsible for the attack?'

'Yeah.'

'And they had told them that he had alerted the police this attack was going to happen, and they had known for some time the attack was going to happen?'

'Yeah, obviously the tout would have had access to the car, so it would have been a case of tracking the car. So, like I say, roundabout tea-time that night there was a phone call made to say it's not going to go ahead because the car had broken down. But the attack did go ahead.'

'And how did the policemen feel about this?'

'Aghast, you know, if that's not too mild a word.'

Jimmy Binns never forgot what he was told in that bar. He wasn't part of the inner team investigating the massacre and knew there was nowhere he could go with what he had been told, at that point at least. He continued with his career, but it haunted him: 'There was a telephone call from a tout a couple of hours before the killings, that the car had broken down and it had been called off, and that's all I got,' he repeated.

The policeman in the bar was telling more over a drink to his colleague than the relatives were ever hearing in their irregular meetings with the detectives leading the investigation. 'I remember a policemen coming into the wake and saying, a few of them actually would have known him personally, known my husband, and said, I'll never forget their words: "We will leave no stone unturned until we get the perpetrators of this." And those words ring in my ear to this day, because I don't think they ever lifted a stone, never mind turned it. It was just an absolute nightmare that we never, ever for one minute ever thought would visit us here. The Troubles were something that happened in Belfast. Yes, we were aware of them and we were aware of all the atrocities and, you know, people losing their lives, but it was something that never touched us and we never, ever for one minute thought that we would ever have to live through that,' said Clare Rogan.

Weeks turned into months and months into years and still there was no respite for the families. 'Any time we had met with the police, when they had come out to us, every question we asked we were told: "Oh, we can't tell you that now, you have to put it in writing,'" remembers Moira Casement. 'No, we can't tell you that, that's national security. We were thwarted all the time. We never were getting a straight answer, or else we were told lies. We were actually told lies.'

***

The Loughinisland families supported the Good Friday Agreement in 1998, although it provided little by way of meaningful support for the families of the 3,500 victims of the Troubles other than the hope that their children and grandchildren would never again experience conflict.

The Omagh bomb, five months later, claimed the lives of twenty-nine people and two unborn children. Republicans in the splinter group called the 'Real IRA', who had broken away from the IRA because of its support for Sinn Féin's political strategy, had targeted the Co. Tyrone town on a Saturday afternoon when it was thronged with shoppers and tourists, their goal to destroy the peace process. Coming four years after Loughinisland, and with so many deaths in between, the world had a new barbarous act to gasp at, as well as condemning the people of Northern Ireland as being unwilling or unable to wean themselves off violence.

The word 'stalemate' and the giddy phrases 'tit for tat' and 'random sectarian killing' had long since been burned into the lexicon of the conflict, and they were rolled out again as shorthand explanations for the latest atrocity. In the early 1990s the British government certainly wanted the people of Northern Ireland, particularly unionists, to believe there was a stalemate. It has been argued that by ensuring the loyalists were rearmed in 1988 and had access to the kind of intelligence that Brian Nelson revealed he had been given, London – and by extension the security forces – were attempting to level the playing field with an IRA that had the slingshot of eager and willing recruits who joined up after the hunger strike and a new cache of arms supplied by Libya. They forced a stalemate, which ultimately helped bring all sides to the table, the argument goes. But at what cost? 'Tit for tat' gave comfort to those who wanted to believe that Northern Ireland was simply a merry-go-round of sectarianism.

However, the truth was much darker, more complicated and sinister. Was Loughinisland a 'random sectarian killing'? Can it really be described as such, particularly if you knew that there were military-trained killers living five minutes away – indeed one of them is working for you – that they have a proven ability to kill and that pub shootings are their favourite tactic? Is it not an inevitability that they'll eventually go for the softest of soft targets up the road, even if you are not controlling them and sanctioning their targets?

At as the new millennium dawned, the families were losing patience with the RUC. Deeply frustrated by the lack of progress in the police investigation, Marie Byrne, accompanied by members of her family, drove to Downpatrick police station where she politely asked for an update. 'When we asked the police if they could tell us what was happening with the murder inquiry, they didn't seem to know what we were talking about. The policeman told me I'd be far better going home and rearing my children. In other words, forget about it. We weren't there to criticise or cause trouble. We were only inquiring about how the murder investigation was going,' she told Barry McCaffrey, still angry at the disrespect they had been shown.

Emma Rogan and her brother, Tony, grew up watching their mother struggle with the loss of her husband. Over the years, as she learned more about what had happened to her father, Emma would find not only her voice but a steely determination to do one thing for her mother: get to the truth behind why her husband had to die.

When she turned eighteen, it was Emma who would bring the families together. 'We needed to get answers. [At the start] ... it wasn't a group that formed, but a few of us, like, maybe even in the pub talked about it; we needed to see what's happening. Nobody had come near us as a family. Nobody from the police had told us in ten years what had happened. It was coming up to the tenth anniversary [of the massacre] and we decided that we had, you know, actually we needed to see where this investigation was at. And then we got together as a group, the different families, and people that were here that night that were injured, some that weren't, you know, were here but weren't physically injured, and we formed a group: the Loughinisland Justice Group.'

***

Of all the changes to society in the North that flowed from the Good Friday Agreement, the overhauling of the policing system was one of the most challenging. The RUC was overwhelmingly Protestant and had never commanded the full respect of the nationalist community, particularly as allegations of collusion with loyalist paramilitaries grew more intense during the 1980s and 1990s.

A former Minister of State in Northern Ireland during the Margaret Thatcher years, Chris Patton, returned to lead a commission on the future of policing arrangements. In the end, he proposed a new force be established, the Police Service of Northern Ireland (PSNI). Ronnie Flanagan, the former Special Branch officer, was the last chief constable of the RUC and the first of the new force when it was established in 2001. There would be new accountability structures to help build community confidence, particularly among nationalists. A newly established Policing Board would have political and non-political members and would provide policing oversight. It would appoint the chief constable and hold monthly public meetings where senior officers were questioned about current events.

The Office of the Police Ombudsman (OPONI) was also established to be an impartial and independent organisation that would handle public complaints into allegations of wrongdoing by PSNI officers. Critically, it would also investigate complaints about the RUC through its Historical Investigation Directorate, examining allegations against the former police force around death or serious criminality between 1968 and 1998. Within months of its establishment, the first complaints of collusion began to be filed with the police ombudsman. Some of the Loughinisland families contacted the ombudsman's office as early as 2001 but did not file a formal complaint at that time.

In parallel to the Loughinisland families organising, a new legal firm opened in Belfast. Kevin Winters had worked for Madden & Finucane, one of the best-known defence firms in the North, founded by solicitors Peter Madden and Pat Finucane, the latter murdered by loyalists in 1989. Winters opened his own practice in 2001, KRW Law. His first hire was an eager young North Belfast lawyer. Niall Murphy had graduated from Queen's University in the summer after the signing of the Good Friday Agreement and went straight into Madden & Finucane as an apprentice, helping the firm in preparations for the Bloody Sunday inquiry that was underway in Derry. Niall became a partner in KRW in 2003, the year before he first met with the Loughinisland families.

In an interview for *Ceasefire Massacre*, he recalled where he was on the night of the slaughter: 'I was seventeen years old at the time. I was a barman in a local bar in Belfast, The Chester. Most of the staff, barmen and waiters, were drunk. We were all drinking, enjoying the craic at the match. Everybody was euphoric. And as the night developed, you could see a depression falling across the bar. People would begin crying and word filtered through that there had been an atrocity twenty-five miles outside Belfast. Nobody had ever heard of Loughinisland, or knew where it was, what type of area it was, but the elation that the football match had presented automatically turned to one of grief and despair.'

The families had gone to a meeting with other bereaved families in the South Down area and it was through this that they were first introduced to Niall and KRW. They had put all their faith in the police and been let down. Some of the families felt a sense of regret that they hadn't spoken up sooner, but once they got together, they drew strength from one another; they had all suffered the same pain, the same loss and had mourned for their husbands, brothers, fathers. They would continue to grieve, but they were no longer going to wait silently for the police to act.

'We were all in shock for so long, it could have been three or four years before the reality of what had happened began to really sink in,' says Clare Rogan. 'Because we were coming to terms with our grief, you know, the grief of loss and burying your loved one and you had to get on with your life. I had two children. I had to get them to school. I had to go to work. Life goes on. But then when the reality sank in, you started to say: But why? The police got the car quite soon after it, they got the balaclavas, they got the guns, they told us all they needed was one hair follicle, one trace of DNA and these people would be brought to justice. But nothing. It just stopped there. That was it. And then you start to question: But why? Where did all this evidence go?'

As for how they were going to get answers, they had no idea, according to Moira Casement: 'We wouldn't have known where to start. When we got Niall and the legal team involved, it was only then we started to realise that there should have been more done in between times. I mean, those ten years were lost. People were busy bringing up their families. It changed everybody's life. I mean, it was a catastrophic thing, never mind when you have a small family, it affected everybody.'

Niall Murphy is a meticulous note-taker. It is his superpower. Regardless of the situation he finds himself in, he will never be accused of not having an accurate – periphrastic, some might say – account of what he witnessed. Right from the first moment he first met the families, at the Millbrook Hotel outside Ballynahinch in January 2005, he began documenting their conversations. 'A series of consultations took place wherein the actual facts, which fed the fears of collusion, were discussed. Unfortunately, there was no firm evidence forthcoming, bar the various stories of local people who related the experience of having been subjected to heavy security pressures and vehicle check-points in the hours prior to the atrocity.'

They set up a meeting with the PSNI to find out what was going on with the investigation, with one of Niall's partners attending on behalf of KRW Law. In July 2005 they met with ACC Sam Kincaid and Detective Chief Superintendent Derek Williamson, who was now the SIO on the case. The families' solicitor recorded the tone, attitude and role of Kincaid, who stated in his opening address that 'none of the detectives could say anything about the role of informers in this case'. The fact that it was the senior police officer who first mentioned informers was noted by the families and their legal representative.

More than the mention of informers, however, the bombshell revelation during the meeting was that the getaway car, the red Triumph Acclaim, had been destroyed less than eight months after the massacre. 'It was commonplace at that time not to retain vehicles involved in murder cases,' one of the RUC officers told the shocked families.

They had destroyed the car? It was, surely, the one piece of evidence that could still yield forensic evidence that would put the killers behind bars. After all, scientific techniques were improving every day; maybe a new tool would emerge that could help police identify the killers through examination of the car.

The families left the meeting with more questions than answers. Still, they had at least agreed with the police representatives to meet again.

At the second meeting, it was revealed that the weapon used in The Heights Bar did indeed come from the South African shipment, a concession they hadn't clearly intended to share with the families prior to them sitting down. Niall Murphy's minutes of the meeting captured the moment: 'A remarkable concession was provided by [PSNI] Detective Inspector Wilson, wherein he accepted that the VZ-58 Czech-made rifle … was one of the weapons that came into NI from South Africa in the late 1980s,' he wrote. This was a remarkable breakthrough in terms of unravelling the facts of this case. Follow-up letters were indeed sent and a reply was received from the PSNI officer stating that he couldn't confirm definitively that the VZ-58 recovered was a part of such a consignment.

Despite their frustrations, the families wanted to give the police all the space they needed to go after the gunmen. So, they held their tongue, they didn't speak to the press, and they waited. And waited.

By March 2006 they'd had enough. No one had been charged, there was no response to the questions that police had promised to answer, so, without alerting the media – thereby providing the police with breathing space to continue their investigation – they formally lodged a complaint with the police ombudsman's office, led at that time by Nuala O'Loan, a former law lecturer who had herself been injured in an IRA bomb attack at the Ulster University outside Belfast. The families wanted a series of questions answered. Primarily, they wanted to know if there was collusion between the RUC and the killers.

The ombudsman's office had already established a reputation for being fearless, rigorous and fiercely independent. This reputation was reinforced when O'Loan investigated a complaint about the RUC's handling of the Omagh bomb inquiry. Finding that the police, through agents, had some prior knowledge that there was to be an attack, she was heavily critical of the quality of the 'defective leadership' in the subsequent investigation into the dissident republican terrorists responsible for the atrocity. The PSNI's chief constable, Ronnie Flanagan, went on BBC Television to respond to the report, dramatically promising to commit suicide if the ombudsman was correct in her assessments. The report stood. Flanagan, not following through on his promise, would quietly bow out, waved off into retirement with two knighthoods from the British government.

The Omagh Report sent shockwaves through the British government and, at one point, a senior official at the Northern Ireland Office (NIO) – the department that governs the North on behalf of London – had warned O'Loan not to publish it. She did anyway. In doing so, she set down the foundation stones of the ombudsman's office and the standards that could be expected from it. She had faced down the chief constable and fiercely defended her findings in private and in public.

In the aftermath, relatives of those who had died during the conflict flooded her office with complaints. As a result, the Loughinisland families would have to wait their turn.

***

A month after they filed their complaint, *The Sunday Times* ran a story that caught the families' attention. The headline read: 'Most senior UVF leaders were "British agents"'. The article was in connection to Nuala O'Loan's investigation into a loyalist paramilitary unit in Northern Belfast. Known as 'Operation Ballast', it would set the standard for OPONI's investigations of allegations of collusion.

Arising out a complaint from the campaigner Raymond McCord about the UVF's murder of his son, O'Loan's investigation revealed a dramatic and damning web of RUC collusion with loyalist killers in North Belfast. John Stevens had carried out three extensive investigations into the murder of Pat Finucane and collusion, but only published a twenty-four-page summary from his third attempt to get at the truth. In contrast, without apology, O'Loan was putting the full, ugly, murderous picture that she had found from the dark underbelly of the conflict into the public domain.

She had discovered that UVF gunmen were working as agents of the state while their handlers knew they were committing drugs offences, as well as battering and murdering their victims, over twenty of them in a decade alone. It was clear that, despite Stevens' report and Nelson's testimony, in the late 1980s through to the late 1990s the RUC Special Branch continued with the same strategies, wrapping themselves in a threadbare comfort-blanket notion that the bigger picture told them they were saving lives.

The ombudsman also found that CID detectives were often treated with contempt by their Special Branch colleagues, who were conducting sham interviews, holding back intelligence and ultimately protecting the murdering agents. She found that 'some serving officers gave evasive, contradictory and on occasion farcical answers to questions. On occasion those answers indicated either a significant failure to understand the law or contempt for the law. On other occasions the investigation demonstrated conclusively that what an officer had told the Police Ombudsman's investigators was completely untrue.'

The OPONI report, published in 2007, accepted that 'intelligence in itself is not evidence. However, it may be possible to derive investigative opportunities from intelligence. There were mechanisms which were used by other police forces within the United Kingdom to prevent the failings of informant and intelligence handling but those strategies were never adopted by the RUC.' One of the most critical sections of the report set out how one UVF informer had been paid almost £80k by the state. 'Prior to 2003, some RUC/PSNI Special Branch officers facilitated the situation in which informants were able to continue to engage in paramilitary activity, some of them holding senior positions in the UVF, despite the availability of extensive information as to their alleged involvement in crime. Those informants must have known that they were not being dealt with for crime. Some RUC/PSNI officers were complicit in the failure to deal appropriately [with informants].'

The *Sunday Times* report detailing the OPONI investigation contained several new revelations, but one line concerning a UVF informer understandably stood out for the Loughinisland families. '[Agent] Mechanic is believed to have taken part in the bombing of a Sinn Féin office in Monaghan and to have, perhaps unwittingly, supplied the car used in a sectarian attack on The Heights Bar in Loughinisland, in which six people were killed.'

The man who supplied the car was an agent? Well, Jimmy Binns suspected it from the moment he had tried to speak to him the morning after the attack, but now the families were learning – not from the police, but from the media – that at least one agent was involved in the conspiracy to murder their loved ones.

They later learned that 'Agent Mechanic' was Terry Fairfield and came to the belief that the article had been strategically placed by a former RUC detective to 'surreptitiously protect' his informant. 'The story sought to portray Fairfield as having provided the car for an innocent purpose, i.e. not a mass murder,' Niall Murphy told the author. 'So he was getting his defence in early. His police handlers knew that the evidence would come back to expose him and were getting ahead of it. It was quite a clever strategy.'

One day, a few months after the article appeared, Murphy took a call from an unknown number. It was Fairfield, now living in England. Like many of his fellow informers, he had left Northern Ireland. 'The most interesting thing that he said was that in the days after the atrocity he received a phone call from RUC detective Jonty Brown to get down to Tennent Street police station, that he wanted to ask him about a car. [Fairfield told him] "I said it was [another UVF man] who sold the car, and I'll come down when I'm finished at the market. He said we'll come down and get you at the market. He came down, I made a statement and that was it."'

The solicitor was now in possession of the other half of Jimmy Binns' story. He hadn't been told anything about the phone call to Fairfield or of the statement taken at the Sunday market by a police officer who had nothing to do with the Loughinisland investigation.

For the Loughinisland families, and many, many more across the North, Nuala O'Loan's report was devastating. For the first time there was documented proof of Special Branch protecting UVF killers. It only invigorated the families' determination to get to the truth behind the massacre in their village.

In 2007 Nuala O'Loan would mandatorily stand down from the role after serving eight years as ombudsman. She had established a culture of rigour and integrity in a vital accountability mechanism. (She would later be appointed to the House of Lords.) The British government wasn't going to make the same mistake again. As her successor, they opted for a quietly spoken Canadian, Al Hutchinson, a former member of the Royal Canadian Mounted Police. The NIO, which appoints the ombudsman, knew exactly what it was doing. There was never going to be another Omagh or Operation Ballast-type report from the office of the ombudsman. The dark forces – those who knew all about, and even allowed, informers to kill and later protected them from prosecution – were now shutting down the only mechanism that could give families the truth behind the death of their loved ones.

***

After the *Sunday Times* report, and the continued lack of evidence that the PSNI were going after the killers, the families decided to hold their first press conference. It was a huge step for them, particularly as they had maintained such a dignified silence for over a decade. Going public to criticise the police wasn't their style. They had put their trust in the police, they had believed they would leave 'no stone unturned' but coming up to the twelfth anniversary, they could not allow the memory of their loved ones to be sullied any longer by their perceived inaction. They were going to tell their story.

However, as they prepared for the press conference, they received a call from a local SDLP representative, Margaret Ritchie, saying the police wanted to meet with them urgently. On 5 June 2006, at the GAA club in the village, they met with the PSNI officers, who raised their hopes that, at last, charges were coming. The following day, two men were arrested, but they were released before dinner time without charge.

This, if anything, only further convinced the families that they had to go public. 'The families considered that their trust and confidence was in fact being abused by the police and indeed that arrests were purely cosmetic and undertaken to offset the criticism the families had decided to make public a week later,' wrote their lawyer. Interestingly, given all that was to come, Niall Murphy also noted: 'the families were also concerned that their strategy was being monitored and that the police were setting their agenda as a self-preservative response to it, rather than being engaged in an earnest attempt to bring to justice those responsible.'

An allegation that the police were 'monitoring' the victims of a massacre so as to allow them to get their defence together was, at the time – even for Northern Ireland – an outlandish thought. But 'self-preservative' were words that would come to the fore much later in relation to Loughinisland.

The press conference was preceded by Clare and Emma Rogan giving Barry McCaffrey from *The Irish News* an exclusive interview, setting out their story and their hopes for justice and truth. The following day, 15 June 2006, in an upstairs room at the Cultúrlann McAdam Ó Fiaich, an Irish language, arts and cultural centre on the Falls Road in West Belfast, in front of the local press corps, and with the baby-faced Niall Murphy at the top table beside them, the families explained how they now wanted a 'rigorous, exhaustive police investigation', as well as an examination of the 'serious and evidenced allegations' of state collusion dealt with in an 'open and transparent' fashion. They also wanted respect from the PSNI for their 'dignified, reserved and patient position' that they believed had been abused.

It was a huge moment. The most dignified families that a police detective could ever wish to deal with had lost their patience with the PSNI. They had been pushed to it by the constant promise of 'no stone unturned'.

The press conference gave them energy, but they were going to need it over the ten years to come.

11 | How to Define Collusion

In the months before the press conference, I had started a television production company, Below The Radar, along with a very talented colleague, Ruth O'Reilly. Prior to setting up the company, we had produced a documentary together for UTV's weekly current affairs series, *Insight*, that had led to a public inquiry into the deaths of babies and children in hospitals in Northern Ireland from a condition called hyponatraemia, caused by an electrolyte imbalance. The health authorities had blamed the deaths of Raychel Ferguson, Lucy Crawford and Adam Strain on an 'idiosyncratic reaction' by the children. Ruth O'Reilly and I had spent two years investigating the cases and UTV had ultimately broadcast the documentary, *When Hospitals Kill*, in October 2004. The documentary showed how the hospitals had, in fact, known the children had died due to being administered too much of the wrong fluid and then covered it up.

Knowing that UTV were going to shut down its current affairs team in order to save costs, Ruth and I left to set up Below The Radar. For the first year we produced investigations for Channel 4 News in Britain before making programmes for the BBC, RTÉ and a number of other broadcasters, including the History Channel. We knew that television current affairs programmes were under attack. The famed *World in Action* programme had already been decommissioned, for example, and the powers at the BBC were beginning the process of diluting its flagship weekly current affairs programme, *Panorama*. Ruth had seen it coming before anyone else. We told anyone who would listen that journalism was under attack and that by shutting down UTV current affairs, Northern Ireland audiences would have to rely on BBC Northern Ireland for hard-hitting investigations. That lack of plurality, or journalistic competition, was unhealthy.

Ruth was constantly feeding me articles, documentaries and alternative perspectives on news stories. She had an innate ability to see the world from a different angle to everyone else. She had worked in *The Irish News*, like Barry, and had covered the Bloody Sunday Inquiry in Derry for the Press Association before returning to UTV in the early 2000s, where we had got to know each other. She was always worth listening to, had a very cultured world view, enjoyed a pint, and had a great, hearty, country laugh. Her family was from Drumaness, up the road from Loughinisland, and she epitomised the South Down softly spoken character who knew her own mind and wasn't afraid of sharing her opinions, no matter who agreed or disagreed with her. She was also a formidable journalist.

During this time, Ruth put under my nose a documentary film called *Enron: The Smartest Guys in the Room*, written and directed by an American, Alex Gibney. The 2005 film, edited by Alison Ellwood, who would become a very dear friend, told the story of the pure greed and corruption at the Enron Corporation, an energy and commodities company that became one of the largest and most successful in US history. The documentary captured beautifully how Enron had abused the energy crisis in California to drive up utility prices at the expense of the average American, with its staff caught on recordings laughing as they hiked up the costs, knowing well the pain it would cause to its subscribers.

Ruth knew what she was doing. Nobody in the UK or Ireland was making feature-length documentaries this way. Alex Gibney and Alison Ellwood were skilled filmmakers who had crafted the story to be seen on a big cinema screen. In fact, Gibney was fast becoming the leading documentarian in the business, with his distinctive accent lending authority to every line of his succinct, punchy narration.

The film was shortlisted for an Academy Award, losing out to *March of the Penguins*, narrated by Morgan Freeman. Gibney was beaten to the Oscar by a man who spoke like the Lord God Himself.

Two years later, in 2007, he was back at the Oscars with *Taxi to the Dark Side*, which told the story of an Afghan peanut farmer, Dilawar, who died after being beaten and tortured by the CIA at the Bagram detention centre in Afghanistan during the American invasion post 9/11. In the searing film, Gibney exposed America's human rights record on torture and interrogation. This time he won the Oscar. In his acceptance speech, he dedicated the win to two people who were now dead: 'Dilawar, the young Afghan taxi driver, and my father, a navy interrogator who urged me to make this film because of his fury about what was being done to the rule of law. Let's hope we can turn this country around, move away from the dark side and back to the light.'

Ruth O'Reilly was the first person I knew to pick up on Gibney and the films he was making. And she told me something else: he was coming to Ireland.

So, on a Saturday morning in July 2008, my wife and I, our daughters and two best friends all piled into a car and drove four hours to Galway so I could hear him speak. Afterwards, over a pint in one of the bars on Quay Street, he agreed to meet with me again in New York when I next visited.

***

After they made the complaint to OPONI, the Loughinisland families had to sit back and let their inquiry run its course. However, as a result of their press conference, new information came to light.

The bereaved father of Raymond McCord Junior, a former RAF radar operator who had joined the UVF and was subsequently murdered by them in November 1997 in a drug dispute, contacted KRW's offices in central Belfast to ask for a meeting. It was at this point that Raymond McCord Senior advised Niall Murphy that Agent Mechanic was Terry Fairfield, and his handler was the CID detective who Niall knew had given Jimmy Binns the runaround when he tried to interview him. Fairfield had been run off the books and was not a formally registered informant, although he still clearly had a free licence to be involved in murder and other serious crime. Murphy passed this information on to the ombudsman.

In another development, Frosty Rogan's brother-in-law was approached by police in his vehicle recovery yard. As part of his business, he was approved by police to collect stolen and crashed cars. A detective, who had no idea with whom he was speaking, showed him a registration for a car that had been lifted from Saintfield police station. It was the Triumph Acclaim getaway car the killers had used. The detective had brought with him an RUC logbook; it was blank in the section where there should have been the signature of the person who collected the car. In other words, the detective had no idea who had removed the car, or where it was taken. 'They were trying to retrace and retrospectively find out what happened to the car. They didn't have a clue,' noted the solicitor. The PSNI knew the car was destroyed but had no idea what the chain of events was that led to the order to have it crushed.

Meanwhile, over the course of 2007 the PSNI changed the SIO in charge of the police investigation a further three times. During the same year, the families were assured by OPONI that their complaint was one of the top six cases currently being processed. But then Nuala O'Loan stepped down to be replaced by Al Hutchinson. By the new year, Hutchinson had a new Senior Director of Investigations, Jim Coupland, who had previously been an officer at Scotland Yard. The chief executive officer at OPONI at the time was Sam Pollock, a former social worker who had spent almost fifty years working in criminal justice.

Eighteen months later, in June 2009, the PSNI told the families that they were effectively shutting down the investigation into the Loughinisland massacre. Niall Murphy, in his notes, drew a line between the PSNI's decision and the UVF's announcement that it was going to follow the IRA and decommission its weapons. 'What aggravated the sensibilities of the families was the fact that the decision to "cold case" the [Loughinisland] file, came days before the UVF carried out, what the *Irish News* described as a "significant act of decommissioning" on 18th June, 2009. The irresistible inference was that a political deal had been done behind closed doors with the UVF, wherein they were assured that there would be no prosecutions for the Loughinisland atrocity in lieu of UVF decommissioning.'

A month later, the families were told by Al Hutchinson that his report was almost complete and he wanted to share his findings with them. The timing all seemed to be choreographed. One month the PSNI puts the file into cold storage, the next OPONI are ready to publish their report?

Niall Murphy had a right to be suspicious. In a meeting on 21 July, the solicitor was told that OPONI had found no evidence of collusion in the Loughinisland massacre. His notes of what the investigators told him were 'suspicion of state collusion in these murders could not be substantiated as there was no evidence of knowledge of prior engagement in the attack or that the RUC were involved, that there was no "preventability". This crude conclusion was completely ignorant to the pre-eminent definition of collusion by Canadian judge Peter Corey.'

Corey had previously been tasked by the British government to advise on calls for public inquiries into the controversial deaths of Pat Finucane and Rosemary Nelson, as well as the UVF leader Billy Wright, who was shot dead by republicans in the Maze Prison in 1997. Corey had come up with a definition for collusion that became widely accepted: 'How should collusion be defined? Synonyms that are frequently given for the verb to collude include: to conspire; to connive; to collaborate; to plot; and to scheme,' he wrote in his report. 'The verb connive is defined as to deliberately ignore; to overlook; to disregard; to pass over; to take no notice of; to turn a blind eye; to wink; to excuse; to condone; to look the other way; to let something ride; see for example the *Oxford Compact Thesaurus,* second edition, 2001. Similarly, the Webster dictionary defines the verb collude in this way: to connive with another: conspire, plot.' The British government supposedly 'bristled' at its breadth, i.e. that it covered inaction as well as action, and patterns of behaviour as well as individual acts of collusion.

Having said his report was ready, Hutchinson had to delay publication due to new evidence coming to light after the PSNI told OPONI they had discovered documents they had thought lost when files were being transferred onto a new computer system. The PSNI admitted in 2011 that in the weeks after the Good Friday Agreement, they had destroyed notes of interviews with suspects between 1985 and the mid-1990s, along with incident reports going as far back as the 1970s. They said that asbestos had been discovered in the room where they had been stored, which left them with no choice but to dump them all in landfill in North Belfast. The Loughinisland families, along with the hundreds of others still seeking justice, were horrified, but not surprised.

One commentator described the PSNI's strategy in dealing with the past as 'deny, delay and death'. Basically, they were playing a long game. Obfuscation was the go-to tactic, where they would do all in their power to make families believe that they were determined to give them justice. It was stalling disguised as progress. The next stage was to bog families down in court action or ombudsman investigations, anything to kick the ball down the road. Finally, they hoped that the generation who were pursuing the truth most vigorously would simply die off.

And, in many cases, it worked. But not in Loughinisland.

***

During this time, someone who heard Ruth and me complain about the unhealthy state of journalism in Northern Ireland was Martin O'Brien. He was managing the Atlantic Philanthropies Fund that had been set up by one of Bill Flynn's colleagues in the Connolly House group, Chuck Feeney. The billionaire, who made his fortune through duty-free stores around the world, was committed to giving away his money by 2016, by investing in education, health care and human rights around the world, but particularly in Ireland and South Africa.

After a lengthy process, Atlantic Philanthropies provided a grant to Below The Radar that allowed it to establish a new current affairs web-based outlet, *The Detail*, which would produce investigations and analysis. All we required were the journalists to help us.

One of the first people through the door was Barry McCaffrey, the reporter who had got the exclusive with Emma and her mother, Clare. A popular reporter with a wicked, self-deprecating sense of humour, he was well known for his journalism at the *Down Recorder* before he joined the *North Belfast News* and latterly *The Irish News*. I only knew Barry by reputation, but Ruth had worked with him and was keen to have him as part of the new team. I found he had an uncanny ability in any situation to say the thing that no one in the room would dare mention. It wasn't exactly an endearing trait, but once you got used to it, you realised it was his way of cutting through any bullshit small talk.

In our first meeting with him, he suggested that we investigate the Loughinisland massacre. We immediately agreed.

Meanwhile, Niall Murphy had been briefed that the delay in the publication of the Loughinisland report following the uncovering of the new information would be only a matter of weeks, but that turned into months, and then years. In fact, it would be May 2011 – almost two years later – when he finally got a message to say that Al Hutchinson was ready to share his final report with the families.

The previous month, the ombudsman's office had been rocked by claims made by Sam Pollock, as he announced his resignation from his £90,000 per year position. Pollock said the independence of the ombudsman's office had been undermined by meddling from senior civil servants at the Department of Justice. Writing for *The Detail*, veteran journalist Chris Moore – the reporter who had broken the story of the UDA having security-force intelligence files in 1989 after the murder of Loughlin Maginn – said there were concerns that 'the appointment of former policeman Al Hutchinson to replace Nuala O'Loan as ombudsman means that two of the top three posts in the ombudsman's office are currently occupied by former police officers – Mr Hutchinson and his chief investigating officer'. Pollock, who had spent forty years in the criminal justice system, said he had been subjected to malicious personal attacks after raising his concerns.

It was a huge blow to Hutchinson and confidence in the office of the ombudsman itself, given that it was such a critical part of the new structures established by the Good Friday Agreement.

When Hutchinson's report finally came, three weeks after Sam Pollock's resignation, it crystallised all the families' worst fears and served to underscore the office's apparent lack of independence. For the families, it was a whitewash.

Murphy had invited the ombudsman to meet with the families ahead of publication, due on Friday 24 June, to which Hutchinson had agreed. Given that he called the meeting for 4.30 p.m. in his office close to St Anne's Cathedral in the centre of Belfast, the former Mountie couldn't have been expecting a very long meeting. It wouldn't end until 2.30 a.m. the next morning.

During the ten hours he spent with the families in the ombudsman offices, the carefully constructed edifice that Hutchinson – along with the PSNI and, indeed, the intelligence services – had cultivated was torn apart. For they had apparently decided that collusion didn't exist. After the embarrassment of Operation Ballast, they were going to ensure that no other such report ever made its way into the public domain. Nuala O'Loan had gone and the waters were now going to close over on the spectre of collusion. The state was going to protect its secrets.

The OPONI chief executive, Sam Pollock, who was serving out his notice period, opened the meeting. 'I have worked in the office as Chief Executive for 10 years in support of the previous and current ombudsman. My responsibility today is to chair this briefing with you, the families of the Loughinisland atrocity. I'll try to do that with the best of my ability,' Niall Murphy noted him as saying in his minutes of the meeting.

Hutchinson had hoped to take the families through each line of their complaint and provide his responses. But Murphy was in the room and, having found their voices, the relatives of the dead and the injured from The Heights Bar were not going to sit in silence and accept Hutchinson's 'factual gymnastics' to arrive at unsubstantiated conclusions.

Within an hour, the wheels had come off the ombudsman's carefully laid plan, with Emma Rogan going toe-to-toe with him across his table. According to contemporaneous notes taken by Murphy's colleagues, there was a key exchange between Emma and Hutchinson at this time.

Hutchinson: 'We're probably going to have to agree to disagree. Because I've said there's insufficient evidence [to find there was collusion in the attack]. You think there is a perception based on the facts.'

Emma Rogan: 'How can it be a perception of something if it's a fact?'

Al Hutchinson: 'What facts are evidence?'

Emma Rogan: 'You say it's a perception, but how is it a perception if it's fact? If the facts are black and white, how is that a perception of something, if it's written down, if it's clearly there for everybody to see? How is that a perception?'

Aidan O'Toole weighed in to support Emma, demanding answers.

After a short tea break, the meeting reconvened at 10.15 p.m. – almost six hours after it had begun. The families were asked if they wanted to keep going or reconvene the following day. Moira Casement piped up: 'We've been waiting for 17 years so we'll wait another three hours.'

And so, it started again, over and over – the families putting the facts that Hutchinson had found together and coming up with irrefutable evidence of collusion, while Hutchinson and his team pushed back.

In wrapping up the meeting after 2 a.m., Al Hutchinson again defended his findings that there was no collusion as he had defined it. Clare Rogan challenged him on his ability to sleep after a meeting where he had defended the indefensible. 'You'll not use the word collusion. You'll not even use the word suspicion. You see when you go home tonight, take your professional suit off and leave it all at the door, and put yourself in our position. Tell me tomorrow if you can lie in your bed tonight and honestly tell me that you wouldn't be suspicious if all these facts were presented in front of you.'

As they were about to leave, Hutchinson reflected on the past ten hours: 'I take on board the sentiments, the feelings, the criticisms; it does rest with me. I fully understand the impact it has on the credibility of the office. My credibility. We try to be evidence-based. If we've missed the mark, I'll try to take the advice of my senior advisers here. I'll just have to consider where we go from here. Fundamentally, I'll have to consider the bottom line.'

Niall Murphy advised him that there were going to be consequences: 'Al, I have to warn you that this will attract the revulsion of 43 per cent of the community in this jurisdiction. That is a serious fear. I'm just the family solicitor, but there will be louder, more influential voices than mine that are going to cause and raise serious concerns.'

It was likely at this point that it dawned on Hutchinson that his report was going to be challenged through the courts and wasn't going to be allowed to stand. His very position as ombudsman was under threat.

***

By morning, the Hutchinson Report had been leaked to Barry McCaffrey and published in *The Detail* under the headline 'Loughinisland – Ombudsman's report published but key issues remain unaddressed'. The article stated that: 'Police Ombudsman Al Hutchinson will say that the RUC murder investigation into the killing of six men in Loughinisland lacked "effective leadership and investigative diligence" and highlight an absence of "co-ordination and commitment" to pursue all investigative opportunities to bring the killers to justice. Mr Hutchinson will further conclude that there were "individual and collective failings" regarding aspects of the murder investigation but will rule out security force collusion in the killings. The move is set to anger victims' families as it is understood Mr Hutchinson has departed from Judge Peter Corey's definition of collusion.' Al Hutchinson published his report the day after Barry McCaffrey had revealed its contents.

At the same time, an NGO, the Committee for the Administration of Justice (CAJ), had doubled down on Sam Pollock's resignation comments in a report. Mick Beyers from the CAJ said it could produce evidence that would potentially call into question the ombudsman's independence. This was due, in part, to 'concerns in relation to the failure of the office to define and apply the term "collusion" in a consistent manner across all investigations and a failure to hold the police to account in relation to historic cases', she said. The report only applied further pressure on an already weakened Hutchinson.

Weeks later, in August, Barry McCaffrey was leaked another report. This time it was from the Criminal Justice Inspector, Michael Maguire, examining the allegations that caused Sam Pollock to resign. McCaffrey reported, 'Dr Michael Maguire has concluded that there had been a "lowering of independence" in the ombudsman's office which means it should now be suspended from investigating historic murders. He also found that ombudsman reports were altered or rewritten to exclude criticism of police with no explanation. Senior ombudsman officials demanded to be disassociated from investigation reports after their original findings were dramatically altered without reason. He also found that ombudsman staff investigating some of the worst atrocities of the Troubles believe key intelligence has been deliberately withheld from them. CJI [Criminal Justice Inspectorate] inspectors uncovered major "inconsistencies" in ombudsman investigations [including] Loughinisland.'

Following this report, and the release of Hutchinson's own report, there were calls from Sinn Féin and the SDLP for Al Hutchinson to resign. He had lost all credibility, they argued. He clung on, only saying he would leave the role six months early.

But the pressure kept piling up on him. Niall Murphy made an 'unprecedented' move in seeking to have the Hutchinson Report overturned in Belfast's High Court. The reporter Vincent Kearney fronted a BBC *Spotlight* documentary in which Sam Pollock gave an exclusive interview, saying that he had lost confidence in the direction of the ombudsman's office and its independence in relation to 'very serious matters'. There were matters 'you cannot fudge', he said.

Within days, the ombudsman said he would now leave office much earlier than planned, ultimately stepping down in January 2012. By the time Al Hutchinson was packing his bags to return to Canada, Niall Murphy decided to send an email. To me.

12 | *No Stone Unturned*

When the new police ombudsman was appointed in April 2012, it was a classic case of poacher turned gamekeeper. The man who wrote the report that brought down Al Hutchinson was to succeed him. Dr Michael Maguire left his position as the Chief Inspector of Criminal Justice in Northern Ireland to take on the role. His challenge was to restore trust in the ombudsman.

While the NIO had been going through the process of appointment, Niall Murphy and the families had taken time to consider their next steps. At a meeting held in Mullaghbawn in South Armagh, they discussed what they wanted to achieve from their campaign. They decided that they wanted to expose the collusion in the death of their loved ones and have the harm inflicted on them publicly acknowledged by the state, which, they hoped, would ensure that it would never happen again. The families instructed Niall to pursue the prospect of a documentary.

The fact that Niall emailed me rather than calling or texting speaks to the extent of our relationship at the time; it was a formal approach.

Arriving on the first working day of 2012, it was a proposal. He asked me to consider a documentary on the events at The Heights Bar. He had previously worked with Barry, and, as the email outlined, 'Barry suggested to me that *The Detail* or Below The Radar might be a vehicle by which such a documentary might be commissioned.'

He also explained why he was bringing the case to Below The Radar: 'We met with and spent two hours with [a local BBC current affairs reporter] setting out the facts. He was shocked and, I think, annoyed that *Spotlight* [their weekly programme] didn't take the case on as a subject matter, advising they were only now interested in "current affairs" issues and were trying to move away from historical matters.'

The email was a reflection of Niall's frustration that the 'process' he had followed to that point was not working. The Loughinisland families, seventeen years after the horror of that evening in June 1994, were still no closer to the truth of how the massacre happened in The Heights Bar than they were the morning after.

He signed off his email to me with 'apologies for the length of this email – in Victorian times, lawyers were paid by the word!' It was a form of self-deprecation that the 'old-school tough guy', as *The Irish News* described him, wasn't known for.

It was clear the full-forward hurler with St Enda's GAC in Glengormley on the outskirts of north Belfast, who had won an All-Ireland medal as part of the Antrim junior squad in 2002, had already come a long way from the press conference in the Cultúrlann. However, he wanted more for the families.

It was still early days, but Niall could see some planetary alignment that was not visible to me, the email's recipient.

***

From experience, Niall knew a documentary wasn't going to happen overnight. However, in the meantime, he was able to get the attention of *The Guardian* in London. Journalist Ian Cobain began investigating the massacre, publishing a seminal story in October 2012 under the headline: 'Northern Ireland loyalist shootings: one night of carnage, 18 years of silence'. The Liverpudlian was able to establish that thirty minutes before the red Triumph Acclaim had been found by the farmer in his field, one of its previous owners had been contacted by police in Belfast.

He also tracked down the Ulster Resistance member who was involved in the South African arms shipment, Noel Little, reporting: 'According to the Armscor source, the UR member who dealt with Bernhardt was Noel Little, a civil servant and former British soldier. Now in his mid-60s and living quietly in an affluent Belfast suburb, Little denies this. "My position is that I wasn't involved," Little says. But he adds: "I would deny it even if I was."

'Noel Little,' wrote Cobain, 'also suspects the British turned a blind eye to the 1987 arms shipment. "It is a theory I can't discount," he says. "Brian Nelson was inserted into the UDA as an agent, he wasn't a recruited member. How could he know about it and not tell his handler?"'

The article was a statement of intent by the victims. Loughinisland was now making national headlines. 'Ian's article has exceptional in its detail on the arms shipment,' said Niall Murphy.

At the time of *The Guardian* piece, the families were going through the courts, determined to have the Hutchinson Report overturned. Barriers were thrown in their way by the authorities, who were equally determined to protect the report and its findings. However, five months after Michael Maguire agreed to become ombudsman, the High Court in Belfast granted the families leave for a full judicial review of the report.

Now, it was Maguire who was in a head-on collision course with the Loughinisland victims. The new ombudsman said he needed time to consider what Hutchinson had produced and how best to proceed.

On the eighteenth anniversary of the massacre, in June 2012, the Irish football team played Italy again, this time at the European Championships. In an unprecedented move, the team wore black armbands in honour of the six men who had died while watching the team play the Italians at the World Cup. The FAI Chairman John Delaney, who had been in Giants Stadium on the night of the massacre, told the media, 'What happened in Loughinisland in 1994 was an awful tragedy and deeply moving for all football fans. I would like to thank UEFA for assisting us in commemorating this atrocity and take the opportunity to remember all those who lost their lives in the Troubles.'

Four days before Christmas the same year, the High Court was told that Michael Maguire had decided not to oppose the application from the families. He invited the court to quash Al Hutchinson's report. Maguire said he was going to start the investigation again.

It was a somewhat pyrrhic victory for the families. Hutchinson's flawed findings weren't going to stand, but now they were back to where they had started when they first filed their complaint. Six years had passed and they had nothing to show for it.

For Niall Murphy, however, they had won a very significant battle that would impact way beyond their fight for truth. 'That ten-hour meeting in Al Hutchinson's office in June 2011 wasn't just about Loughinisland. It was about a conspiracy to deny the truth. The Loughinisland families ended that conspiracy. In that room, they were speaking for every single one of those victims who had died as a result of the South African arms shipment; every one of the victims of state collusion. If they had given in, or given up, the state would have steamrollered its narrative through. Their strategy died in Al Hutchinson's office,' he argued.

***

Since our pint in Galway, I had met with Alex Gibney several times in his offices in what is known as the 606 building on the Lower West Side of Manhattan. We had very quickly found common ground, primarily bonding over a compulsive need to tell stories. A very intense and impressive figure with a dry sense of humour, Alex was building his own company off the back of his Oscar success. During these meetings, we had fallen into conversation about working together.

Some time later, Alex began editing a new film, *Mea Maxima Culpa: Silence in the House of God*, the story of sex abuse within the Catholic Church. We set up a co-production arrangement for the documentary, which would go on to win three Primetime Emmys, and raised finance from the Irish Film Board. A collaboration had begun.

Early in 2013, I visited Alex in his office overlooking the Hudson River. By this stage, I had created a new company that was going to be focused on the American market: Fine Point Films. I had been in New York, having a series of pitch meetings, talking to potential funders for our films, and was due to fly back to Belfast later that evening.

Gibney was, as usual, behind his desk. He had a bag full of ideas for films that he was going to make, and every producer in America wanted to pitch their documentary to him, hoping he would direct. He arguably didn't need another film idea, while he juggled *Mea Maxima* and several other projects in development and production with running a company.

Still, I had his attention for this moment and needed to make the most of it.

'Have you seen the *Two Escobars* film, the ESPN 30 for 30?' I asked, referring to the sports series that was renowned for telling stories that transcended a sporting storyline.

The Two Escobars examined how the lives of Colombian footballer Andrés Escobar and drug lord Pablo Escobar had become intertwined. The rise of Colombian football was credited to the money that was coming into the game from Pablo Escobar's drug money, but after scoring an own goal costing his team the game against America at the 1994 World Cup finals, drug dealers lost a huge amount of money that they had gambled on Colombia winning. Andrés Escobar was murdered as punishment.

'Love that film,' he responded, never saying more than was absolutely necessary.

'I've an idea for the Irish version of that movie.'

I told Alex the story of Loughinisland and the Irish team.

'That's a 30 for 30,' he said. 'I'll call ESPN and pitch it.'

He did and they wanted to hear more. The 2014 World Cup was coming up, in South Africa, and ESPN wanted to commission a series of documentaries that would be primarily aimed at its core US audience, something to help build interest ahead of the tournament. Alex knew they were going to do one feature-length documentary and a series of shorter, twenty-five-minute films. Despite everything else he had going on, he pursued ESPN with the zeal of a director that desperately needed the gig. But ESPN had already committed the ninety-minute slot to another project and didn't have the budget for a second.

As a result, it became Fine Point Films' first commission. A twenty-five-minute documentary directed by an Oscar-winning director. Ireland hadn't been at a World Cup since 1994 – missing out on this most recent outing thanks to a certain handball from Thierry Henry – but the story of their famous victory over Italy and the Loughinisland massacre was going to be told around the globe ahead of the tournament.

It was a huge moment for us, and the beginning of a journey that would ultimately end, for Barry and myself, in a police cell.

***

Once Michael Maguire got his feet under the desk at the ombudsman's office, Loughinisland was high on his agenda. However, he had another problem, one all of his own making. Because he had discovered that the office was compromised while under Hutchinson, the PSNI had decided that they were not going to hand over any more sensitive intelligence documents for examination. They didn't inform the ombudsman as to what they had decided, they just stopped responding to requests, including those coming from the investigators who were now digging back into the Loughinisland massacre.

Regardless of this – or perhaps even because of this – in January 2013, while I was pitching to Alex Gibney in New York, and almost eighteen months after the CJI report that helped bring about Al Hutchinson's downfall, Michael Maguire was announcing that he was resuming investigations into more than 150 historical events in which RUC officers had been accused of criminal activity and misconduct, many of them allegations of collusion. A fresh CJI report had paved the way for the ombudsman to begin reopening inquiries that had been shut down.

The PSNI chief constable, Matt Baggott, had been in Northern Ireland since 2009 and was now entering the final year of his contract. He made clear in a *Belfast Telegraph* interview his views on the past. 'The past is toxic to the PSNI and a huge drain on resources ... the past is a huge dilemma that has to be resolved,' he added. It was Baggott who had allowed senior members of his team to rescind their co-operation with the ombudsman, although it wasn't his idea. On his way out the door he urged the politicians to grasp the nettle of the past, despite having permitted this action, which hurt those who had suffered most.

His successor came from within. George Hamilton had served in RUC Special Branch during the Troubles and had risen through the ranks of the PSNI. He was seen as a coppers' copper; one of the boys who retained an emotional attachment to the RUC.

The new chief constable told *The Irish Catholic* that his tenure would be guided by God and that he was deeply influenced by Old Testament prophet Micah, whose words had inspired him in his own policing and human journey. 'There is a passage of Scripture from Micah [6.8] which talks about what God requires of us, and it says to act justly, to love mercy and to walk humbly and if you can do that, justice, mercy, have some compassion and a bit of humility, those are three things that make a pretty good cop in my experience,' he said.

As Hamilton prepared for duty, ESPN broadcast *Ceasefire Massacre*. Alex Gibney had flown into Dublin in October 2013 to spend four days in Loughinisland, meeting and interviewing several of the family members and victims, including Clare and Emma Rogan, Aidan O'Toole and Brenny Valentine. They all agreed to speak with him in the very bar where the shooting had taken place almost twenty years before.

Hugh O'Toole gave us the run of the pub for filming, with the interviews all shot in the lounge bar. The section of the pub where the shooting took place had been turned into a pool room. With Ruth's fastidious attention to detail and her knowledge of the area instructing the shape and tone of the interviews, Alex went back to New York safe in the knowledge that he had the film in the can.

But it turned out that the shoot had only whetted his appetite. He knew twenty-five minutes wasn't going to tell the story we wanted to tell. 'Let's talk,' he said.

We all agreed that we needed to find a way to make the longer film. Tell the whole story. The only problem was we didn't have an ending. There were too many unanswered questions, too many gaps.

I was still at my desk late one evening when I got a call from Bill Flynn. Every time I was in New York, we would have lunch at his private members' club where the waiter knew to set him up with a shot of vodka on arrival. Every single meal ended with him making the same statement: 'Loughinisland was not a random attack. There was nothing random about it.'

After one such get-together, when we were joined by Mark Thompson from the RFJ victims group, I had an epiphany. Flynn was harbouring a concern that his attachment to Gerry Adams and the peace process had led to his family's home village being targeted. He had previously told me how he had introduced himself at meetings with UVF leaders as a son of Loughinisland. Did one of them decide to send a message to Irish-America by attacking the village?

During a subsequent phone call, Flynn brought me into his confidence. He admitted that he had indeed considered the theory. In fact, he had spoken to the former British Secretary of State to Northern Ireland, Mo Mowlam, about his concerns. He refused to break the confidence of their conversation, but it was clear he still carried a burden. We talked for some time and he agreed to be interviewed for the documentary.

When we spoke to him on camera about him being a potential reason for the attack on Loughinisland, he responded as if it was the first time he had heard such a theory. He couldn't bring himself to go there publicly, which we understood. We included the exchange in the short film, as we knew there was more to mine with Bill Flynn, but we never did get the chance to follow up. The former CEO and chairman of Mutual of America insurance company died in 2018, aged ninety-one. Whatever Mo Mowlam had told him, he took to his grave.

In an interview with *The Hollywood Reporter* ahead of the documentary's broadcast on ESPN on 29 April, Gibney admitted that we still didn't have answers: '[An] interesting aspect of the story is that a lot is still unknown. There is a sentiment of "let's move on", but also a disquiet of not knowing what really happened.'

At the same moment, Michael Maguire was dealing with similar issues. He was unable to give families the truth if the PSNI remained unprepared to give up their files. In that moment of the late spring in 2014, the paths of Alex Gibney, Barry McCaffrey, myself, Michael Maguire – and Ronnie Hawthorne – were converging. *Ceasefire Massacre*, Maguire's appointment, Barry's doggedness, and the RUC's protection of the file that named Ronnie Hawthorne as the chief suspect in the

Loughinisland massacre were all beginning to move in a direction that would lead to a new film, one that told the whole story.

One that Michael Maguire would never have been able to tell.

***

In June 2014 the ombudsman announced that he had launched an unprecedented action against the PSNI over its refusal to hand over sensitive intelligence files. In an interview with the BBC, Maguire explained his case. 'At this point in time, the police have refused us access to 100 pieces of information involving investigations surrounding in the region of sixty murders. I find that unacceptable and we have no other choice but to take legal action against the chief constable. We're talking about complex investigations into over sixty murders where there have been allegations of police criminality and misconduct in relation to their failure to investigate those murders; the fact that they may well have been protecting individuals involved in those murders,' he said, doing well to keep in check his obvious growing frustration at the position the PSNI had adopted.

At a hearing that June, counsel for the PSNI, Tony McGleenan QC, complained that there had been an 'exponential growth in requests for sensitive information, which was quite radical in the past two years [under Dr Maguire]. When the volume was identified by police, they had concerns about the nature of it and how it is to be handled.' In other words, they didn't care for Michael Maguire's drive for the truth.

The facts and figures revealed during the hearing supported the thesis that Al Hutchinson had simply been uninterested in holding the police to account. In 2011 he had made just four requests in the whole year for sensitive information. In 2012, when Maguire was appointed, the number rose to twenty-three and further rose to sixty-nine in 2013. In the first quarter of 2014 he had already made thirty-nine requests for files.

Maguire's argument was that the police couldn't simply decide whether or not to hand over the materials – under the law, he argued, they must. 'The police have taken the view that they will decide whether or not to provide us with information and in many cases have now decided not to. We cannot have a situation where any public body, and particularly the police, can decide whether or not it will co-operate with a criminal or misconduct investigation, particularly where legislation requires them to do so,' said Dr Maguire.

Niall Murphy summed up the families' observations at this point in the process: 'The reasons for the refusal to engage with the new ombudsman were quite obvious, in that he was doing his job properly and was asking the difficult questions, seeking the sensitive information which led to the doors closing. Doors which had not been pushed by Al Hutchinson.'

After the hearing, George Hamilton and Michael Maguire held talks on how to resolve the dispute and, three months later, the PSNI capitulated, settling the case by conceding all the points made by the ombudsman's legal team. It was humiliating for the police but, ultimately, the dark forces had delayed the process of truth recovery by a further two years. They had denied the truth until the evidence was insurmountable; now they were on to the tactics of delay, knowing that every year, more and more of those who hungered for truth were going to their graves without ever being told why their loved ones had died.

***

Around this time, a large brown envelope arrived in our offices at Linenhall Street, addressed to Barry McCaffrey. Its contents would unlock the secrets that George Hamilton and the PSNI were determined the families of those who were murdered and injured in Loughinisland would never know.

Barry later recalled his reaction to what he had been sent: 'One morning I get a brown A3 envelope through the door of the office. Ninety-nine point nine per cent of the time they're boring reports or the rantings of disgruntled employees or blinds-twitching nosy neighbours. This envelope was different. It was, I think, seventy pages long. The more I read, the more details started to reveal themselves.'

Concerned at what he read, Barry decided to spend some time away from the office while he fully considered the impact of what he had been sent by an anonymous admirer of his work on the case. He spent several days in Donegal, working his way through each line, each paragraph and page, building a picture that was simply explosive. He told no one what he had been sent until he had fully considered the implications.

The working week in the office never provided the time to sit down and shoot the breeze. Weekend mornings were when Barry and I spent time together, walking our spaniels in Belvoir Forest on the outskirts of South Belfast. The phones would be left in the car and the rest of the world forgotten about, while we walked and talked through the forest. It was on one such walk, on a damp and cold autumnal morning, that Barry revealed what he had received in the post.

The first question, we both agreed, was – is it real or is it a fake? Hitler's diaries were mentioned once or twice in passing reference. How could we know the documents were indeed authentic? We discussed the motivation of the person or persons who could have sent them. Why now? Who could have had access to them? They clearly fell into the category of 'top secret' – the envelope pulled back the curtain on the Loughinisland massacre, revealing names of suspects and details of events before and after the attack. It was highly unusual in Northern Ireland for sensitive security documents – which it appeared these were – to be leaked.

We decided that we would sit tight for the moment and do nothing. There would be a moment to share these with the world, we agreed, but the time wasn't right.

If we hadn't already had the motivation to make the feature version of *Ceasefire Massacre*, someone out there had very kindly but decisively just strapped booster rockets to the project.

I decided I would brief Alex Gibney on my next visit to New York. He was already to find the money to fund the project. There were some financiers nosing around, but we were a long way from getting the cameras back up on the sticks. That was, until Nick Fraser, a titan in the documentary film world, came on the scene. He ran the *Storyville* strand at the BBC in London and had backed a previous project of ours. This meant that, with my colleague Eimhear O'Neill, who would become indispensable to us throughout the production, we had an opportunity to pitch Loughinisland to him.

'I'll do it if you can tell the full story of the fleas on the back of the loyalist paramilitary dogs. I want you to get down to that level of detail. Can you do it?' he asked us over a coffee during the Tribeca Festival.

We promised that we could. Leveraging Nick's support, we quickly found the rest of the finance, including support from BBC NI. From the off, I knew that the sixth floor at the BBC offices in Belfast, where all the top executives had their offices, had been buoyed by Nick's backing. They really hadn't given the pitch their full attention. It felt that they were led by what getting involved would do for them, for their careers, rather than caring what was best for their audience.

Still, we had our finance. Now the feature-length documentary about Loughinisland could move into production.

**

A year after the attack at Loughinisland, rumours had swept around the village of a letter. The families picked up on something about a vexed girlfriend of one of the killers having sent his name to a local councillor. But the years rolled on and no one was ever able to prove the letter existed or, if it existed, discover what it actually stated.

But we now had another document in our possession. When Barry opened the brown envelope that fateful day, he was amazed to find a document with two reports: 'Scope 1' and 'Scope 2'. The innocuous-sounding titles belayed the significance they would have for the Loughinisland investigation, for Alex Gibney and, ultimately, for the two of us.

The document set out the full facts of the RUC's failures in the Loughinisland investigation. It had been written in the years leading up to Al Hutchinson's report by an ombudsman investigator. The difference between the detail Barry was reading and what had ultimately ended up in the Canadian's findings was night and day. Maybe that had been the point for whoever had sent it to Barry?

'The document contained a list of all the named suspects who had been arrested; the dates of their arrests, and whether or not they had been fingerprinted, etc. In a lot of cases they weren't. We weren't to know it then, but those small details would help us to unlock the final pieces of the jigsaw much later on. Even more important was the fact that the report identified the names of the suspected killers and the roles that they carried out in not only Loughinisland, but previous attacks. I knew that this was explosive, but I also knew that it was also highly dangerous to be in possession of this document,' said the reporter, who isn't known for hyperbole.

During our walk in Belvoir Forest, Barry had given me the bullet points of what he had read. Later, back in the office, I had the first chance to read it for myself. Barry recalled my reaction: 'I could see that he was visibly shaken. He had just read the report and now he realised exactly what was in our hands and how explosive, literally, it was. Apart from the names of the suspects, it had given us leads of the names of the detectives involved and their roles in the investigation – or lack of it,' he said.

In Clare Rogan's interview for *Ceasefire Massacre*, she had talked about the commitment given to her by the RUC: 'They would leave no stone unturned.' That had stuck with us. Clare's experience was one we had encountered in so many homes across the North. Victims' families being given commitments, being assured and promised over tea and biscuits that the police would bring them justice. It made them resentful, full of remorse, that they had been taken in by the detectives who knew full well that these promises would never be honoured.

The phrase would be the title of our feature documentary. And with the documents we now had in our possession, thanks to the brave, public-spirited whistleblower, we had the evidence that would take the film beyond the usual round-the-houses telling of the story.

Many, many names bounced off the pages of the seventy-page document, lighting up the dark corners of the events leading up to and following the massacre in June 1994. But one stood out, one that Barry recognised.

Patsy Toman was born and bred near Loughinisland and was very proud of it. Known as a gentle, witty soul, he worked for the moderate nationalist SDLP party in the area for many years before later becoming a councillor, representing the Ballynahinch electoral ward area in Down District Council. The year before Loughinisland, loyalists had targeted him: 'My wife's a nurse and she was working night duty this particular night. I heard my son coming in about half past eleven and he knocked on my room door and he says, "Daddy, there's something on our doorstep, the front doorstep." And I says, "What like?" He says, "I don't know," he says, "it's suspicious looking." So we opened the door from inside and we looked at this thing sitting on the step of the door, and it was like, you'd have thought it was like a dynamo of a car or something like that. So we looked down and we seen batteries and we seen wires. And I says, "Niall, we better get out of here, and not come back."

'So we rang the police. And the road suddenly was filled with jeeps; the tanks coming up our lane and everything. But anyway, they looked at it and they seen it and he says, "Yes," he says, "it's a bomb. Now," he says, "what we're going to have to do, the only thing we can do is put an explosion on the bomb and try and blow these things off, not blow up the whole bomb, you know. But," he says, "You will lose your front door and maybe your windows in the front." He says, "If the real bomb goes off you could lose quite a bit of your house." I remember this was going on during the night, middle of the night, and they put this soldier down on the ground and they put this suit on him, belts and all. And I said to the policeman that I knew well, I says, "Does that save his life?" And it was a little bit not very funny; he said, "No, but it'll make him easier gathered up." So any way, he didn't [blow up], they got it off and we lost the front door and that sort of thing, not as much as we could have lost. But nobody was got for it either, nobody was ever arrested,' he said in an interview for *No Stone Unturned*. It was clear that, many years later, he was still dealing with the attempt on his life.

On St Valentine's Day 1995, eight months after the massacre, Patsy received a letter which wasn't as physically dangerous as the device left on his doorstep, but was, all the same, explosive. 'Whenever the shooting was over and everybody was trying to settle down, I was afraid that people would get bitter about it. It was a great place to live and there's great friendliness between the two religions. And I got this letter on Valentine's Day. I just pulled it open and it started off about my name, address, it had my name at the top, Patsy, and all that sort of thing. And I say to myself, maybe somebody's sending me a Valentine card. But, as I read down it, I found out that it was serious, and very serious. And it seemed to be, I thought it was a lady's writing,' he said in his interview.

Unbeknownst to Patsy Toman, the anonymous letter was actually written by the wife of the chief suspect for the Loughinisland massacre, Ronnie Hawthorne. Whatever motivated Hilary Hawthorne, she had decided to unmask her husband, several of his accomplices and herself in the Loughinisland massacre. The letter read:

Dear Mr Toman,

I am writing to advise you of certain facts that I think would be of interest to you in your quest to cage the Loughinisland murderers. When I saw you on TV after the inquest I felt that I had to let someone know what I was privy to.

The men arrested after the murder were indeed close to the culprits. The commander of the operation went on holiday after the event. He was local and so were the accomplices. The gunman was one Ronnie Hawthorne, a married man from Clough. Gunman two was Alan Taylor, single from Dundrum. The driver of the getaway car was Gorman McMullan, a convicted terrorist from Belfast and a leading light in the Belfast UVF. I was privy to this info because I was in the original planning of the murders. I pulled out of the attack due to a prior engagement that I couldn't cover up. The police indeed had the boys in for questioning but, as a policeman told me, we know who done it but we can't prove it, and without proof or statements they'll go free. Hawthorne and Taylor, they took part in the attack on the Thierafurth pub in Kilcoo a few years ago, and various other incidents in the area.

This information will somehow ease my conscience, but will never fully clear my name. But I do this for the family and children of the men who were slaughtered in Loughinisland.

Contributed, may we all live in peace.

When he read it first in 1995, Patsy Toman immediately realised its significance and how important it could be for the RUC investigation. 'She didn't sign it in any way. So I thought about it and I went and I showed it to a couple of friends outside the family, my family, and they read it. And they're right sensible guys and they says, "Patsy, you should take that to the police."' This is likely how rumours of such a letter spread around the village. 'So I done that, I went to the police with it, Downpatrick, showed them the letter and the police were round it like a hive of bees, you know, everybody was looking at it. And they were very happy to read it and look at it, and I says, "It's maybe somebody playing a trick or something." They said, "No, this is a breakthrough."'

It was indeed a detective's dream. But not if you were working for the RUC, it seemed. Toman continued, '[The detective] says to me: "Have you showed this letter to anybody?" And I says, "Yeah, two friends and my family." He says, "Would you bring them into us, we want to get their fingerprints off the letter, because there could be fingerprints on it." [He told me] there could also be something written on the pad, on the sheet above, a groceries list or something, and that would [be] very useful. It seemed to be very important then. So I says, "Okay, fair enough." So I, my wife went in, whatever time she went in, and all the family went in [to give their fingerprints]. When we were coming out the road that night from the police barracks, we nearly thought that there'd be arrests the next day, you know. The way they were talking, you know what I mean, but nothing happened.'

It wasn't until nearly twenty years later that Barry McCaffrey discovered the existence of the letter. When he read the document that had been leaked to him, he knew he had to see Patsy Toman. 'As I had known Patsy since my days as a cub reporter in Downpatrick, I jumped in my car and drove to his house, determined to jog his memory for anything he could remember of that letter sent to him twenty years earlier but since, purportedly, lost by police,' recalled Barry.

'After a short time of him showing me his prize canaries, I brokered the subject: "Patsy, it's about this letter you gave to police about the Loughinisland killers, the one they've now lost," I said.

'"Lost?" Patsy replied. "The police may have lost their copy of the letter, but I kept [a copy of] the original. I'll get it now."

'With these words, he reached into a drawer. "Here it is here," he said, handing me a photocopy of the original.'

***

We had had two significant breakthroughs in the research, meaning we were now in possession of a document that gave a full picture of the murders, the suspects and the failings by the RUC investigation, and also a letter that we knew the police had been handed only a few short months after the massacre. Putting the two documents side by side, we knew exactly who the author of the letter was; it could only have been Ronnie Hawthorne's wife, Hilary. The next natural step was to track Hilary down. Surely, we thought, she couldn't still be living with the man she had tried to have jailed?

Barry picks up the story. 'After trawling through phone records and hundreds of public documents we finally found the house where Hilary lived. Trevor and I drove down to the house to approach her. The house was only a few miles from Loughinisland, close to the loyalist village of Clough. As we sat in a car outside the house, trying to build up the courage to knock on the door, a van pulled up in the driveway. A tall, middle-aged, grey-haired figure with a peculiar, hooked nose stared back at us with an inquisitive look. We froze as we came face to face with the chief suspect in the Loughinisland massacre, Ronnie Hawthorne.'

In the passenger seat in the van was Hilary. My God! They were still together. Barry and I turned the car and pulled out of the lane, trying to cause the least suspicion possible. But there was no doubt, Ronnie had seen us. He would have clocked the number plate of my car.

Barry set about building a picture of Hilary's life and discovered that she was selling Disney toys online and in markets around Down and Antrim. He contacted her through social media and, after exchanging a series of messages, Hilary agreed to meet at a garage in the town of Lisburn so Barry could ostensibly buy toys for his niece, but she didn't turn up. Later, he visited a Christmas Fair not far from Clough and found that she was indeed doing a roaring trade in soft toys. There was no sign of Ronnie.

By this stage, Dr Michael Maguire was well into his investigation into Loughinisland. We decided that we should ask to meet him to enquire whether he was prepared to be interviewed for *No Stone Unturned*.

The most senior press officer at the ombudsman's office was Tim Gracey, a former BBC journalist and much-respected figure in Belfast media circles. Barry would have been in constant touch with Tim and his colleagues on a range of stories, not just Loughinisland, so when Barry called him, Tim knew it wasn't a courtesy call.

Barry followed up with an email to Tim in July 2014: 'Would be much appreciated and really helpful if it was possible for us to look towards yourselves from time to time for guidance while we're making the documentary. I think our goals and aims are ultimately the same, as in getting to the truth. I have attached the link here for the ESPN documentary. As I said earlier the one we are working on now will be feature length.'

And that was it, we had advised the ombudsman's office what we intended, and hoped that Dr Michael Maguire would agree with our sentiment. There would be stresses and strains as we pulled and pushed in different directions doing very different jobs, but we genuinely believed we could work together.

There was some back and forth, but ultimately we reached agreement on how Michael Maguire could participate.

***

Then, out of nowhere, we thought we had lost Barry. It wasn't good. He texted me on a Wednesday evening. He wasn't downplaying his situation:

'Trevor – it's very doubtful in the extreme that I'll be back in Belfast on Monday. I'm in Altnagelvin Hospital after I got chest pains. I will probably have to have a stent in. Anyway, the reason I'm telling you this is you'll know I'm not messing you around but there's not much chance of me working on anything in the foreseeable future.' In the end, he learned that a stent wasn't going to do it; he needed a triple heart bypass.

We knew we would have to protect him from himself and not allow him to worry about the documentary. It would work out; after all, his health was the priority. He had the operation in the Royal Victoria Hospital and was soon back with us, having lost a lot of weight but none of his charm.

In October 2015, with Barry in the room, Alex interviewed the ombudsman for the first time, ironically in the now derelict former UVF Hospital in East Belfast where First World War victims had recovered. It was clear the two men had great respect for each other, which would help significantly in the time ahead. At this point, Michael Maguire was still several months away from publishing his new report into Loughinisland, so the interview was more about hypotheticals and generalities than specifics. It was agreed that when the ombudsman knew he was going to publish, Alex would return for the major interview for the film.

Delay followed delay, but then we got word in early 2016: the Loughinisland report would be published in April. Then it slipped again, it would be May. No, more delays, now it would be June. Finally, it was locked in: 9 June.

We moved up a gear, knowing this was the critical moment for the Loughinisland families and for the film.

As the date for publication of the ombudsman's report approached, we had one key outstanding request for Dr Maguire – that he would allow us to film him when he met with the families privately to share his findings. He was planning on doing this the day before he went public. Eventually, it was agreed that we could be in the room. We had no idea what he was going to say – he could back up Al Hutchinson's findings of no collusion – but whatever he would tell them, we would be there to capture it.

The weather in June is as unpredictable as the other eleven months of the year in this part of the world, but when the day came, we were blessed with summer sun. We all gathered in Loughinisland GAC, trying to keep our nerves under control. Ultimately, all the work that we had done would be framed by what Dr Maguire would say. Despite the leaked documents and Hilary's letter, we needed the ombudsman to ratify what we had found. He had no idea what we had got and, equally, we were blind to what he had discovered during his three-year investigation. Just as it should be. We were journalists and filmmakers doing our job, he had to do his. There was professional respect between us by this point; it was obvious that whatever conclusions he came to, he would defend rigorously. But, due to Barry's work, we had a couple of aces up our sleeve for the film if Maguire couldn't find the evidence to back up what we believed was at the dark heart of Loughinisland: collusion.

Ten years after the families had first filed their complaint, Dr Maguire arrived at the GAA club and was now finally in front of them in the room and ready to tell them his findings. As the families arrived, Barry, Alex, Eimhear and I shuffled around at the back, ensuring the crew were ready to record.

Loughinisland GAC is like hundreds of others across the island: the walls covered in photographs of past glories, the tables dark wood, the chairs tubular brass with patterned cushions. The club had set the room up for the meeting, with a top table for the ombudsman and his team. The families were positioned in rows of chairs in front of him. The Rogans sat in the front, Clare and Emma nervously holding hands. Moira Casement, Marie Byrne and Malcolm Jenkinson's family were there. Paddy McCreanor, Dan's nephew, was at the back, listening intently to every word. Brenny Valentine had been in hospital, where he was being treated for cancer. So determined was he to be there for the moment of truth, that he had left his hospital bed that morning and was driven to Loughinisland by his daughter, taking his seat along with the other families. 'Brenny still had his ward details and hospital number of plastic dog tags on his wrists. It was a humbling experience to observe and be part of,' recalled Niall Murphy. 'There was nothing that would stand in Brenny's way of getting to the truth of what happened to his friends.'

The atmosphere was intense. Niall Murphy walked around trying to give comfort, guidance, leadership, when he had no idea of what was to come and what he would be dealing with in just a few short minutes.

Dr Maguire took his seat at the front and opened the meeting with 'Okay, ready to go,' to which, like an obedient classroom of teenagers, the families responded in unison in their soft South Down accents: 'Good afternoon, Dr Maguire.'

He set out how this was the day they had been waiting for. It had been a long journey, longer than it should have been, and he was very aware that there were people linked to the tragedy who had died during the previous decade, no longer around to hear the truth. 'Thank you for sticking with me. I appreciate your patience, even though I recognise that at times we didn't deserve it, but I am grateful for the fact that you have worked with me while we have inched towards the publication of this document.

'I now intend to report on my independent investigation into the events leading up to that awful night ... It's not an easy read. It's 160 pages, 44,000 words, with a lot of detailed information. It's the result of 200-odd interviews, 700 investigative actions, all of these numbers fly off the tongue. I am going to tell you my conclusion and then I'm going to tell you how I arrived at that conclusion based on the information that we have received.'

Maguire continued, getting straight to the point: 'When I looked at all the information, which I will spell out this afternoon, I have no hesitation in saying that collusion was a significant element in relation to the killings in Loughinisland.'

Emma Rogan's chin dropped first, followed by a flood of tears. It was raw relief, emotion. Frosty's daughter, eight years old when he died. The wee girl who had cried 'I want my daddy' over his grave had, finally, reached the end of a long, torturous journey. She had her truth. Her mother, beside her, sat up strong, staring straight ahead, the calm exterior hiding the effect of such soul-destroying news.

The RUC had not honoured their commitment to leave 'no stone unturned'; instead, they had colluded with the killers and covered up their crimes. One police officer had even called Ronnie Hawthorne to alert him of the plan to arrest him the next morning, allowing him time to destroy any evidence or clothing that may have incriminated him. It was truly shocking, even to us as journalists who thought we had heard it all.

All through the room there was a silence. Each in their own way computing the shocking news they had just received.

Collusion. There was collusion. They had been right all along. They hadn't manufactured it through grief and paranoia. It was now an established fact.

Dr Maguire spelled out how and why he had reached this conclusion: 'A critical element of my investigation has been the police use of informants within loyalist paramilitaries. The investigation considered the extent to which the Covert Human Intelligence Source (CHIS)/police relationship undermined policing prior to the Loughinisland murders and the investigation into that attack. It is my view that the nature of the relationship between the police and informants undermined the investigative process in a number of ways. There were many examples of failures to pass on intelligence to investigators. This meant that investigative lines of inquiry were not followed and individuals, who might have been subject to detailed and robust investigation, were effectively excluded from consideration. In the case of the incidents prior to the Loughinisland murders, limited action was taken against the UVF unit suspected of a series of serious crimes.

'It is of particular concern that Special Branch continued to engage in a relationship with sources they identified in intelligence reporting as likely to have been involved at some level in the Loughinisland atrocity. If these individuals were culpable in the murders they took every opportunity to distance themselves by attributing various roles in the attack to other members of the UVF. The continued use of some informants who themselves were implicated in serious and ongoing criminality is extremely concerning. Many of the issues I have identified in this report, including the protection of informants through both wilful acts and the passive "turning a blind eye" are in themselves evidence of collusion as defined by Judge Smithwick. When viewed collectively I have no hesitation in unambiguously determining that collusion is a significant feature of the Loughinisland murders,' he told the families.

Niall Murphy could sense the mood and asked for a break to allow the families to get a breath of fresh air, take it all in.

I exchanged glances with our cameraman: 'Keep the cameras rolling,' the glance said.

'This is unbelievable,' Niall told Emma, as the families huddled together in the main hall in the club, where dances are held at weekends and prizegivings at the end of every season. It had never hosted an event so emotionally charged as that summer afternoon.

'At least we know we're not imagining things. It got to the stage where you're thinking that didn't really happen,' said Emma Rogan.

'It's a fact,' the lawyer reassured her.

Later, having read the report, Niall said, 'I keep saying things like unbelievable and incredible; it's not, because it's what we always suspected. But to read it, it's just mind-boggling. And then, you know, this is difficult. You know, we entered into this process to recover as much truth as possible. We know that, we know that there's not going to be justice, because justice is jail and, you know, there will be no jail here. So it has been about truth recovery and we've got it.'

13 | Hear No Evil, Speak No Evil, See No Evil

The day after speaking with the families, the police ombudsman delivered his report into the world in a first-floor function room at the Crowne Plaza Hotel in South Belfast. His detailed understanding of his brief was clear. Since the debacle of the Hutchinson era, he had rebuilt confidence and trust in the ombudsman's office. This report would define Maguire's time in the role. And he didn't pull any punches on the failings of the police, despite the first paragraph of his conclusions: 'The persons responsible for the atrocity at Loughinisland were those who entered the bar on that Saturday evening and indiscriminately opened fire. It is also important to recognise that despite the failings identified in this report there have been many within the RUC and PSNI who have worked tirelessly to bring those responsible to justice.' Still, over 160 pages, eight separate sections and six appendices, he tracked the origins of the VZ-58 weapon; the murders and attempted murders by the same gang in the years preceding the 1994 massacre; the intelligence available prior to the attack and the RUC investigation that followed, and, finally, he tackled issues relating to resourcing and further developments in the investigation.

In terms of the importation of the weapons, he concluded that the RUC was aware of the plans by Ulster Resistance, along with the UVF and UDA, to ship the consignment of weapons into Northern Ireland in 1987 and had known about its arrival after it landed at Belfast docks. He found there were 'significant failures' in the 'intelligence-led' operation, which resulted in so many of the weapons ending up in the hands of loyalist killers. 'I also believe that there were informants involved in the procurement and distribution of the weapons, including individuals at the most senior level of the organisations responsible for the importation.' And, of course, intelligence was not shared with the detectives investigating the largest haul of weapons ever brought into Northern Ireland by loyalists.

Turning to the actions of the UVF gang in South Down, Dr Maguire said he had concluded that there was a 'strategic failure' by the RUC to counter its 'escalating activities', including failing to disseminate all relevant intelligence; an unwillingness by Special Branch in Belfast to support and advise their colleagues in South Down; and a lack of 'sustained rigour' in the investigation of the Thierafurth Inn attacks, which left Peter McCormack dead, and in the murder of Martin Lavery. 'I believe in the case of one officer involved, [he] was influenced by what he believed to be the republican background of victims,' he said, damningly.

Maguire further outlined how there had been no 'proactive policing response' to the threat that emerged from the UVF against the nationalist community in South Down following the Shankill Road murders. There was also no evidence that informers who might have helped the RUC identify where and when the retaliation was going to occur were 'tasked' with doing so by Special Branch at a strategic or local level. In fact, even though the UVF was riddled with agents at all levels, little intelligence emerged that could have prevented the murders. This, according to the ombudsman, was due to the value some Special Branch officers placed on 'strategic' intelligence or, in other words, 'picture building' over the prevention and detection of crime.

In a mind-blowing conclusion, Dr Maguire said it was his view that Special Branch didn't ask difficult questions of their informers so as to avoid exposing their knowledge of the murders to come. He described the relationship between members of the security forces in South Down and the UVF as 'corrupt'. The failure to investigate the role of agents in a range of criminal activities, Maguire surmised, effectively meant that they were protected. Which meant they could continue with their campaign of murder. 'There was a "hear no evil, speak no evil, see no evil" approach to the use of some informants,' he wrote.

The British Prime Minister, David Cameron, released a statement in which he said he 'fully accepted' the findings and said he took allegations of police misconduct very seriously. South Down MP Margaret Ritchie called on Cameron to make an official apology to the families, but it never came.

With the Maguire Report now published, we knew we had the keys to unlock the cyphers that littered it. The ombudsman had explained that he couldn't name names. 'I have been required to consider competing interests relating to national security, human rights and the public interests,' he said, adding that he couldn't disclose information that could result in any person's life being placed in jeopardy. As a result, each of the suspects and police officers involved were only identified by a letter or number.

Barry and the rest of us went back to an empty office building with the Maguire Report, Scope 1 and 2, and also the Hutchinson Report. We spent hours cross-referencing all the reports to come up with a clear picture of the UVF and RUC personnel that were hidden behind what Alex would go on to describe in the film as a 'thicket' of letters and numbers. Barry was way ahead with his knowledge and intimate understanding of the case, and he won the award for cracking the code first, allowing us all to see the hideous jigsaw picture of collusion that had previously been hidden, and would have remained so if not for his tenacious journalism.

We now knew that 'Person A' in the Maguire Report was Ronnie Hawthorne and his accomplice in the McCormack, Lavery and Loughinisland murders was 'Person M', Alan Taylor. The UVF man in East Belfast who operated under the control of the Shankill Road leadership was 'Person I', Gorman McMullan. 'Person K' was Trevor Watson. Albert Carroll was 'Police Officer 4'.

With the code broken, we knew our responsibility. Dr Maguire had set the table, our job was to serve the meal. The film would set out the RUC's failures in fine detail. We would name the chief suspects, including

Hilary, and report the fact that one of the three men in the car was an informer at the time of the massacre.

The next day, we would interview the ombudsman, along with two senior members of his team. We knew they were not going to be able to go further than what was in the report. And although they knew nothing about the document we had been leaked, we planned to push them as far as we could to help us corroborate the information we had in our possession.

Late into the night, we prepped for the key interviews ahead, poring over the documents, worried we had missed something, while also confirming the key questions and areas we wanted to pursue inside the allotted time we would have with the three men. First into the chair was the ombudsman himself. Alex, with great skill and patience, poked and prodded, but Maguire failed to yield a single new fact. I then interviewed Paul Holmes and his colleague Phil Dennison. It was during the second interview that we pursued the subject of what police knew in the build-up to the attack. We knew the Triumph Acclaim supplied by the UVF on the Shankill Road was little more than a wreck. Several hours before the attack, it had broken down. An eyewitness had seen men working on it on a side road outside Clough. We knew from the Maguire Report that Ronnie Hawthorne, Gorman McMullan and Trevor Watson had been seen on the main promenade of Newcastle that same afternoon. But who had seen them? Who told police they were there?

Maguire said two members of the UVF gang had been in Clough's only pub, Frenchies, when a third member of the gang called. I asked Phil Dennison how Special Branch knew about this call. 'I can't tell you that. I know how they get to that, but I can't tell you that, sorry,' he answered. I pushed further, asking if the phone was bugged. 'It's not.'

Jimmy Binns had told us that the detectives he'd had a late-night drink with said police were aware of the plans for the attack, but their agent had told them the car had broken down and it had been called off. The Maguire Report had confirmed that Special Branch knew where the gang was on the afternoon and knew about the phone call to Frenchies Bar. We could, therefore, only draw the inference that one of the gang was an informer and had been briefing his Special Branch handlers in the hours prior to the killings. Which led us to reach the ghastly conclusion that police had failed to step in and prevent the massacre.

One other question bugged us. The leaked Scope document had alerted us to an anonymous phone call to the police after the massacre, one that named the killers – now we knew this was Hilary's first attempt to draw police attention to the fact that her husband was involved. But how did police know it was Hilary Hawthorne who had called the RUC's anonymous phone number in the days after the attack? 'I would ask the same question if I were in your shoes,' said the investigator. 'I can answer that question, but I know what your next question is going to be and at that point I would shut you down completely.'

Hilary worked for the RUC in the same police station in which the Special Branch in South Down was based. The wife of a known UVF paramilitary. From Dennison's answers, or lack of answers, we came away with the distinct impression that Hilary Hawthorne should have been arrested after sending the letter to Patsy Toman, and the fact she wasn't only raised further serious doubts over the RUC's attempts to bring those responsible for the massacre to justice.

At this point in the production, the plan for the film was to premiere it at a major festival in the US – which at that point looked to be the Tribeca Festival in April 2017 – before it would return to Galway for the annual Film Fleadh in July and then roll into cinemas the length and breadth of the island. After an agreed length of time, the film would then screen on the BBC across the UK. That was the agreement between all the funders.

Around this time, we started to feel a cold draught blowing around the film. When we advised the BBC that we intended to name the chief suspects, the draught became a howling wind. The central issue was the naming of Hilary Hawthorne as the letter writer. For us, in the letter to Patsy Toman, she had clearly confessed to being involved in the planning of a massacre. Our analysis was that the RUC hadn't arrested her then because they had to protect their agent in the gang. For the BBC, however, it strongly felt that she shouldn't be named in the film in case her husband didn't know she had written the letter. The conversations about how to resolve our differences became increasingly frustrating, leading to a feeling on our side that the BBC was trying to find a way out of the film.

We decided to focus on attempts to clarify whether Ronnie had, in fact, known about the letter. The natural first step was to ask a man who should know – one of the senior RUC officers in charge of the Loughinisland investigation.

***

We first became aware of Albert Carroll's name in the leaked Scope documents. When we read the Maguire Report we had realised that we were going to have to track him down at some point. Now, with the BBC wavering, it moved to the top of our list of priorities.

Barry made a few calls and discovered how, after his retirement, the former detective, with his wife, Victoria, retired to France. Being the resourceful investigative journalist that he is, he turned to the French phone book, where he discovered three listings under the name 'Albert Carroll'. He called the first number and, once he heard the soft southern Irish accent on the other end of the phone, he knew immediately he had got the right one first time. We had already been told by one of his former colleagues that Carroll had been an 'outsider' from Wicklow, who had moved North after marrying.

Barry has a patter, which he uses with great skill. He puts people at ease through a mix of humour and genuine interest in them, their families or their dogs. He seeks out a connection, a bond, and once he's established their trust, he begins pursuing answers to his questions. And it works. No matter their profession, background or level of trust of journalists, Barry can open them up and, in the end, have them thanking him for taking the time to call. By the time he finished with Albert, he had an invitation to visit him in France.

We made a plan to go, but Albert backed out at the last moment, saying he had been advised by the PSNI not to speak to us. What the

PSNI was doing, advising former detectives with whom they should or should not speak, was a question that would be left hanging. But Barry kept up the contact, and a month after Michael Maguire published his report, we were on a flight to France.

We flew to Toulouse, hired a car and drove the one hour to the village Albert Carroll now called home. We arrived the night before the meeting and were still somewhat concerned that he wouldn't show up, never mind shed light on his investigation, or lack of it, and particularly the relationship between the Hawthornes.

He had agreed to meet us at the Commercial Hotel just off the village's main square at 11 a.m. My notes documented his attitude on arrival: 'He immediately asked sarcastically if we were police officers. When we laughed, he said, "Well this is going to be a very short meeting." There was something of a dawning realisation about the ambition of the film when we told him that it would be shown in France and that we were going to record the "fact" that he had been involved in the Loughinisland inquiry.'

It wasn't exactly an auspicious start. 'So what can I not tell you?' he asked repeatedly at first, defensive and belligerent.

Barry turned on the patter, while I suggested his attitude would be seen as insulting to the families of the six dead men, who would expect former officers like himself to help them get to the truth. 'This did have an impact on the conversation, and he did try to be more responsive,' I noted after the meeting.

When he began to talk more openly, Albert Carroll revealed a picture that had us both enthralled yet horrified. After everything we had learned from Scope and the Maguire Report, the former RUC detective would add texture to our understanding of the UVF in South Down and the police failings to bring them to justice.

He began by telling us about his career. When he left the RUC, he said flatly, he left behind 147 unresolved murders. Loughinisland was just a number. He had worked the beat in Belfast in the 1970s, at the time the UVF Shankill Butchers were prowling the streets, and, later, he went on to work as a detective. He told us that the ombudsman's team had visited him twice in recent years and he had also had two separate visits from senior officers at the PSNI. He didn't explain why the police had been to see him or why they had warned him not to talk to us.

To ensure we had his full attention, and that he understood exactly what we knew, I laid the Scope documents, which we had brought with us, out in front of him on the table. Barry succinctly recorded Albert Carroll's response to the documents in *No Stone Unturned*: the retired detective had 'shit himself', he said, when he realised the level of detail we had.

Once we turned to Loughinisland and the suspects, Albert Carroll was extremely forthcoming. He began to talk about the getaway car, the red Triumph Acclaim. He said police knew the 'back end' of the car was gone before the attack, which meant it would 'have sounded like a tractor', a situation that was hardly ideal for terrorists trying to make their escape without attracting attention. We put it to him that Ronnie Hawthorne would have been disgusted at the quality of the 'getaway' car provided by Gorman and the UVF in Belfast. Albert said he knew exactly what Ronnie had said when he saw the car – that he was angry but had decided to go ahead anyway. 'That was the mentality – they had a shit getaway car, but they still went ahead and got it done. That's the way it was with them: they got things done.'

He said the car was so fragile that the forensic officers had been forced to 'lift it' out of the field. The former RUC detective also suggested that the original getaway plan was for the whole team to drive to a pub in Saintfield to meet with other UVF members, who would take the guns from them, and then they would travel on to Belfast in a different car.

Then Albert's focus narrowed in on the UVF gang in South Down, explaining how he had been aware of their threat. Hilary Hawthorne had been employed at the RUC's station in Newcastle, he told us, working in the canteen. Her husband, we knew from another RUC source, had been kicked out of the same barracks in the late 1980s because one of the detectives there was concerned that he had been taking the information from security briefings and bringing it back to the UVF. The same police officer had been disturbed that the UDR didn't immediately discharge him, taking months to fire him. But his wife continued to work in Newcastle and was very friendly with the Special Branch officers.

He described Alan Taylor as 'thick' but dangerous and under the control of Ronnie Hawthorne, who, he said, had been thrown out of the family home by his father. Albert believed that Hawthorne had formed a relationship with Gorman McMullan after they met at a club in East Belfast. 'There were only three active members of the UVF in South Down – Ronnie Hawthorne, Trevor Watson and Alan Taylor,' he advised us.

But then the former detective made an audacious claim: he had brought Ronnie Hawthorne's career as a sectarian killer to an end. He had 'turned him off,' he said.

'Well, did he ever kill again? Have you seen or heard him linked to any killings after Loughinisland? Was he ever arrested for anything else?' he challenged us.

It was clear, we noted at the time, that Albert Carroll was proud of the fact that he had 'turned off' Ronnie Hawthorne, whom he described as a 'bad boy'. Hilary was in love with Ronnie, Albert explained, even though she knew that he was 'involved' in terrorism, an action with which she disagreed. He described their relationship as being akin to that of a battered wife who stays with her husband; the detective believed that she would never give evidence against him in court. She loved him too much.

Albert told us how, in the days before the Loughinisland attack, Hilary had seen people 'coming and going' at their home in Clough. She had witnessed the preparation on the Saturday morning of the massacre and knew an attack was being planned. At one stage, she had left her husband and taken their young son, apparently disillusioned with her husband's involvement with the UVF. Albert thought this happened after the Loughinisland massacre but before she made the anonymous phone call to the RUC in January 1995.

It was clear Albert wasn't comfortable talking about the events of the mid-1990s but, as we pushed and prodded, he did answer more of our questions. We pushed him on his knowledge of Hilary's role. We had known from Scope that Hilary had been arrested in November 1995, ten months after she had made the anonymous call to police identifying her husband as being among the suspects. But the former detective revealed to us that he had been the one behind her arrest. It was just weeks after the call, clearly frustrated by the RUC's lack of interest, that she had written to Patsy Toman.

Carroll told Barry and me that while Hilary was in custody, Ronnie Hawthorne had been allowed to visit her – something which was unheard of when suspects were being held and questioned about terrorism offences. The only person a suspect would see was their solicitor. But Albert Carroll told us he had engineered the situation. Ronnie Hawthorne's wife had left him; she had called the police; she had written a letter. Now she was in custody. Carroll's strategy was to put the fear of God into Ronnie that his wife was going to be charged, and, given that she had already made at least two attempts to have him prosecuted, he could be in no doubt that she would implicate him and the other gang members. The same tactic had been used on Delbert Watson when his sister-in-law, Doreen, was arrested for the Jack Kielty murder. Delbert had cracked and told police everything.

Although Hilary was released without charge and her husband would never face a court, Albert took great satisfaction, over twenty years later, that Ronnie Hawthorne hadn't killed in the previous two decades. He had evaded a life sentence and the families had been denied justice, but he hadn't killed again.

After ninety minutes, Albert left the hotel, saying his wife was waiting for him. Barry and I compared notes. Then we returned to our hotel, packed our bags and left for home, leaving behind a retired cop content with his life's work.

***

The Albert Carroll meeting had provided us with key missing details. We were much more confident of our story as we relayed everything we knew to Eimhear and Alex. In October 2016 Alex sent us a rough cut of the film. We watched in stunned silence in a suite at our offices as the film played on our large screen. We already knew that Gibney was a master storyteller, but this something else. Watching him pierce through the layers of the story with such craft, clarity and precision for the first time was a moment for us all in that room.

By this time, the BBC had added another executive producer – we had five in total during the process of producing the film – and it was safe to say that they were now only fully appreciating what they were dealing with. We had been advising them of our research and interviews all along the way, of course, but now, with this rough cut, they were witnessing for themselves the gut punch of an Alex Gibney film. It floored them.

But the BBC became entrenched on the Hilary Hawthorne issue. Did her husband know what she had done? Could the film live without this storyline?

No! It spoke directly to the RUC's collusion with the killers. They had the very wife of the chief suspect admitting she was involved in a massacre and naming her husband and the rest of his gang as being responsible. Why did they not prosecute?

Our job at this point was to provide evidential back-up to every single statement contained in the documentary. We also had the legal support of a very senior barrister in Belfast who was going over the film, line by line, providing assessments to the BBC. In turn, their in-house lawyer, David Attfield, was calm, collected and always on top of his brief. He was just the kind of collaborator filmmakers want in their corner, telling us clearly what he required from a legal point of view to allow the film to be broadcast.

The issues were among the executives. In the end, we were able to deliver a signed letter from a former RUC officer who had worked in South Down, stating that Ronnie knew about Hilary's phone call and letter. So that was it – the confirmation they were looking for. But then new issues were found.

It was time for a big move to break the deadlock. I spoke to Alex, Barry and Eimhear and told them that in order to keep the BBC on board, we should go the PSNI and advise it of what we were going to do.

It was risky. If the PSNI decided that it didn't want the film to come into the public domain, it could injunct it, which would drag us into a lengthy and costly legal battle. However, by telling the PSNI, we were discharging our responsibilities to protect the safety of the suspects. They may have not cared for the human rights of those they had murdered, but by briefing the PSNI, we were advising the only organisation that could decide whether we were going to put lives in danger, including Hilary's, as to what was going to occur.

The BBC supported the idea and so did the team, albeit while voicing some very understandable concerns. To give the BBC even greater comfort, we promised to invite John Ware, who had been their man in the North for thirty years and someone they had put huge trust in, to any potential meeting with the PSNI. In some ways, this was only a minor adjustment, since we had already briefed Michael Maguire's team that we intended to name names. They had told us that they had passed on notice of our intentions to Deputy Chief Constable Drew Harris.

On 31 March 2017 I emailed the head of the press office at PSNI headquarters in East Belfast:

> Hi Liz,
> We'd like to set up a meeting in relation to the film, in particular the naming of suspects. I understand OPONI have briefed Drew Harris on same. Would this be possible early next week?

Four days later she responded:

> Hi Trevor,
> I have spoken with the DCC and ACC [Stephen] Martin, Head of Crime Operations, to check on their availability for a meeting ... We will get back to you once we have a date for the meeting. I appreciate you will want the meeting as soon as we can facilitate it so will work on that basis.

Deputy Chief Constable Harris wasn't mentioned the next day when the PSNI came back to offer a meeting for the following afternoon at police headquarters.

John Ware, Eimhear O'Neill and I attended the meeting on 5 April 2017. We were met at reception and led to a large meeting room where the ACC positioned himself at the top of the table with the PSNI's press officer and legal adviser on his right. Eimhear had become central to the production and very much a key voice in terms of the decisions that we were facing. She would ensure there was a contemporaneous record of the meeting.

According to the PSNI's own minutes of the meeting, the ACC said the 'PSNI values press and the role of the media and freedom of the press and would not seek to undermine the role of the press'. This is a statement that would come back to haunt both the police and the officer who said it.

The minutes record that I told the ACC that we intended to identify four suspects – Ronnie Hawthorne, Alan Taylor, Gorman McMullan and Hilary Hawthorne. The forty-five-minute discussion hinged on whether it was the PSNI's legal duty to warn the four of our intentions to name them. If they said they had no intention of warning them, then we could deduce that they didn't believe naming them in the documentary would place any risk on their lives.

We knew going into the meeting that Deputy Chief Constable Harris had been kept abreast of the documentary and our intentions to name suspects and potentially an informer by OPONI officials. ACC Martin confirmed they had been advised by the ombudsman that we intended to name an informant, to which I responded that we were still doing our due diligence, but, at that point, we didn't intend to do so, even though we knew there was an informant in the gang. The senior police officer had come to the meeting with that as his only direct question. I also told him that it was helpful to know that the office of the ombudsman was passing on information to the PSNI that it was gleaning from our meetings.

The rest of the meeting went back and forth on the legal obligations of the PSNI as regards the protection of individuals. 'I am not going to comment and I'm not going to answer and am not going to seek out answers,' was how the PSNI's own notetaker recorded Stephen Martin as responding to a direct question on Hilary Hawthorne and her husband's knowledge of her actions. The police solicitor in the room told us that 'if we felt we had an obligation, we would manage it'. That was as far as they would go.

The ACC pointed out several times the potential risk to Hilary Hawthorne if her husband didn't know she had written a letter and called the police to inform on him. What he refused to say, time after time, was if the police, now with foreknowledge, would do anything to mitigate that risk, i.e. by advising the Hawthornes of what was about to occur.

In the end, we shook hands and left PSNI headquarters with very little new knowledge, but a sense of comfort that we had at least given the police forewarning of our intentions. They would have to account for their own decisions, should anything happen to the four suspects once we named them.

We redoubled our efforts to keep the BBC on board and, in August 2017, they agreed that we could write to each of the suspects – Ronnie and his wife, Alan Taylor, Gorman McMullan – to advise them that we were going to name them in the film and it was going to be broadcast on the BBC. None of them responded. The BBC then asked us to hand deliver the letters in case they had failed to arrive, despite us having signatures on Royal Mail documents showing they had been signed for. So we did. I drove to Ronnie Hawthorne's home and posted it through the letter box outside his home. Again, no response. We had tracked Alan Taylor to separate addresses in South Down and in Leeds. My fearless friend Benny, who lives in Yorkshire, visited the Leeds address but could find no sign of him.

We then received an invitation to premiere the film at the prestigious New York Film Festival in October. We accepted, even though we were locked in discussions with the BBC at very senior levels. There were fraught meetings as they continued to demand that Alex compromise his film.

Before we locked the film, we had one more lead we wanted to chase down. Where was Ronnie Hawthorne now? What did he do? With the help of a private investigator who went above and beyond, we found an answer that took our breath away. We found the loyalist in republican West Belfast where we filmed him getting out of his van, cigarette in hand, Hilary by his side. Ronnie Hawthorne was still in the business of killing, it turned out. He was now a rat exterminator.

***

Accompanied by Clare and Emma Rogan, Moira Casement and Aidan O'Toole, we flew to New York for the screening, still with no agreement with the BBC. As we checked into our hotel, I got the call – the BBC was out. They were not prepared to support the film any longer.

It was devastating for the families, who wanted the vindication of witnessing their story on their television screens. They wanted their friends and neighbours to fully appreciate what they had come through. It was a huge blow, but it wasn't terminal. We were now simply more determined that the film be seen by audiences at home and abroad; that the families' story would be heard.

While we watched the credits roll on the film at the Lincoln Center for the Performing Arts on the Upper West Side in Manhattan, Michael Maguire opened up a video link back in Belfast to watch the film for the first time. We had honoured our agreement; he would get to watch it at the same time as it premiered in New York.

When, two weeks later, *No Stone Unturned* premiered in London, we had still heard nothing from the ombudsman's office. We were relieved that he hadn't found anything he disagreed with, but we were still uneasy. There was relief, therefore, when the ombudsman agreed to take part in a panel discussion, chaired by journalist and our good friend Susan McKay after the film screened for the first time in Belfast. It was a huge moment for us all. He knew that his appearance would, as far as the audience was concerned, at least, act as an endorsement of the film, even if he was only standing over his report. He always said that we would have to do the same for the film; that it was none of his concern.

When the PSNI issued a press release on the morning of the Belfast screening, stating its determination to open an investigation in relation to Loughinisland, it made complete sense. Surely the police force had no other option, given the weight of evidence, the power of Dr Michael Maguire's report and the fresh evidence showcased in our documentary. However, we quickly realised that it wasn't Ronnie Hawthorne or Alan Taylor that the God-fearing chief constable, George Hamilton, was determined to bring to justice. It was us.

'You're the subject of a criminal investigation. That's serious,' whispered Niall Murphy to Barry and me as we prepared for the screening at the Queen's Film Theatre in South Belfast.

What Niall was particularly concerned about was the statement earlier that day from the ACC that we had met six months earlier, Stephen Martin: 'We are aware that sensitive documents relating to the Loughinisland investigation, which we believed originated from within the Office of the Police Ombudsman of Northern Ireland, are suspected of being used in the *No Stone Unturned* film.' He was investigating the 'theft' of the sensitive material and had asked Durham Constabulary, which the PSNI had called into Northern Ireland two years earlier to lead an unconnected investigation into documents that had been leaked from the ombudsman's office to the family of a murdered RUC officer, to extend their existing investigation.

At this point in time Chief Constable Hamilton had decided that resources should be focused on finding journalists' sources. It was an insult to the memories of the men who died in The Heights Bar, sending a signal to the victims' relatives as they watched the film, some of them for the first time, that going after journalists was far more important than pursuing those who perpetrated mass murder.

In truth, apart from Niall, none of us really took the statement seriously. Leak inquiries are announced all the time and, after time, they normally fade away. However, our lawyer could see that something was on the horizon; he knew the impact the ombudsman's findings had had on the 'RUC family', the former Special Branch officers out there who disliked the fact that Michael Maguire had uncovered and disclosed the truth. A truth that was now about to go on cinema screens right across Ireland in glorious technicolour.

Our Donegal-born, long-term friend, Patrick O'Neill, released the film through his company, Wildcard Distribution, and soon we were getting reports of long queues outside cinemas in Downpatrick. By any metric, the film was a success at home and abroad, winning a Royal Television Society award and being nominated for a News and Broadcast Emmy. It was the biggest documentary released in 2017 in Ireland, with a box-office taking of over £150,000. Amazon subsequently stepped in and bought the rights to stream the film. Its release created headlines in newspapers both North and South.

But the BBC ignored it. Having first refused to investigate the Loughinisland massacre itself, and having withdrawn from the film, it failed to report on *No Stone Unturned*, despite its revelations, carried across several days by *The Irish News*, and the positive response from the public. Some of the reporters contacted us to express their embarrassment and acknowledge the damage the BBC was doing to itself. It was a scandalous undermining of its journalism and caused further hurt to the families. Still, it failed to undermine the documentary's overall success.

Even if the documentary's legacy was about to take an unexpected turn.

14 | Offences

For all of us involved in *No Stone Unturned*, we had to move on, work on new projects and try to put behind us the toll of getting the film out into the public domain. But an afternoon screening for students in Belfast had a huge impact on Barry. Véronique Altglas was born in Paris, and was a lecturer in sociology at Queen's University Belfast, with a particular interest in religion. 'The first time I saw Barry was on the big screen when I went to see *No Stone Unturned*. I really remember everyone laughing when he said Albert Carroll had shit himself.'

The petite Parisienne decided to watch the film again when it screened for Queen's students. Before the screening, she introduced herself to Barry. 'Later, we would see each other socially at the Duncairn Centre in North Belfast and that's really where I got to know him. I found him very inquisitive! He would always ask questions. What was my favourite movie? I learned quite quickly that he didn't share my love for Woody Allen films, but I liked his curiosity.' Having been brought together by *No Stone Unturned*, Barry and Véronique began to see each other.

'He came over to watch another documentary – but we never did get to watch it. The rest is history!' They married during the Covid pandemic in 2020 and later held a reception in Newcastle, South Down. In his speech, Barry's father, Gabriel, welcomed Véronique into the family, joking he had worried that I would be the only partner his son would ever have.

There was no such love between the Retired Police Officers Association (RPOA) and the ombudsman, so it came as little surprise when the former officers took an action in the High Court that sought to have the ombudsman's Loughinisland report quashed.

It wasn't unusual for former RUC officers to defend their force in the media and push back on the growing number of allegations of collusion. In December 2017, two months after the film's release, Mr Justice McCloskey found that the authors of the report were 'careless, thoughtless and inattentive in the language and structuring of the document', adding that the police officers who were deemed to have colluded with the UVF were 'in effect tried and convicted without notice in their absence'. In an interim ruling, not his full judgment, Mr Justice McCloskey also said that the findings of collusion were 'unsustainable in law'.

A BBC report on the ruling described it as 'a damning attack on the report and on the office'. DUP MP Jeffrey Donaldson and TUV leader Jim Allister both called on Michael Maguire to resign. The ombudsman said he stood over his report and had no intention of resigning. Emma Rogan told the press outside the hearing: 'Last year we felt we were given truth ... and dignity was restored to our loved ones, and this year it has been suffocated once again. We will go home, celebrate Christmas, and we will regroup and focus our energies on our campaign.'

In the New Year, a week before the final ruling in the case, the veteran BBC reporter John Ware wrote an article for *The Irish Times*. 'Inquiries, "collusion" and seeking truth in Loughinisland killings', read the headline. Underneath, he set out the background to the court case and why the former RUC officers were so aggrieved. He told the readers of the newspaper that although the PSNI Chief Constable, George Hamilton, had previously accepted Maguire's report 'in full', the PSNI chief now said he had reservations 'consistent' with those that Mr Justice McCloskey had found in his December ruling. 'Hamilton said he expected the Ombudsman to be held to the same evidential standards as the PSNI and wondered why, if Maguire was so convinced there had been collusion, he had not recommended prosecutions. The answer to that is the quagmire into which the battle for control of the story of the Troubles has sunk. For a start, there is no clear definition of collusion, so it cannot be defined in law,' wrote Ware, who went on: 'Collusion has become a wink-wink, nod-nod approach with a "Need I say more [attitude]," says RPOA's chairman Ray White, a former RUC assistant chief constable and a senior Special Branch officer. Behind the RPOA's attempt to get Maguire's Loughinisland collusion finding quashed lies a seething frustration over what former RUC officers see as the rewriting of the narrative of the Troubles.'

In a further two paragraphs, Ware revealed something unknown to the ombudsman. At the time of the Omagh report by his predecessor, Nuala O'Loan, Mr Justice McCloskey had represented the RUC: 'Then, as now, Raymond White [a former RUC ACC] tried to quash O'Loan's report, represented by QC Bernard McCloskey, before he became a judge.' The judge had represented the former head of RUC Special Branch in the attempted quashing of a previous report on collusion.

The following Friday, with one of Northern Ireland's most senior judges now at the centre of the row, came a showdown in the fight for the narrative control of the very history of the conflict. 'This was a court hearing like no other,' wrote the BBC NI Security Correspondent, Vincent Kearney. 'In thirty years of journalism I have witnessed nothing like it before. The judge and legal teams involved all described the proceedings as unique and unprecedented.'

The ombudsman's legal team used Ware's revelations to request that the judge recuse himself from the case. In response, Mr Justice McCloskey said the test for recusal was not met. However, he agreed to step down because of the 'unique and unprecedented circumstances' of the case.

There was pandemonium in the court. Outside, Emma Rogan told reporters: 'We are delighted that our report still stands in its entirety – the report that we got in 2016 is still the report that's on record. All we ever wanted was the truth – that's it, bottom line. Everybody deserves it, it's human decency for people to know and for people to acknowledge what happened to their loved ones.'

Niall Murphy was there and was clearly stunned by what he had just witnessed, describing it as 'the most unprecedented' outcome to a judicial review he had ever seen. 'What we have now is an opportunity for the police ombudsman and the families, as interested parties, to re-engage in a brand-new reflection of the legal issues raised, and we look forward to doing that as quickly as possible,' the lawyer told the waiting press.

The decision by McCloskey to step back from the case was a huge blow for the retired officers and to the chief constable, particularly considering his U-turn from accepting the Maguire Report to then supporting attempts to have it overturned.

What we had no idea of was that, at that very moment, the Durham investigation into the leaking of the documents was being stepped up a gear. Barry McCaffrey and I were criminal suspects. The battle over the ombudsman's report, and Michael Maguire's established narrative on collusion in the Loughinisland massacre, was about to enter a new phase.

***

The summer was almost over. My wife and three daughters had gone to France to spend time with her family, while I remained in Belfast working. One Saturday afternoon I glanced over my shoulder to the road in front of our home and saw a police car. I thought at the time that it was odd to see the PSNI patrolling in our street, which is a five-minute walk from their headquarters. I watched as they slowed down at the junction facing the house. For a moment, I thought they were going to come in, but they turned left.

Six days later, on Friday 31 August, my family were home and the police were back. In hindsight, I realised that the drive-by had been a scouting mission. I had all but forgotten about the investigation announced by Stephen Martin ten months earlier, although I did know that it was causing huge frustration at the ombudsman's office. Now, having exhausted their investigations and found nothing, ACC Martin had ordered the arrests of Barry and myself. The same senior officer who had spoken to me of his appreciation for the role of the press sixteen months previously, had now sent dozens of officers to my home at 7 a.m. in the morning to arrest me in front of my wife, young daughters and family from London.

After being arrested, I was driven to Musgrave Street Police Station in central Belfast. The journey through the early morning traffic didn't take long. When we arrived at Musgrave, I had to wait in the car for a spell, which I thought was odd. Were they not expecting us? Afterwards, I was led upstairs and put in a room with a young constable, who had obviously been tasked with monitoring my behaviour. He tried to engage me in chit-chat, but I wasn't really in the mood.

I was then led out to stand in front of the custody sergeant, who sat behind a glass partition. I wasn't wearing my hearing aids so struggled to understand what she was saying. At one point, I thought I heard her mention a co-accused. *They've arrested someone else?* I thought.

Following this, I was invited to go into another room to the right, where I had my mugshot taken. The officer then said he wanted to take my DNA through a buccal swab. *You didn't take Ronnie Hawthorne's*, I thought. He asked about my health and if I had taken any drugs. 'Unfortunately, none this morning,' I joked. He didn't laugh.

Five minutes later, I was walked past a row of cells by another officer, who told me to take off my shoes and belt. As I did what he asked, I looked to my right and saw a pair of instantly recognisable brown walking boots outside the next-door cell. Barry was the co-accused! I heaved a sigh of relief that it was him and not anyone else. On the worst morning of my life, I was in the best possible company.

At around 8.20 a.m., the cell door slammed shut behind me. The day had taken a dramatic turn. I was incarcerated for the first time in my life. There was a blue plastic mattress on a shelf to my right and a toilet and wash-hand basin to my left. On the wall in front of me were forty-two glass bricks. I counted them repeatedly as I began to consider just what had happened.

I began to pace the cell. I started banging on the wall to try to get Barry to respond. I sat down on the mattress, thinking of my eighty-year-old mother in Enniskillen and wondering how she would find out what was going on. It wasn't easy to concentrate with so much swirling around my mind.

In the next cell, Barry was having similar problems. He had slept in and had been rushing to get ready for the day ahead when the knock came on his door. 'I'm in the bathroom just about to start shaving when the doorbell rings. Immediately I know there's something wrong. No one rings my doorbell at 7 a.m. No one actually ever rings my doorbell,' he later told me. 'I go to the top of the landing and look down the stairs to see through the glass panel in the front door that there is a large male in a dark blue boiler suit and matching baseball cap with his finger on the bell. That's no postman, I think. He doesn't even have a bag.

'My first thoughts are that someone's had an accident. But deep in my heart I know exactly what is about to go down. The choice was either I was going to be shot or be arrested. The caller at the door is dressed in a boiler suit. The police don't arrest journalists just for doing their job. Do they? In that split second at the top of the stairs I decide that, if it is the police, resistance is going to be futile. They are going to be coming through that door one way or another. The only thing I have left now is self-control, self-composure. I decide my only weapon to hand now is indifference, show no emotion, give nothing away, kill them with kindness and say nothing.

'My heart is pounding as I open the door. There's a little voice in my head, telling me to make a run for it. "You can make it to the trees," the voice keeps telling you. Then I hear the adult voice in my head telling me to wise up and calm down. The six foot plus sergeant introduces himself. I don't immediately take in his name. He has a piece of paper in one hand and a clipboard in the other. *You're a big lad*, I'm thinking, as I survey the rest of his search squad. It's the full *Line of Duty* show. All the bells and whistles. Squad cars, vans, uniformed officers, plain-clothed detectives. No expense has been spared, it would seem. "Mr McCaffrey. We've a warrant to search your property. Can we come in?"'

He'd had a similar start to the morning as I had, feeling emotional when the cell door locked behind him. He remembers surveying his new surroundings: 'There is one threadbare blanket folded neatly on the bed. There is a camera up high on the wall, which I suspect is watching my every move. I consciously remove my shirt, trousers, socks and T-shirt and fold them neatly beside my bed. For the first time that morning I try to properly assess where I am and what is happening. I am in serious trouble. I pull the blankets up over my head and I cry. Am I on my own? Who else has been arrested?

'I am shaken out of my self-pity by a booming voice coming down the corridor. I have no idea what time it is as they have taken my watch from me. But I instinctively know the owner of the voice. Like anyone with hearing difficulties, Trevor Birney has to speak loudly. I immediately know it's him and almost at once feel a big wave of reassurance. I hear a banging on my cell door. "Are you singing like a canary, McCaffrey?"'

Back at home, Sheila was struggling with having our home invaded. Using her sarcastic sense of humour to best effect, she reminded the officers that there were children in the house who had never experienced armed police in their home or seen their father arrested. The search officers were going through our books, personal effects, cupboards, children's rooms, taking her mobile phone without explanation along with a small pink handset that belonged to one of our daughters. However, they failed to find the single sheet of paper for which they were apparently looking.

***

Over the course of the next twelve hours, the day descended further into farce. I don't know how long it was until a custody officer came into the cell to say that my solicitor was here. He waited while I put on my shoes and walked me back past the cell doors and through a series of non-descript corridors to a small, dark room where Niall was waiting. 'Alright?' we both said in unison.

I couldn't sit down, so we walked around the room, trying to make sense of it all. He confirmed that it was only Barry who had also been arrested, and that no one else had been, thank God. Niall told me two other things. 'One, this will be a no comment interview, you will not answer any question. Two, you are going to witness a very different me in the interview. This is what I do, and you've got to trust me.'

I did trust him, so there was no issue with that.

By then, Niall had examined why we had been arrested and said he needed me to fully understand the implications. There were four separate offences. The first was theft of the Scope documents. The second was handling stolen goods, i.e. the Scope documents. There was also a charge of unlawfully obtaining personal data, which turned out to be Albert Carroll's phone number. But it was the fourth that most worried him. 'Unlawful disclosure of information entrusted in confidence contrary to Section 5 of the Official Secrets Act 1989.' Niall broke the bad news. If found guilty of a breach of the OSA, we could be jailed for ten years. The good news was that there had never been a successful prosecution in the UK of anyone alleged to have breached the OSA. Indeed, to his knowledge there had never even been an arrest under the legislation in Northern Ireland. But the very fact that the PSNI and Durham had arrested us on this basis was an indication of the seriousness of their intent.

It wasn't until after midday that I was again led from my cell and taken to the first interview session. There were two police officers on the other side of the desk. A camera was on a wall above us. One of the detectives had obviously just been on holidays and was sporting a tan and a tight, light-coloured shirt. The other was older. He, I discovered, was from was Durham Constabulary. The tanned one introduced himself; he was from the PSNI.

The opening exchanges, later transcribed from the recordings made in the interview room, tell a story of how the defence lawyer operates in such circumstances. Very quickly, I knew I was in safe hands.

> Durham Detective: Mr Birney, you have your solicitor here, and if at any time during this interview you wish to stop the interview to consult privately with him, let us know and we will get the interview stopped, alright. Just a bit of the layout of the interview room, just to your left is a microphone ... if you are going to speak to us, or if you have any questions could I ask that you speak loudly so that the microphone picks you up. On the wall there you will see a light illuminated, [this indicates there is] downstream monitoring, that means that when that light is illuminated somebody from outside

this interview, an authorised person, may be watching in, listening to what is said and done, okay.

Niall Murphy: Who is that?

PSNI Detective: I'm not in the room, so I don't ...

Niall Murphy: You don't know?

PSNI Detective: I don't know who is watching right at this minute, no.

Niall Murphy: Do you know [directed to second officer]?

Durham Detective: No.

PSNI Detective: Mr Birney, you have been arrested this morning in relation to two secret documents stolen from the offices of the Police Ombudsman for Northern Ireland and their use in a film *No Stone Unturned*. The offences for which you have been arrested for are Theft contrary to section 1-7 of the Theft (Northern Ireland) Order 1969, Handling Stolen Goods contrary to section 21 of the Theft (Northern Ireland) Order 1969, Unlawful Disclosure of Information Entrusted in Confidence contrary to section 5 of the Official Secrets Act 1989, Unlawfully Obtaining Personal Data contrary to section 55 of the Data Protection Act 1988.

Niall Murphy: Just in relation to the fourth matter, Unlawfully Obtaining Personal Data contrary to ...

PSNI Detective: Section 55 of the Data Protection Act 1988.

Niall Murphy: What does that relate to?

PSNI Detective: Mr Murphy, I haven't even done the ... I haven't even done the caution yet so we're not going to discuss that at this stage.

Niall Murphy: You're not going to discuss what he has been arrested for?

PSNI Detective: I have informed you of the offences, the interview will [now begin].

Niall Murphy: Who's personal data is it? Do you know?

PSNI Detective: Do I know?

Niall Murphy: Yeah.

PSNI Detective: I'm not willing to discuss that at this stage, you know yourself that these interviews are phased. We'll be going through a series of questions, I'm not going to disclose that at this stage before I've even cautioned your client. Okay, Mr Birney, before I ask you any questions in relation to that I'm going to caution you: you do not have to say anything but I must caution you if you do not mention when questioned something that you later rely on in court, it may harm your defence. If you do say something, it may be given in evidence. Okay, Mr Birney, so what that means is during this interview you may or may not answer any of the questions that are asked [by] myself, or by [Durham Detective] here. If you choose to do that and this case goes to court further on down the line and you present a version of events in court that you fail to provide to us now, then a judge or jury in that court might draw other conclusions from that. Do you understand what I mean?

Trevor Birney: I do.

Niall Murphy [to Durham officer]: What is your rank?

Durham Detective: I'm the investigating officer.

Niall Murphy: Oh, are you, yeah? Constable, sergeant, inspector, a superintendent?

Durham Detective: I'm a member of Durham Constabulary police staff.

Niall Murphy: Is there a problem with you averring as to your rank? Are you a detective? What's the problem?

Durham Detective: I haven't got a problem.

Niall Murphy: Why can't you tell me what your position in the police is?

Durham Detective: I've just told you what my position is. I'm a civilian member of staff of Durham Police and I'm the investigating officer.

Niall Murphy: A civilian member of staff. Are you sure you're authorised to conduct an interview under PACE 1?

Durham Detective: Yes.

PSNI Detective: Okay, during this interview Mr Birney will be asked a series of questions and pre-interview disclosure has been given to your solicitor, Mr Murphy. Basically, you're going to be asked in relation to your knowledge of Police Ombudsman Northern Ireland documents that are outstanding, your involvement and history in journalism and interest in Loughinisland, your employment history, what firms you've been involved in and your relationship with males Alex Gibney and Barry McCaffrey.

Niall Murphy: Just to put my advice on the record, I will be advising

Mr Birney to make absolutely no comment during this interview and to retain his right to silence.

PSNI Detective: Okay, Mr Birney, just before we ask you any questions, I'm just going to ask you if you have anything you want to say or add. I'll remind you that this is your chance to give your version of events.

Niall Murphy: No, no, no, no, no, you have deprived him of his liberty. It's not his opportunity to do anything, it's your obligation to put evidence to him in respect for which the crimes he's been arrested.

PSNI Detective: Right.

Niall Murphy: So don't try to controvert what the actual circumstances are. We can do all this 'history', 'how long have been a journalist', 'what are your interests'. That's nonsense and you know it is and you're wasting time, so I'd prefer if you got to the evidence in this case.

PSNI Detective: Mr Birney, this is your opportunity ...

Niall Murphy: It's not his opportunity.

PSNI Detective: Mr Murphy, I'm going to speak, now I've let you have your say, so if you would let me have mine. [To me] This is your opportunity to answer any questions that we put to you. It's your opportunity to give us any version of events that you want to talk about. It's not Mr Murphy being interviewed, it's you and I would remind you of that and although you have been advised by your solicitor, it's your interview so ...

Durham Detective: Mr Birney, you made a *No Stone Unturned* documentary. Tell me about your involvement and knowledge of this production.

Durham Detective: Are you aware of the Police Ombudsman of Northern Ireland documents that are contained in the documentary *No Stone Unturned*?

Durham Detective: Do you have them in your house in any format? If so, where at?

Durham Detective: Are those documents stored at your place of work? If so, where at?

Durham Detective: Tell me about your employment history, Mr Birney. Have you studied journalism?

Durham Detective: Where did you study journalism?

Niall Murphy: Well, just, I would like to say something. I would like to put on the record that this arrest is unlawful, is malicious. I would request that Mr Birney is immediately released and I want that confirmed and put on the custody record as there will be civil litigation commenced immediately, due to this malicious arrest. Can I enquire whether either of you two have watched the film *No Stone Unturned*?

Durham Detective: I'm not prepared to comment on that.

Niall Murphy: Have you [to PSNI detective]?

PSNI Detective: What relevance has that got to do with Mr Birney being interviewed?

Niall Murphy: Because line one of the pre-interview disclosure states that it is in relation to the use of allegedly 'a secret' and allegedly 'stolen documents' from the police ombudsman's office in the film *No Stone Unturned*.

PSNI Detective: And what does it matter if I've watched it?

Niall Murphy: Because Durham Police issued a press release saying that they would 'follow the evidence wherever it leads us' and I would've thought that if one had followed the evidence which arises from *No Stone Unturned* that they'd be investigating a murderer of six people, rather than a journalist who has portrayed the truth. So, I'm going to ask you directly have you watched the film?

PSNI Detective: Whether we have or have not watched the film, we don't have to tell you.

Niall Murphy: Has Ronnie Hawthorne been arrested today?

PSNI Detective: Ronnie Hawthorne?

Niall Murphy: Yeah.

PSNI Detective: Not that I am aware of, no.

Niall Murphy: No. So you're not following the evidence. Who prepared this press release? You're the Durham police officer, who prepared the press release? Could you make inquiries about that?

By the end of the first session, I knew that, whatever the outcome of all of this, there was something very sinister behind my arrest. Since ACC Stephen Martin announced the criminal investigation, I had never doubted for a moment that we had done anything wrong. Now I knew police also knew that but had still mounted this operation against us. Why? What really was behind our arrest?

I was allowed to meet with Niall again before being taken back to the cell. I could feel anger swelling up. He was trying to keep me calm. What the fuck had they arrested me for? To ask me if I was a journalist? If I was a member of the National Union of Journalists (NUJ)? What was this all about?

Barry, meanwhile, was having a very similar experience in a similar room across the corridor. He recalls his own first session: 'It quickly becomes clear that the questions being asked of me aren't designed to bring the killers to justice but are being carefully co-ordinated to put myself and Trevor behind bars. I am distinctly aware that detectives in front of me are merely the mouthpieces. They read a series of carefully pre-prepared questions from a paper sheet. They need to get me talking so that their faceless superiors watching on television cameras in some adjacent room can unpick and unravel any morsel of evidence which I might inadvertently give. Having sat through dozens of murder trials I am very aware that no question is ever as innocent or throwaway as it seems. I know that discretion is the better part of valour when you're in the massive hole that I now find myself in. Less is more, loose lips sink ships, mum's the word, snitches get stitches … I meet question after question with the same polite reply. "No comment at this time, thank you." Over the next number of hours, I repeat it again and again, like a meditative mantra.'

The day had already provided many surprises, but the most shocking was yet to come. As recalled by Barry: 'The repetitive monotony of the questioning is unexpectedly broken when Detective 1 asks if I regret the hurt and pain which I have caused to Ronnie Hawthorne? I look at John [Finucane, his solicitor] – John looks at me. Both of us are mystified. Have we just heard him right? I am stuck in my no comment mantra, but thankfully John is not bound by the same need for silence. "I'm sorry. Are you asking my client if he regrets causing hurt and pain to a man who the police say murdered six people? Are you seriously putting that question to my client?"

'Like a bully who has just been challenged in the playground, Detective 1 tries to ignore my solicitor and repeats the question. "Are you seriously going to ask him that?" a now-irate John asks again. PSNI 1 butts in and defends their right to protect the reputation of their mass murderer. Finucane grows visibly angrier. He turns to me: "Get your coat. We're leaving." I am confused. Coat? My coat is locked up in some police evidence bag somewhere down the hall in this building. I'll never find it, I think. The PSNI officer interjects, pointing a finger at John and then me. "You [John] can go where you like, but he is under arrest. He's not going anywhere." John's voice rises an octave, growing even more irate. "That's it, we're out of here." My head is now in a spin, more than a little unsure what is going on here. A testy silence ensues until one of the detectives suggests a break for lunch.'

The shocking discovery made in Barry's interviews was repeated during my own. It turned out that Durham and the PSNI had gone to the home of Ronnie Hawthorne to take a witness statement. Not about his involvement in the Loughinisland massacre. No, they had asked about the hurt and pain he had suffered because of being featured in *No Stone Unturned*. It took a moment for that fact to sink in. The PSNI had turned the man who had massacred six men into a victim. He was the wronged one, not the Rogans or the Byrnes or Barney Green or the other men slaughtered in The Heights Bar. No, it was the UVF leader in South Down who had suffered.

While we were alone, Niall said he wished for me to listen seriously to what he had to say. He said he had spoken to his colleagues. As well as coming to my home, police were now raiding our offices, no more than a ten-minute walk from where we were being held. He said the advice was that we should immediately launch a judicial review against the police operation. I nodded in agreement; it sounded exactly like what we should do. Fight back.

However, and this is where he got very serious, this was going to be at my financial risk. If we lose, you lose. It could cost hundreds of thousands of pounds in legal costs. 'Do you still want to do it?'

I didn't have to think. The financial implications would have to be thought through later. We needed to take action now. 'Do it,' I told him.

With that, Niall was out of the room and I was put back in my cell. In that moment, it was the opportunity to assert some sort of control; to take a decision in a day when all the decisions were being taken for me and Barry.

The interview sessions in the afternoon continued in a similar vein to the morning. I had lost all track of time when Niall came back into the dark room to deliver good news: 'We've been in the High Court and we've been granted an interim injunction. The police have to stop the searches and put everything they've taken from your offices in bags until there can be a full hearing,' he told me with a real sense of achievement in his voice.

The mood changed from that moment. We were still under arrest but now the police had had their day ruined.

As a reminder of what this was all about, Niall took his mobile phone out of his pocket to show me a picture that had been circulating on social media. It was of the Loughinisland families holding a vigil for Barry and myself outside The Heights Bar. We stared at the picture for a moment, taking in the compassion and humanity of a group of people who had suffered so much over the previous twenty-four years. It was humbling. But in that black box of a room, we agreed that their thoughtfulness, fortitude and stoicism was in stark relief to the amoral actions of the PSNI.

While Barry and I were back in our cells, Niall and John were called to speak to the most senior officer in the station. They came back to tell us that the police wanted to continue to hold us into the evening. However, they had fought it and won. We were going to be released.

I was led to a room where Barry was already waiting. We gave each other a hug and exchanged obscenities. It was over. We could go home.

Niall told us there were television cameras waiting outside. We joked about our dishevelled appearance as we walked out the door of the station. But, once the lights of the camera hit Barry, he folded into tears. 'This man has been arrested in front of his children,' he complained through sobs. A moment ago, he had been laughing and joking at the absurdity of the situation; now he was railing at the injustice. 'I have been on the other side of the cameras all my life,' he said. 'I have watched this scenario play out so many times I can write the script with my eyes shut. I am not meant to be in front of the camera. We are not meant to be the story.'

Barry later recalled, 'Faced with the TV lights, I find myself unexpectedly launching into a mini tirade with a broken voice, fighting to hold back tears. It is embarrassing and verges on car-crash TV. Thankfully, it is over in a matter of seconds.

'When the cameras are turned off, we get handshakes and hugs from the reporters and cameramen. As we walk through town, we are unexpectedly joined by the rest of the guys from the office. They have been fighting their own battle all day, trying to prevent the police from taking away all the computers. We are shell-shocked at what has happened over the last fourteen hours. Someone suggests we all go for a drink. I make my excuses that I have to go to a cash machine to get money. I disappear around a corner and walk as quickly and as far away as I can,' he added.

'I finally find myself at a bus stop. I feel as if people are looking at me. Somewhere in the back of their heads, I think, they recognise my face from somewhere. I keep my head down as I board the bus.

'We were free, but I knew that there was a long road ahead.'

15 | Shooting Crows

While Barry and I had been settling into our cells, at our offices on Upper Arthur Street, our colleagues were holding the line. In co-ordinated raids, dozens of PSNI offices in boiler suits were already tearing through our first-floor base just a street back from the City Hall. Tipped off by Niall Murphy, his colleague Joe McVeigh and then junior counsel Stephen Toal had gone to the office to confront the police. When they got there, Managing Director of Below The Radar Michael Fanning, and Editor of *The Detail* Kathryn Torney were already questioning the legality of the police search.

Fanning later recounted the reaction by the SIO from Durham Constabulary, Darren Ellis, when he told him he had called Niall Murphy's legal firm. 'At this point Detective Ellis became agitated, asked who the solicitor was and said that in any other circumstances ... he wouldn't allow him into the building. He expected the search to progress unhindered, that it was in our best interests to allow them to get on with it and nothing would stop it bar a document signed by a judge.'

In this moment, Ellis likely felt that he was top dog, believing his many months of meticulous planning was going to see Barry and myself facing a lengthy prison term. 'I'm a straight guy. Ask me anything, I'm an open book,' he told the two highly experienced lawyers. But when they began to question the legality of the warrant, Ellis abruptly told them to 'Get out!' As they made their way out of the offices, their experience told them that they had already learned enough to mount a legal challenge against the raids.

The court application for the raids had occurred two weeks earlier, on a Friday afternoon, when the High Court in Belfast was traditionally empty. The court officials and lawyers who weren't on holiday had long since left the building for the weekend. But County Court Judge Neil Rafferty was going to have to wait a little longer to get away that Friday afternoon. He had an urgent application from the PSNI to hear.

PSNI Detective Sergeant Arnold Henderson would be the witness. Counsel for the police would be Mark Robinson, a junior who, according to his CV, specialised in judicial review, legacy inquests and litigation, medical negligence, commercial law and personal injury. Henderson and Robinson laid out the case against us in front of Judge Rafferty. We were completely oblivious to the proceedings, just as the police had ensured we would be.

'Your Honour, this is an application for four search warrants under PACE Schedule 1,' explained Robinson. 'Your Honour, there are two subjects, Mr McCaffrey and Mr McBirney, sorry Mr Birney,' he added, making his first mistake in the hearing.

Robinson invited the PSNI officer to explain our background and how we were involved in the film before he moved on to the application itself. The judge had already read the documents sent to him, explaining the background and how the purpose of the warrants was to recover the Scope documents that had been leaked to Barry. 'There does seem to be, at least on the balance of probabilities,' the judge said, 'the existence of material marked secret. Is that the material you seek?' The barrister confirmed it was. The court was told that it was the ombudsman's office that had made a complaint about its missing documents, something Dr Michael Maguire would later contend was untrue.

Later, Mark Robinson revealed that the chief suspect in the Loughinisland massacre was part of the PSNI's prosecution case. 'Ronnie Hawthorne, named as the gunman and ringleader of the gang. His business [rat extermination] was identified and pictures of his home address are shown. Mr Hawthorne provided two statements ... where he comments upon finding comments online where people are trying to find where he is. He also mentions the fact that his business has suffered and is concerned about his safety,' the PSNI's barrister explained, failing to advise the judge that the filmmakers had gone to the ACC Stephen Martin seventeen months earlier to raise this very issue – the safety of those we intended to name. In fact, there was no mention of that critical meeting at all in the lengthy hearing that day.

'Article 2 [of the Human Rights Act – the right to life] weighs heavy?' asked the judge at one point.

'It does indeed and not only for the individuals named but generally when there is a leak of such nature,' replied Robinson, again failing to reveal that we had been so concerned about the Article 2 rights of those we intended naming that we had gone to the PSNI six months before the film premiered.

Then the judge sought to reassure himself given all he had been told by the police: 'Do I really take into account, for example, this is not being done as an exercise in shooting a crow to warn other crows about landing in the farmer's field?'

To which Robinson replied: 'Yes.'

The judge then asked: 'Without access to this material [Scope], your case is this goes no further, we're stymied and that's the end of the investigation,' to which Detective Sergeant Henderson said, 'It is indeed.'

As a result, Judge Rafferty granted the application for the warrants to raid our homes and offices. There was no one in the room to represent Barry or myself; to tell the judge the other side of the story.

After that point, our arrests had only been a matter of time.

***

Our first appearance in the High Court came a week after our arrest. We were challenging the legality of Judge Rafferty's decision to grant the warrants. Niall had secured Barry MacDonald QC to lead for both Fine Point Films and myself. Barry had John Finucane, who had been with him during questioning, and they had brought on Peter Girvan as junior and the highly experienced Gavin Millar QC as senior counsel. The NUJ held a protest outside that was joined by many of our friends and colleagues, which gave us huge comfort as we arrived.

The week since our arrest had been a blur. Barry and I had gone for a long walk down one of Belfast's leafy avenues in East Belfast, just a stone's throw from PSNI headquarters, to try to make sense of it all. We were concerned for others. Could there be further arrests? Who could they target? We both thought of Eimhear O'Neill. She was born and bred in Bellaghy in Co. Derry and brought a fierce and steely attitude to her work. But could she be next? She hadn't been mentioned during our interviews, but Barry and I agreed that we would do nothing to worry her and do all we could to deflect any further police attention away from her.

Ironically, the hearing was in front of Mr Justice McCloskey, the same judge who had to recuse himself from the RPOA case, in a small court on the first floor of the Royal Courts of Justice in Belfast. It was standing room only as our case was called. Junior Counsel Stephen Toal set out the case for a full judicial review of the granting of the warrants. 'We are conscious that this application gives rise to serious issues concerning freedom of the press and abuse of police powers, which, in our submission, have been used to intimidate journalists and prohibit not only journalists but whistleblowers,' he told the court, succinctly summing up our case.

The hearing was adjourned.

In the weeks that followed, the PSNI began to disclose documents relating to our case. They usually arrived by email at the end of the day on a Friday, meaning the weekend would be lost as we pored over every single page. Slowly, a picture began to emerge of how the PSNI and Durham had gone about their investigation. It was like reading the diary of a house burglar as he put together a meticulous plan to rob you of all your worldly prized possessions. It was the intrusive nature of it all that was most unsettling. The picture – a hugely erroneous one – that police had built up in their minds as they set about their flawed investigation was detailed and forensic.

However, there was one statement that stood out above all others. It was here that we first discovered that the PSNI and Durham had a complainant, someone who had provided them with a statement of the impact that *No Stone Unturned* had made on his life.

'I was shocked at what I read about myself. I was shocked at the venom of it,' Ronnie Hawthorne told detectives who visited him twice at his home outside Clough. Hawthorne revealed that on the day the film premiered in London, PSNI officers had visited and 'advised me regarding my personal security at home'. Hawthorne admitted that he had watched the documentary. 'In the film they're trying to say that I was a paid informer for the Royal Ulster Constabulary or British intelligence. They are saying my role in Loughinisland was [that of] the gunman. In one part of the film they actually call it The Hawthorne Gang. From that I take it they are trying to make out I was running the whole show. I say that all of that is a total lie.'

Later, in a second statement, he made it clear what the detectives were seeking from him and it had nothing to do with his involvement in terrorism. 'I know that Durham Police have been directed by ACC Martin to investigate the ombudsman's office. I've been asked how I feel about documents from OPONI in a film which names me as a gunman at Loughinisland in 1994 and alleges I was conspiring to murder. Well I don't know that there are enough words to describe it. OPONI is a public service and they obviously don't take care of their documents.'

Hawthorne's main complaint was that his business had been affected by him being publicly identified as the chief suspect in a mass murder. 'I've been brought into the limelight because of the film. My business, Building Cleaning Services, has also been affected. Before I was named in the film I had a cleaning business in all areas of Northern Ireland, including Kilcoo, Castlewellan, West Belfast, and the Gaelic-speaking school in the Falls Road area of Belfast. Now as a result of the film and the publicity, all of that has been shut down in a total loss. Since this all started I haven't received many phone calls for work. I'd say 90 per cent of my work was for or in nationalist communities. I can say that contractors have not been phoning me. I've been asked [by the detectives] how this affects me. I know myself that I am stressed. I hear every creak in the house or every floorboard or every time the dog barks. I'm up checking to make sure there's nobody in through the gates. I'm a proud man and I'm not going to the doctors for pills. I blame the film, the filmmaker, people that appear and the people that backed it, it's just a whitewash job. I'm just a wee cog in a big wheel. It's taken all the way back to the British State and nothing said about me other than being arrested is true.'

The PSNI, with the help of Durham, had turned its chief suspect in the Loughinisland massacre, and in the murders of Martin Lavery and Peter McCormack, into the victim.

When we discovered Ronnie Hawthorne's statement among the bundle of disclosure, it cast a new light on the investigation against us. It was difficult to comprehend how morally corrupt the PSNI had become that rather than go after the killers, it had turned its own chief murder suspect into the injured party. If we were ever to go on trial, Hawthorne was going to have his day in court, giving evidence against us. The PSNI had decided it had no issue with that. It was incomprehensible what it was prepared to put the victims of UVF violence through to pursue its case against us.

We were still coming to terms with our arrest; knowing that the police had gone to such lengths made us realise just how dark and sinister the PSNI investigation was.

***

In November we had to go back to Musgrave Street Police Station to answer our bail conditions and for what police told us would be another series of interviews. The Loughinisland case seemed to be forever commanding news headlines but, for the families, it was never for any of the right reasons, i.e. those responsible for the atrocity being held accountable. We were always very conscious that while the spotlight was on us, the families were the real victims in all of this. Our arrest was only the latest attempt to deny them the truth they deserved.

The NUJ again mounted a large protest outside the main entrance while we went inside. When we did, there was no sign of Darren Ellis or Arnold Henderson. The custody sergeant, who was constantly on the phone to someone – who appeared to be Darren Ellis – didn't seem to know what to do with us.

When they did call us forward, the police attempted to impose new bail conditions, demanding that Barry and I not communicate in any way while the investigation was ongoing. Niall and John got to work and the attempt to try to prevent us from communicating was dropped. The PSNI was clearly intent on humiliation rather than putting any evidence to us. We were bailed to return to the same station three months later. I was frustrated and angry and felt the need to make a protest, so I signed my bail document 'Darren Ellis'. The custody sergeant failed to notice.

Outside, we spoke to the press. I said that the day had been 'quite clearly [a] punitive attempt to restrict both myself and Barry and the work that we're trying to do. Ultimately this is all about the Loughinisland families, this really isn't about us and I think this farce today has just added to their grief and added to their concern that they're corks in the ocean being bobbed about by forces here and in Durham.'

Niall went one step further, saying the investigation was 'a malicious farce conditioned by a paranoid hysteria in the senior ranks of the police. Not one Durham police officer dignified the custody suite with his presence today,' he said. 'I think it's remarkable, I think it belies the real situation here – that this is a PSNI-inspired police investigation.'

In February 2019 we were back in court, this time in front of the Lord Chief Justice himself, Sir Declan Morgan, who would sit with two senior judges – Seamus Treacy and Siobhan Keegan. The three judges granted us the permission to challenge the legality of the search warrants and set down a date for a full hearing during the last week of May.

Around this time, we became aware of a malicious whisper campaign against us coming from the PSNI. A senior Irish government official advised us that they had been warned by the police to be careful lending us support as there was a lot more to come out in our case. We knew we had to get out ahead of the insidious briefings emanating from the PSNI, to tell our story and explain why it was such an important case for journalism and free speech.

With the help of an incredible press officer at the NUJ, Sarah Kavanagh, we visited London to meet with a range of MPs, including Durham MP Grahame Morris, deputy Labour leader John McDonnell and his Labour colleague Tom Watson. We bumped into former journalist Boris Johnson in the tearoom at Westminster, who was very quick to lend his support and have his photograph taken, without clearly having an iota of understanding of our case. We also met the former Brexit Minister, David Davis MP, who was very engaged and committed to coming to Belfast for the judicial review. He wouldn't have been a natural bedfellow for Barry or me, but he had a strong track record on issues of civil liberties, having previously opposed the Tory–Lib Dem coalition's plans to allow police and security services to extend their monitoring of the public's email and social media communications.

Journalists in Ireland and the USA began to take up our story. Patrick Radden Keefe, whom I had met on several occasions in Belfast and New York, wrote an article for the *New Yorker* magazine in which he remarked, 'The United Kingdom prides itself on being a liberal democracy, but, to Alex Gibney, the reaction to *No Stone Unturned* feels dismayingly in keeping with our times: when confronted with a film that identified prime suspects in a massacre of unarmed British citizens, the authorities made no apparent effort to further question those suspects – and arrested the filmmakers instead.' Susan McKay, the Derry-born writer and journalist managed to speak with Darren Ellis on the telephone for her *Irish Times* story, which ran under the headline: 'Why were two journalists investigating Loughinisland arrested?'

Six months after our arrest – and despite the best efforts of the Durham Constabulary – I found myself at a rooftop party in Santa Monica, Southern California. The director J.J. Abrams was giving a speech at the Oscar Wilde Awards, an annual event to celebrate Irish success in the film industry. It is a champagne and canapes type of affair held at Abrams' offices, with Oscar winners mingling with wannabes who have somehow managed to blag a ticket to the best party in town that week. Abrams is a rock star in the film industry, having created and directed some of the best-known television shows and movies of the last twenty years. The February 2019 Oscar Wilde Party honoured the actors Glenn Close and Chris O'Dowd, but Abrams also used his speech to voice his support of another issue.

I was standing with some friends when the *Star Wars* director said my name. 'That's you, that's you he's talking about,' a colleague said. I craned my ear to hear Abrams tell the audience of the importance of *No Stone Unturned* and the travesty of our subsequent arrest. Our case was now attracting attention way beyond Belfast, it seemed. Some of it we had sought, of course, but most of it came from a genuine response to the PSNI's attack on press freedom, coming as it did at a time when journalism around the world was being challenged from forces old and new. 'Now more than ever, investigative journalists need to be supported,' Abrams concluded.

After the Oscar Wilde event I flew to Chicago, where I met Barry and Niall for a lobbying trip through Boston, New York and Washington DC. We sat down with Democratic Congressmen Brendan Boyle and Richard Neal, who both gave us their full support. Having reported and worked with Irish-American leaders since the mid-1990s, I had built up a significant network of contacts, one of whom challenged ACC Stephen Martin when he visited Washington in the weeks after our arrest. He likely wasn't expecting to be ambushed at a private dinner attended by senior US police officers, where he was seeking to win friends and influence people as he prepared for a life after he left the police.

It was an easy story for Americans to understand in the years after the election of Donald Trump, a president who was attacking and undermining journalists on a daily basis. We just had to tap into their concerns and highlight that it was happening in the North of Ireland too.

We had pictures taken outside Capitol Hill on a bright, frosty DC day. When we posted them online, the podcaster Blindboy tweeted that we looked like veteran comedians about to perform at the Edinburgh Fringe! He did add that our case was a 'huge, worrying injustice' that needed support, although that bit of the tweet was largely missed by our friends and comrades in their fits of laughter.

***

Back in Belfast, the financial risks that Niall had alerted me to when under arrest were becoming very real. The judicial review dates were set in stone and I was running up huge legal bills. Fine Point Films, whose offices were raided due to the warrant, was the lead applicant in the review, with Barry and I tagged on. This was because it was thought that the High Court would not accept Barry and I being the leading applicants, as it would be viewed by the judges as so-called 'satellite litigation', designed to slow down or halt the police investigation.

The NUJ had come in to help cover some of Barry's legal costs but not all of them, leaving him financially exposed. But even though our company and *The Detail* employed several NUJ members, they refused to underwrite our costs. If we lost, the legal bill could be, Niall Murphy warned, well over £2 million, as in that case we would also be liable for the PSNI's legal fees. The case would bankrupt Barry, me and the company, close the business and put up to thirty people out of work. Despite the void that we could be sucked into, we had to put the ramifications to one side and trust in our legal team's ability to win.

We went into the High Court on the Tuesday morning, 28 May, ready and prepared for a hearing that would determine the legality of the warrants for the searches of our offices and homes. None of the legal teams had made any promises on the outcome.

As promised, David Davis travelled to Belfast to be in court for the hearing. Also in the packed court were members of the Loughinisland families, back in the same building where they had challenged the attempts by the retired police officers to quash the Maguire Report. My wife, Sheila, and daughters Ella and Mia sat beside our friends and colleagues from Below The Radar, Fine Point Films and *The Detail*.

The PSNI QC was Peter Coll, an experienced barrister who had acted on behalf of the British government and various authorities on previous occasions. His junior was Mark Robinson, the same barrister who had appeared in front of Judge Rafferty in the warrants hearing. It was going to be an uncomfortable week for Robinson, as the three judges and our own legal team unpicked the PSNI and Durham evidence presented at the warrant applications hearing.

Peter Coll had barely got going on the first morning when the Lord Chief Justice himself interjected, going straight to our meeting with ACC Stephen Martin six months before the premiere of *No Stone Unturned*, pointing out that we had gone to the lengths of advising the PSNI of our intention to name suspects. The tone had been established from the outset; the PSNI would be on the back foot throughout the week. We felt that Declan Morgan had dismantled Coll's case throughout the first morning, but when we broke for lunch there was no sense of relief or celebration. We huddled together in small rooms off the 140-foot-long central hall, Barry and I constantly seeking clarity from our lawyers on the legal points that had just been debated in court.

In the afternoon, both of us took our seats on the front row of the benches facing the judges, with our legal team in front of us in the body of the court. Niall Murphy and John Finucane, at that time a Sinn Féin councillor who had been elected Lord Mayor of Belfast just a few days before, sat below the court clerks facing us, their expressions giving us a sense of how they felt we were doing.

Throughout that first afternoon, it became clear to all that this was the domain of Barry MacDonald, one of the most significant legal figures of the late twentieth century in Northern Ireland. Armed with a wry smile, he was coming to the end of his career in the courts. Oblivious to the campaign we were waging outside the court, MacDonald's only concern was winning the legal argument.

MacDonald told the three judges that our arrest had set off alarm bells in Britain, Ireland and the United States. He said media organisations from each of the countries had intervened to support the case, including the Reporters Committee for the Freedom of the Press (RCFP). Alex Gibney had played an influential role in encouraging the RCFP's intervention, which had resulted in them filing a twenty-six-page argument in support of our case.

'Over the last half century, the US Supreme Court has repeatedly affirmed the right of the media under the First Amendment to the US Constitution to publish any material they lawfully acquire, even when it may have been unlawfully acquired by a source in the first instance,' the

RCFP counsel, Eamonn Dornan, wrote. 'This is an essential American civil liberty and has led to a vast array of journalism in the public interest, particularly in national security matters where government secrecy is at its zenith. The First Amendment prevents both federal and state governments from enacting any laws that "abridge" the freedom of speech and of the press. As a result, some of the most impactful national security stories of the past 50 years would not have been possible were it not for robust legal protections for the publication of information that has been lawfully acquired by a news organization but may have been disclosed illegally by a whistleblower or other source.'

Barry MacDonald said the police search operation had been outrageous. 'Under cover of a warrant that was obtained without giving the applicants the opportunity to be heard, and which should never have been granted, the police raided homes and business premises of two journalists and a film company. They rifled through all their confidential files, accessed literally millions of documents, and then seized computers, phones, media storage devices and documentary materials which they still retain – most of them completely unrelated to the pretext on which the search was carried out. This was the kind of operation associated more with a police state than with a liberal democracy that does have in place laws designed to protect investigative journalists and their sources from this kind of intrusion,' said the QC, adding that 'an ulterior motive [for the arrests and raids] was to undermine journalists and whistleblowers from exposing misconduct of the police'.

The Durham SIO, Darren Ellis, sat at the back of the court on the same benches as Barry and myself, getting more and more agitated, passing notes to the lawyers as MacDonald tore through his investigation. At one point, as the skylights raised the temperature inside the court, the veins in his head could be seen to swell as the police counsel struggled to make any coherent responding arguments. Ellis had spent ten months planning our arrests only to have been stopped in his tracks by our legal team. Now, in front of his eyes, the very tenets of that investigation were being torn away by Northern Ireland's most senior judges.

In his investigation diary, some of which was disclosed to us, Ellis had expressed his opinion on *No Stone Unturned*, describing it as 'sensational' – a producer's dream quote for a promotional poster, although we didn't think the detective used the word in the way we understood. He said our work was a 'clandestine pseudo murder investigation'. The families of those who died in The Heights Bar may have thought, at least someone was conducting a murder investigation!

As Emma Rogan listened in the back of the court, Barry MacDonald turned to the detective's diary and read to the court one note Ellis had made showing concern for Ronnie Hawthorne, who had been 'put in danger for merely having the misfortune of being involved in terrorist atrocities at whatever level'. The QC described Ellis's stance as 'a staggering proposition' and evidence of the 'warped mindset' of the police officer driving the investigation, which was 'nothing less than outrageous'. Ellis, he added, was 'a man on a mission' against the ombudsman and investigative journalists, who had 'put words in the mouth of a suspect'.

Going back to Judge Neil Rafferty's decision to grant the police the warrant for the searches, MacDonald told the court that Rafferty had asked if this was 'an exercise in shooting a crow so as to ensure that other crows don't land'. Despite police denials, MacDonald said that this was 'exactly what this is'.

Peter Coll QC admitted that Mr Justice Rafferty had not been taken through legislation relevant to the granting of warrants in relation to investigative journalism. To undercut this error, he said the PSNI and Durham case against us was still at an early stage and 'other potential offences' might emerge. In response, the Lord Chief Justice told Coll that he was confined to dealing only with the evidence put before Justice Rafferty. In other words, the PSNI could not now come up with new reasons for the searches and our arrests.

The police lawyer also admitted that the OSA had been engaged for the purpose of getting the warrant, arguing that this referred to the importance police attached to the management of informants. It was 'absolutely essential' that their identity be protected.

The British government first introduced an OSA in 1889, aimed primarily at foreign spies and civil servants who had notions of handing over sensitive documents. In 1911 it was updated and became a much more powerful tool. According to Dr Paul Lashmar, author of *Spies, Spin and the Fourth Estate*, as feared, journalists and whistleblowers became targets. The Newspaper Proprietors Association at the time protested the bill's 'far-reaching liabilities ... upon the public and the Press'. An even tougher act came in 1989, in reaction to the government's embarrassment over a series of well-publicised intelligence scandals in the 1980s.

In the documents disclosed to us ahead of the judicial review, Darren Ellis and the senior officers at the PSNI had concluded that 'both men [Barry and I] ... have openly disclosed sensitive and secret information contained within [the Scope documents]. In doing so they would have known or reasonably believed that the disclosure would have been damaging.' The key word is 'damaging'. Who was damaged by the film? In order to prosecute us under the OSA they had to find someone who said they had been damaged. Darren Ellis thought that person was Ronnie Hawthorne. By taking statements from the chief suspect in a mass murder, the PSNI had a 'victim' who was impacted by the publication of the Scope documents in *No Stone Unturned*.

'A constituent element of the offence requires harm to have been incurred,' Niall Murphy told me. 'Ronnie's statement, that his rat-catching business had been harmed, satisfied that constituent element.'

As we filed back into court after lunch, David Davis was the first to say out loud that he thought we were going to get a quick, positive result. Sure enough, he was proven right on his 'quick' prediction when, after 3 p.m. on the second day, the Lord Chief Justice said he wanted a short adjournment to consider the judgment.

Over the past two days, we hadn't witnessed the PSNI winning a single point against MacDonald, Millar or the three judges. However, we were also aware of the limitations of our legal knowledge. And none of our team was exhibiting any signs of confidence. It was quite the opposite, in fact; they were managing expectations, advising that it was likely the judges would tell the court they were going to take some time to consider their verdict.

Within an hour, we were called back to the Judicial Review Court.

With Seamus Treacy on his right and Siobhan Keegan to his left, the Lord Chief Justice took his seat and allowed the court to settle, before speaking. Sir Declan Morgan was coming towards the end of his time in the courts. Born in Derry, he studied in Cambridge at Peterhouse College but during the summers returned home to work in a butcher's shop where one of his colleagues was Martin McGuinness, who would leave the job to lead the IRA in the city. Now, almost fifty years later, he was about to make a ruling that would impact on the rest of our journalistic lives.

Sir Declan cut to the chase. The warrants issued by Judge Neil Rafferty in August 2018 that led to our arrest and the raids on our homes and offices were unlawful and should be quashed. He said that a fuller judgment would come in due course.

We had won!

Barry and I could only nod to each other with muted smiles as we were surrounded by our family and friends. Out of the corner of my eye, I could see Niall Murphy, John Finucane, Stephen Toal and the rest of the lawyers allowing themselves a moment in the body of the court. I walked down towards them and shook Barry MacDonald's hand. 'It's a ten-nil win,' he said. 'We've won on every single point.'

It was clearly a huge moment for them too. Stephen Toal, who had worked so hard on our case from the very moment he first challenged Darren Ellis in our offices, was key to getting the case over the line. It was an important moment for journalism in the United Kingdom, one that allowed myself and Barry to breathe for the first time in nine months.

We gathered ourselves and headed outside, where the media was gathered beyond the old, cranky turnstile gate, a throwback from the Troubles when the High Court had been a target of IRA bomb attacks.

Surrounded by family and friends, NUJ members, Amnesty International's Patrick Corrigan, Belfast Lord Mayor John Finucane and former Brexit Minister David Davis, we gave a short press conference, trying to find words to properly explain our relief and the importance of this victory for press freedom.

'It's not very easy to explain what the last eight or nine months have been like for myself and Barry, and our families, friends and colleagues,' I said to a BBC reporter. 'I want to thank everyone who gave us support – we've had tremendous support from home and abroad, from people we've never met before to people very close to us. Today restores our faith in the checks and balances of the court system. It's a damning indictment of the police investigation.'

Seamus Dooley, the Dublin-based leader of the NUJ in Ireland, said the decision to quash the warrants was 'a good day for journalism and a good day for human rights in Northern Ireland'.

Barry put the pressure back on the PSNI, calling for an apology from Chief Constable George Hamilton.

John Finucane told the BBC, 'This is a tremendous news day for my client and for Trevor Birney, and for all journalists. This will be a very important judgment for the freedom of expression, for the freedom of journalists to do their job.'

David Davis told the Press Association chief reporter, David Young, that 'protecting press freedom is not just about protecting journalists, it is about protecting their whistleblowers and their witnesses, it is about protecting the ability to expose wrongdoing and expose failure and that is what these journalists are doing and they don't deserve to go through what they are going through now. Their cause is so important, it should be known throughout the whole of the UK and the rest of the world.'

Niall Murphy also made a statement to the press, speaking of the 'warped mindset' of police who pursued me and Barry rather than the killers. 'Senior police must now reflect on their actions and stop this farce of an investigation.'

We had won the judicial review, but Darren Ellis was still leading a criminal investigation into us. Our victory hadn't changed that fact.

16 | Truth and Justice

I was at our dinner table in the kitchen of our home in East Belfast on the following Monday evening when a strange number appeared on my mobile phone. Two minutes later, Niall Murphy's number popped up. He had answered a call from the same number. It was Arnold Henderson from the PSNI. The investigation was over. The chief constable had taken the weekend to consider the judicial review and had decided to bring a halt to it. The detective told Niall that the computers, documents and notebooks that police had taken from our homes and offices could be handed over the following morning at Castlereagh Police Station.

Barry called to say he'd had the same good news. We agreed that it was only because of our legal action that police had ended the investigation. It wasn't due to them coming to their senses. George Hamilton had less than a month left to serve as chief constable. Barry had called on him to apologise for going after us instead of the Loughinisland killers, but while he had called off Darren Ellis, he wasn't ready for *mea culpa*.

Overnight, we made the press aware that the investigation had been dropped and we were getting our journalistic materials back. The PSNI had offered to deliver them to the office, but we knew going to Castlereagh Police Station, which had become so notorious as the barracks in which terrorist suspects had been interrogated, would be much more of an event for the media. We arranged for the hire of a white van, which our colleague, Michael Law, would drive.

When Niall, Barry and I arrived at the gates the following morning, we were escorted into a ground-floor office, where Detective Henderson and the detective who arrested me were waiting. Our computers, notebooks and documents were littered around the office. I spotted the pink iPhone belonging to my daughter that the police had taken from our home. We packed them all up into see-through plastic bags and walked out through the gates where the reporters and cameras were ready and waiting. Michael had backed the van up so the media could film us in front of the station, loading our bags.

Barry and I even climbed into the van at one point, after being asked by photographers for another shot. When I look back at the pictures now, I can see the stress on both of our faces. We had been under immense pressure for months. Barry wanted to protect his partner, Véronique, from what was going on. I had a business to run, as well as supporting Sheila and the girls. Having to constantly explain that I wasn't a thief and that we hadn't stolen documents had taken a heavy financial toll. We were suffering from a distinct chill from some of our broadcast and finance partners. Every interview, court appearance, video opportunity, had been an attempt by the two of us to explain our story; to ensure that there was no ambiguity; that anyone who was interested couldn't help but appreciate that we had been at the wrong end of a malicious police operation designed to undermine press freedom in Northern Ireland and the UK. The judicial review and the support from the across the political divide had gone a long way to restoring our good character. The decision to drop the investigation allowed us to get on with our lives without the threat of imprisonment hanging over us.

A few days later, outgoing Chief Constable George Hamilton was to make his final appearance in front of the Northern Ireland Policing Board, the oversight body that appointed him and held him to account. It was decided that Barry and I should attend and, on the afternoon of the meeting, many of the Loughinisland families turned up to support us.

It was early June 2019 – the twenty-fifth anniversary of the massacre was only a couple of weeks away, yet here they were coming out to support a couple of 'clowns', as Barry had taken to calling us.

Hamilton decided he couldn't face the meeting alone and so brought with him his chief constable counterpart from Durham, Mike Barton, who was also about to leave the role he had held for seven years. In an interview with *The Daily Telegraph* to mark his retirement, Barton said he didn't want 'anyone to think I am a trendy, pinko liberal. I'm a straightforward, Northern [English] bloke.' Despite being one of the smallest forces in the UK, Durham, according to the Her Majesty's Inspectorate, was one of its best performing. Now, however, he and his force were immersed in a scandalous investigation in Northern Ireland and had to account for its unlawful actions.

Ahead of the meeting, two members of the Northern Ireland Policing Board, Dolores Kelly from the SDLP and Sinn Féin's Gerry Kelly, were both critical of the PSNI's chief constable. 'I think an apology is owed to these journalists,' Kelly told the BBC. 'I think freedom of the press has to be protected and the chief constable has made a huge error of judgement.'

Despite the damning verdict against them in the High Court, the two chief constables opted to get through the meeting with a mix of bluster and bombast. Incredibly, in his first public utterance on our arrest, never mind the High Court verdict, Mike Barton admitted he didn't know the law. 'I've got to say that I thought the law was in a different place, until the Lord Chief Justice corrected me and I stand corrected and I have now changed my mind on what the law is,' Barton, dressed in full dress uniform, told the meeting. 'I absolutely respect press freedom, but I do not – in my view and I have been corrected by the lord chief justice – I do not think it appropriate that secret documents that put people's lives at risk are put out there in the public domain – I think those discretions should be fettered.'

Gerry Kelly asked if he would apologise to us, but Barton refused. Hamilton said there had been nothing easy about the investigation, which, he admitted, had cost over £300,000. He stuck to the same ridiculous line as Barton, saying that leaked documents were a serious matter. Hamilton, in short shirt sleeves, tried to stick to the line that there was theft involved, even though he knew now that no such crime had been committed.

Barry and I listened to them both, frustrated that they were not put under more scrutiny by the body whose job it was to hold them to account. At one stage, Barry threw up his hands in despair at the lack of candour from either chief constable.

After the meeting, Niall Murphy summed up our reaction in an interview with the BBC: 'We are very disappointed at the abrasive attitude adopted by both chief constables. An opportunity has been lost to attempt to rebuild and restore the confidence of the families and certainly the community from which they come. One would have thought that an apology in this case would have been immediately forthcoming, first and foremost to these families, but also to Trevor Birney and Barry McCaffrey.'

It was not to be.

***

While we had received all the physical materials taken in the police searches, there remained one vexing outstanding issue – the data that had been downloaded from our server.

At a hearing on 24 June 2019, the Lord Chief Justice issued an order that the PSNI should not review the material it had taken from our servers. It later transpired that the SIO, Darren Ellis, hadn't been pleased with this latest court ruling. In emails to senior PSNI officers, which were later disclosed to the Policing Board, he launched an attack on 'another quite stunning decision by the LCJ', Sir Declan Morgan. 'I think the situation is an outrage. The general judicial oversight and management of this case including the "performance" of the LCJ, beggars belief,' he wrote. In an email, to ACC Barbara Gray, he said he was going to contact his former boss, Mike Barton. 'I would sense he would like to take advices [sic] from the Home Office given the national implication of what I personally consider to be the most perverse judicial decision I have come across in my thirty-year policing career. It is preposterous.' The PSNI ACC wrote back, describing his email as 'totally unacceptable' and said it would be raised with Barton. The release of the emails by the PSNI was seen as an attempt to put distance between them and the Durham officer who had led a highly sensitive investigation on their behalf. But it only served to further damage the limited credibility the two police forces had in the case.

Back in the High Court, the PSNI displayed little embarrassment as they insisted that the data taken from our offices could not be deleted. Our data, our films, documentation and company records, were now on PSNI microfiche stored at one of its bases off the Lisburn Road in South Belfast. The police admitted that it was an archaic system, which had not been updated due to lack of funds. In layman's terms, it was explained that they couldn't cut anything out of the microfiche as it would mean the loss of other highly sensitive material. We called in an expert, who went to the police base and examined the storage system. In the end, it was agreed that our data would remain on the system, but it would not be accessed and at any point we could seek a report from the PSNI to prove that it hadn't been tampered with.

It was not an easy compromise to make – to allow our sensitive information to remain in the hands of the PSNI – but it was the only way to conclude the judicial review without causing frustration among the judges who were urging both sides to find a resolution.

Soon we were faced with something that helped put all our difficulties in context. Niall Murphy, as usual, was pushing himself to the limits. He had been invited to New York by the Brehon Law Society to speak at their annual St Patrick's Day dinner on 10 March and flew there following some engagements in Glasgow. When he got home, he was straight into court on Friday 13 March for an application by former British soldier Dennis Hutchings to vacate his trial for the killing of John Pat Cunningham, due to the impending pandemic. John Pat, a vulnerable adult with learning difficulties, was shot dead by Hutchings on 15 June 1974.

On that Friday evening, Niall began to feel ill, and by the Saturday morning he had a temperature of over 40 degrees Celsius. He was sapped of energy to the point that he couldn't get out of bed, had no appetite and seemed incapable of getting the temperature down. He was bedridden for eleven days, until Wednesday 25 March, when he was admitted to Antrim Area Hospital suffering from Covid, one of the first people on the island to officially have the virus. He spent sixteen nights in a coma. At one point his wife, Marie, was told there was only a fifty-fifty chance he would survive. A man known for his strength of character and determination, it was little surprise that he ultimately pulled through. However, when he was wheeled out of the intensive care unit on Good Friday, he had lost significant weight. He was later told he was the first person in Northern Ireland to make it off a ventilator alive in the pandemic. It was 'Niall's Easter Rising', as Susan McKay described it.

During the distractions and hardships of those early months of the pandemic, I was advised by a source that the PSNI would be prepared to pay compensation to both of us. When I raised this with the legal team, they were initially unconvinced; understandably, given their knowledge of the courts. But my source was insistent, and so, despite his reservations, Barry MacDonald approached Peter Coll in the High Court about the issue. He was told that my source was correct. First, however, the Lord Chief Justice and his two colleagues had to deliver their full judgment.

This came in July 2020 – via video, of course, due to the Covid restrictions. In a twenty-six-page judgment, Declan Morgan, Seamus Treacy and Siobhan Keegan denounced the hearing overseen by Judge Neil Rafferty when he granted the warrants. 'We concluded that the conduct of this hearing fell woefully short of the standard required to ensure that the hearing was fair,' read the Lord Chief Justice.

During the judicial review, the PSNI had claimed in court that I had destroyed evidence by telling colleagues to delete anything that would have revealed our source. At the time, the PSNI's barrister had been shut down by the judges. In their full judgment, they went further: 'The material [that I ordered be deleted] consists of email traffic in which there is discussion by Mr Birney and Mr McCaffrey about the risk of steps being taken by the police to try to establish the source of the leak. Unsurprisingly both of them were anxious to ensure that they should take all steps to try to protect the identity of the source including the deletion of material. There is nothing suspicious or inappropriate about this. It is exactly what one would expect a careful, professional investigative journalist to do in anticipation of any attempt to identify a source. It does not lead to any inference that such a journalist would commit a contempt of court [i.e. by destroying evidence].'

The judgment stated that by meeting ACC Stephen Martin ahead of the premiere, we had acted responsibly, raising the issue of risk and 'refraining from naming an informant'. It said there was 'no overriding requirement in the public interest which could have justified an interference with the protection' of our journalistic sources.

The judgment was hailed by the NUJ and Amnesty International, which described the police actions as 'outrageous'. Patrick Corrigan said the judgment 'should mean this sort of undue interference with press freedom never happens again'. David Davis said the judges had 'set a strong and authoritative precedent for press freedom across the whole of the UK'.

Following the judgment, Simon Byrne, who had replaced George Hamilton as chief constable, let it be known that he wished to write to us and to deliver a message via video conference call. This was set up for mid-July. In his letter, he offered an 'unreserved apology for the distress and upset caused to [Barry and myself] and [our] families'. With this message, Byrne had done what Barton and Hamilton refused to do.

It was deeply appreciated, as Barry and I told the journalist William Crawley on his BBC *Talkback* programme. 'We need assurances that this won't happen again and that no other journalists or their families should be put through what we've gone through in the last couple of years. There has been a shadow that's been cast across myself and Barry, our careers, our family life, our personal life, our professional lives as a result of the actions that were unlawful back in August 2018,' I said.

Barry added: 'The chief constable says they are going to look at the lessons that need to be learned; we think it's obvious the lessons that need to be learned. This was bad policing, this should never have happened, this was an attack on press freedom.'

Two months later, Barry and I and our legal teams were invited to the Resolution Centre in Belfast for a mediation session. From the outset, it appeared that the PSNI was ill-prepared and had no interest in finding a solution. However, on day two, the mood changed, due mostly to the work of our counsel, led by Barry MacDonald, who was at his most impressive. Implacable, determined and detailed, he wanted a resolution no matter the difficulties the PSNI position posed.

The PSNI agreed to pay Fine Point Films £600,000 in compensation. On top of that, Barry would get £125k and I personally would receive £150k. All our legal costs would also be paid. It was a fair settlement, although we were very aware that the families of the six men who died in Loughinisland and those who had been injured had not received compensation, like thousands of others who had suffered during the conflict.

It was over. We went back to the south Belfast home that Barry and Véronique shared. Sheila soon arrived and the four of us reflected on everything we had come through together. Before *No Stone Unturned*, Barry and I enjoyed a very good working relationship; now we were as close as brothers. We were an odd couple thrown together by circumstance but, maybe because of our very different life experiences, we got on. Critically, we trusted each other implicitly and valued and respected each other's judgement. But it was Barry's ability to find that cutting humorous comment, no matter the situation, that, for me, was his strength. And his eye for detail, of course.

***

Our arrest and the court battles would never be far away from our minds, but by March 2023 it wasn't something we dwelt on, apart from slagging each other on a good night out. It all got very real again, however, when Niall Murphy and John Finucane contacted us to say they had received notification from the Investigatory Powers Tribunal (IPT) in London.

Back at the end of the judicial review, Sarah Kavanagh, who was working for the NUJ at the time, had advised us to lodge a complaint with the IPT. Sarah approached Gavin Millar, who suggested we bring in a colleague of his in London, Ben Jaffey, who was an expert in the tribunal and its workings. We asked the IPT to investigate if there had been any unlawful use of surveillance during the police investigation.

We all met to go over the communication. In the letter from the IPT's counsel, Jonathan Glasson QC, he said that the tribunal had found matters it wished to disclose to us. The tribunal hadn't got to the substance of the 2018 investigation but had discovered that there was an incident in 2013 where Barry's communication data was examined by the PSNI without his knowledge.

Our immediate reaction was that it must have had something to do with Barry's investigation into Loughinisland. We pored through our notes and records to match up the dates on the disclosure documents we were sent, before coming to the realisation that it had to do with an altogether different story Barry had written. He had received a tip that the PSNI were investigating an allegation of corruption within its own ranks. The case had commenced after a bank official told a DUP representative that they had seen strange payments going into the account of a senior civilian who worked at the PSNI. Just as any other journalist would do, Barry called the PSNI press office and asked for confirmation. Were they investigating the civilian official? It was a straightforward request.

The head of the PSNI press office asked Barry for three days' grace while police carried out a covert operation against the suspect. When the seventy-two hours had passed, the press officer went to ground. Barry couldn't get an answer from the PSNI. Eventually, *The Detail* ran Barry's story under the headline: 'Senior PSNI figure at centre of financial allegations', writing: 'The PSNI has been pressing for an indefinite blackout of the story. It asked *The Detail* not to publicly identify or approach the person at the centre of the allegations, claiming it would jeopardise "an ongoing covert investigation".'

No one had ever been arrested, never mind charged. As with Loughinisland, rather than focusing on the suspected guilty party, the PSNI turned Barry into a criminal suspect.

In the weeks after the initial notice from the IPT, we were provided with disclosure from the PSNI that documented exactly what the police had done in 2013. Although heavily redacted, it was clear they wanted to know who had told Barry about the corruption scandal, so harvested three weeks of his outgoing and incoming mobile phone calls. Under the

Regulation of Investigatory Powers Act 2000, a PSNI constable from the Professional Standards Department stated in his application for three weeks of Barry's data that he 'is a suspect in the above investigation and the information sought is needed to identify the suspect and other criminal associates'. A detective superintendent granted the request within twenty-four hours.

It seemed that the PSNI were dragging their heels again, delaying further disclosures each and every time the IPT ordered them to hand over documentation. When a new disclosure did eventually occur it alerted us to a second harvest of Barry's phone data, this time in 2011, when Barry had been leaked the CJI report that led to Al Hutchinson's early departure from his job as police ombudsman.

The Canadian had complained to the PSNI about the leak and they had, in turn, called in Scotland Yard to investigate. Detectives from the Met had written to *The Detail* editor, Ruth O'Reilly, seeking our co-operation, but we had politely declined, advising them that, if they wanted access to any of our materials, they should go to court and apply for a 'production order', which, if granted, would mean us having to hand over whatever materials the police were seeking. Police across the UK have gone to court regularly to seek such production orders. Indeed, the PSNI and Durham could have chosen to go down the same route rather than arrest us, but in the warrant application in front of Judge Neil Rafferty, they had told the court that because we had refused to comply in 2011, a production order wasn't going to work.

Following on from these disclosures, Niall Murphy, John Finucane and Stephen Toal were back representing us again, with the highly experienced Ben Jaffey leading the team. Over the course of twelve months, we began to pull back the curtain on the PSNI's surveillance of journalists in the North.

For a period, it appeared that Durham and the PSNI were acting together; however, the English force broke away over several months in 2024 and began to act in its own interests. Durham flooded the IPT with documents relating to our arrest. Just hours before one IPT hearing, Durham disclosed over 700 pages in one tranche. From this, we discovered that Darren Ellis and his team had applied to go after our communications data prior to our arrest. It was likely to this he was referring in a document he had written, which we had come across during the judicial review, in which he referred to a 'covert operation' against us.

We could also now see in black and white how Ellis had concluded that a press officer at the ombudsman's office had been the source of the leaks to us. His application for our data was turned down by the PSNI, so he opted to go after the OPONI press officer and, this time, the PSNI chief constable, George Hamilton, agreed. When we were arrested, the ombudsman's chief press officer was put under twenty-four-hour surveillance for two weeks. Ellis had sought and been granted a Directed Surveillance Authorisation (DSA), seemingly having come to the conclusion that after we were released from Musgrave Street PSNI Station, we would go straight to see the press officer and he would hand over more documents.

It was laughable. Ellis clearly had no understanding of how leaks occur; furthermore, in my experience, the last person in the world who would decide to leak secret documents is a press officer. Their role is to liaise with the press, to explain sometimes complicated situations, and to generally help journalists in the best interests of whatever organisation they represent. They aren't the kind of people who put their jobs and their very freedom at risk by leaking. But Ellis and his PSNI colleagues were convinced that's exactly what had happened. And George Hamilton backed him, agreeing to the DSA. All in the hope that they would identify Barry's sources.

Poring over the newly disclosed documents – usually at weekends, what with them having been delivered at 5 p.m. on a Friday – we could get a glimpse into the Ellis's mindset through his copious notes. It became clear that during his investigation he didn't have just Barry and me in his sights; he was also after Niall Murphy. He had met with the Law Society to discuss KRW Law and, in one note, described Niall as 'loud, verbose and aggressive'. In a statement to the IPT, Ellis went further, saying the defence lawyer was 'combative, unreasonable and threatening'. It was frightening to see a senior police officer targeting a professional for doing nothing more than his job.

Through disclosure, we also discovered that Barry and I were not the only journalists in the PSNI's spying sights. Reading between the redacted lines in part of Durham's disclosure, we realised that former BBC journalist Vincent Kearney also had his phone data culled in 2011, when he was examining Al Hutchinson's time as ombudsman for BBC NI's current affairs programme, *Spotlight*.

The BBC had always given the impression that they were off limits; given their status as the UK's leading public service broadcaster, they projected the sense that the police and MI5 wouldn't dare tamper with their journalists. But for the PSNI – and Scotland Yard – we could see now that this was not the case at all.

It was clear, too, from everything we had seen, that the PSNI had been going after 'troublemaker' journalists. We had opened up a Pandora's box.

***

The IPT held its first public hearing into our case in February 2024 at the Royal Courts of Justice (RCJ) in London. Amnesty International's Patrick Corrigan was there to stand alongside us, along with Daniel Holder from the CAJ in Belfast. We had briefed the Alliance Party, SDLP, Sinn Féin and Unionist parties, some of which had representatives in court, including the then North Down Alliance MP Stephen Farry and his South Down counterpart, Chris Hazzard from Sinn Féin.

The president of the IPT, Sir Rabinder Singh, would oversee the case. Sitting with him was Lady Carmichael, a judge in the Supreme Courts of Scotland, and Stephen Shaw, a Northern Ireland KC who sits as a temporary judge in Belfast's High Court.

It was clear the PSNI was trying their patience by its refusal to deal with the IPT in the professional manner expected. To underline this, Ben Jaffey told the court how the case was a shambles. In front of the packed press benches, he explained how we had received another eighty-six-page redacted document from the PSNI and Durham that morning, the

Metropolitan Police Service having also handed over new disclosures just a few days before. We had had little time ahead of the hearing to digest all the documentation and appreciate its significance.

Three months later we were back in London for a second hearing, by which stage the BBC was in court to support its former journalist, Vincent Kearney. Having trawled through hundreds of pages of disclosure, we had realised that the incidents against Barry and Vincent were just the tip of a very dark and deep iceberg. The PSNI had been running a six-monthly 'defensive operation' against all the journalists for which it had telephone numbers. Ostensibly, this was to see if PSNI officers were speaking to reporters. The operation had temporarily ceased in March 2023 – the same month the IPT first revealed to us that we had been spied on. As Ben Jaffey pointed out, the police were evidently obsessed with finding the sources of stories in Northern Ireland. At neither the February nor the May hearings in London's RCJ did the PSNI's KC ever once speak to challenge anything Ben was putting into the public domain.

As news of the so-called 'defensive operation' broke, the PSNI found itself at the centre of an emerging spying scandal. The chief constable who apologised to us, Simon Byrne, had left and been replaced by another Englishman, Jon Boutcher, in October 2023. His force's continued tactics of denial and delay at the IPT were only heaping further pressure on him to explain what exactly had been going on.

Boutcher had presented a report to a private meeting at the Northern Ireland Policing Board in April 2024, stating there had been fewer than twenty incidents of data communication harvesting against journalists and lawyers. Members of the board said the report was vague and called on the chief constable to give far more detail, which he promised to do.

In June 2024 Boutcher dropped his follow-up report. It turned out that there were not fewer than twenty incidents involving journalists and lawyers, as previously stated. Instead, the PSNI admitted in a fifty-six-page 'Covert Powers Report' that over a period of thirteen years between 2011 and 2024, there had in fact been 320 applications for journalists' data in Northern Ireland. On top of that, they had made over 500 applications for data belonging to lawyers. The report also detailed the use of informers within the ranks of journalists and lawyers on four separate occasions.

Amnesty International and the NUJ called for a full public inquiry. Boutcher, supported by the Northern Ireland Justice Minister, Naomi Long, wasn't in favour of more public scrutiny. Instead, he said he would call in another highly experienced KC, Angus McCullough, to examine the PSNI's surveillance operations against journalists, lawyers, NGOs and activists. This climbdown was a reflection of both the pressure he was under and the realpolitik of modern-day Northern Ireland. After all, unionists were never going to back a public inquiry, despite their private reservations about the PSNI's wrongdoings. Even the DUP were concerned about their phones being bugged, but publicly backing an inquiry that could expose all sorts of ugly truths remained unappealing.

Ahead of a third hearing in July 2024, we received further disclosure. We learned that in 2011, the PSNI, with the support of another English police force which can't be named at time of writing, harvested 4,000 separate pieces of communication data (texts and phonecalls), between twelve journalists, including Barry and myself, in Belfast over a four-month period. They also used cell site analysis to record where we were when we communicated with each other. As far as I was concerned, there was no explanation as to what exactly the PSNI was looking for, but it was further evidence of how far they were prepared to go to track reporters doing nothing more than going about their jobs.

At the time of writing, Angus McCullough is continuing his investigation. A full hearing into the complaint that Barry and I brought in 2019 is scheduled to be held in the autumn of 2024.

In our first meeting with Ben Jaffey, he said that we had pulled at a dark thread and that we had no idea of the full mosaic picture we would expose by the time our case was heard. With the support of Ben, our legal teams, Amnesty International, CAJ, NUJ members and all our friends and colleagues, we had uncovered the PSNI's unlawful criminalisation of journalism in Northern Ireland.

After all, it goes without saying that Barry was not a criminal suspect, as the detective had described him in 2013. He is one of the finest investigative reporters to ever work in Northern Ireland. He had turned over every stone in the Loughinisland story to reveal the truth behind the murders of six innocent men: Barney Green, Dan McCreanor, Malcolm Jenkinson, Eamon Byrne, Patrick O'Hare and Adrian 'Frosty' Rogan. Nothing the PSNI had done to Barry and myself would ever come close to the pain and the suffering of their families and of the injured, like Brenny Valentine, who passed away in 2017, and the barman, Aidan O'Toole, who lives every day with the horror that shattered the peace of a beautiful South Down village on 18 June 1994.

On the thirtieth anniversary of the massacre, Barry and I, along with my wife, were in the graveyard adjoining St Macartan's church in Loughinisland for a memorial Mass. On a long summer evening, the families stood in a dignified silence to remember their dead. Also attending was Niall Quinn, the Irish footballer who had never forgotten the victims murdered on a night of such celebration for the country, the team and the Irish supporters. He was later welcomed into The Heights Bar, where stories were told and songs were sung.

Over three decades, the dignity of the people of Loughinisland as they fought for the truth has been in stark contrast to the morally vacuous actions of the RUC, the PSNI and the British state. There is no doubt that they have been appalled that their carefully curated official history of the conflict has been torn asunder by victims from across Northern Ireland's political divide and by investigative journalists such as Barry McCaffrey, all of whom are simply not prepared to accept anything but the full, ugly truth of our past.

The legal facts of that truth have been judicially endorsed time and time again in Northern Ireland's courts. Despite this, the British state remains so concerned by the emergence of the real picture of systematic collusion and the role of the security forces in the deaths of so many victims that it introduced the Legacy Act in the spring of 2024 to shut down access to truth and justice.

The Loughinisland families have led by example. With the help and bravery of both Michael Maguire and Barry McCaffrey, they got their truth, although they would never have the justice of seeing the UVF gang responsible behind bars. For thousands of others, their quest continues, passing down through generations as the years roll on.

And one thing is certain: no British government or legislative act will ever extinguish the blazing fire of injustice that still burns in hearts, homes and villages across the North.

Postscript

On the way to Barry and Véronique's wedding reception in Newcastle, we spotted a roadside café. The Thirsty Herd was in a lay-by on the Dundrum Road, just beyond the village of Clough. It was little more than a souped-up horse box but appeared to be doing a decent trade from passing motorists. I stopped to get a coffee and thought I recognised the woman behind the counter. I realised it was Hilary Hawthorne. She and Ronnie had diversified and were now in the service industry. I paid for my drink, walked back to my car and drove on.

The *Sunday Life* newspaper had picked up on their new venture. One of their reporters called but was told to 'piss off' when they challenged Ronnie about his role in the attack on The Heights Bar. At the time, he was busy putting up gaily coloured bunting around his café.

Life stood still for the Loughinisland families on 18 June 1994. But for Ronnie and Hilary there is money to be made, and their notoriety after the release of *No Stone Unturned* clearly did not daunt them. The families of the six men who died regularly drive pass the Thirsty Herd. Life has also moved on for Gorman McMullan, who, in the summer of 2024, married a Thai bride. The *Sunday World* reported that 'serial jailbird Gormy McMullan (71), a leading suspect in the shocking Loughinisland massacre, is to tie the knot with [a] stunning Asian beauty'. The newspaper published a picture of McMullan firing a high-powered rifle during a visit to Vietnam. When a relative of one of the men who died in The Heights Bar had their bathroom renovated, Alan Taylor was one of the tradesmen who turned up. He only learned of Taylor's past when he watched *No Stone Unturned*.

Darren Ellis is no longer a detective. But he did respond to the IPT when he was asked to answer questions about the requests he made to bug phones belonging to Barry and myself, and to put surveillance on a press officer at the OPONI. He clearly wasn't happy that the decisions he took in Belfast were still being scrutinised. 'The applicants and their legal teams operate in a community where no one ever holds them to account,' he wrote in an email to the IPT, 'in a system that simply allows them to ride roughshod over people who "dare" challenge them. For too long, they shout and they brawl and intimate [sic] others. I consider it to be a strategy to frighten and softly intimidate, and hence place a ring of steel around corrupt activity. Their growing legal teams simply seem to look to rewrite history and have an innate ability to be unable to accept clear explanation and correction of their superstition and innuendo,' the email continued. 'This isn't "sport" for them. This isn't "payback" time. This is serious stuff which has serious implications.'

After seven years in charge, the former Police Ombudsman, Dr Michael Maguire, left the ombudsman's office in 2019 and was a visiting professor at Monash University in Melbourne before becoming a lay member of the Committee of Standards at the UK Parliament. Inquiries that Maguire led into loyalist attacks on a bookmaker's on Belfast's Ormeau Road in 1992 and the 'trick or treat' massacre in the village of Greysteel the following year were published by his successor.

At the time of writing, the full hearing into our complaint to the IPT is yet to be heard. But the evidence we have uncovered during the disclosure process in the case has far-reaching implications for journalists in Northern Ireland and beyond. The PSNI spying operation on journalists, with the willing support of Scotland Yard, was undeniably widespread and industrial. It is now clear that no journalist's data was beyond their reach. Solicitors and human rights activists were also caught up in their dragnet. The case has pulled back the curtain on the dark heart of policing.

Barry McCaffrey and I are in no way surprised by what we have discovered, but there is a realisation, right across the political divide, that, despite the accountability and oversight mechanisms that flowed from the Good Friday Agreement and the Patton review of policing, the PSNI had given itself unfettered access to the data of those deemed to be of interest. The Policing Board, which is supposed to hold the PSNI to account, was at the very least misled about the spying operation, and through disclosure we have learned that the OPONI was only given documents the PSNI allowed it to have. There has been a fundamental failure to appreciate or question the scale and scope of the PSNI's spying, never mind hold its leadership to account.

There are many stories buried in the thousands of documents we have received through the work of our legal team, led by Ben Jaffey KC and Stephen Toal KC. Each time we turn up in London we make the long walk to Court 72, which seems to be the farthest room from the imposing entrance of the Royal Courts of Justice. Each time, we are exasperated at the foot-dragging tactics of the police.

But nothing prepared us for the appearance of Mr Andrew Byass on 18 July 2024. The tall, bald gentleman in the sharp suit advised the court that he represented 'respondents three', or, in other words, MI5. He said that MI5 had such vast amounts of material on BBC journalists that they would not be able to brief the court on what they had until December. MI5 intended to hire two junior barristers and put them through a rigorous security vetting process before they began to wade through the documentation. So there was no way they could respond to the court ahead of its planned full hearing in October. We were then all told to leave as the courtroom went into closed session, which lasted for two hours. Only the three-judge panel, Mr Byass and the PSNI's representative, Kathryn McGaughey, remained in the room. When we were allowed back at 3.30 p.m., the President of the IPT, Lord Justice Rabinder Singh, advised the BBC that its submission for the complaint of its former reporter, Vincent Kearney, to be conjoined and heard alongside ours, had been turned down. The BBC was dismissed from the courtroom with little more than a 'don't call us, we'll call you'. No date was suggested never mind considered for when the BBC would hear what MI5 had found amongst its records.

Many former BBC journalists have been suspicious that there was an MI5 agent within the broadcaster's Belfast headquarters on Ormeau Avenue. Those suspicions have only grown after an IPT hearing on 22 July. We know that many of those who have worked at the BBC are also concerned about what their editors and managers knew of the relationship with MI5. We have been advised that the BBC has worked alongside the security services on issues of national security. That is not something of which the BBC's own journalists appear to be aware.

It appears that the post-conflict strategy adopted by the British government is to shut down all of those who seek truth, be they victims' families, the OPONI or, indeed, journalists. They want to protect the dominant narrative: it was all a dirty war between two warring sectarian factions.

The PSNI and Durham constabulary decided to go after truthseekers, with the support of the rat catcher turned barista Ronnie Hawthorne. By doing so they inadvertently lit a fire under a magic porridge pot that continues to spew out their darkest secrets.

Select Bibliography

Books

Bowman, Timothy, *Carson's Army: The Ulster Volunteer Force, 1910–22* (Manchester: Manchester University Press, 2012)

Brewer, John D. and Higgins, G., *Anti-Catholicism in Northern Ireland, 1600–1998: The Mote and the Beam* (London: Palgrave Macmillan, 1998)

Edwards, Aaron, *UVF: Behind the Mask* (Dublin: Merrion Press, 2017)

Glennon, Kieran, *From Pogrom to Civil War: Tom Glennon and the Belfast IRA* (Cork: Mercier Press, 2013)

Potter, John, *A Testimony to Courage: The History of the Ulster Defence Regiment, 1969–1992* (London: Leo Cooper, 2001)

Urwin, Margaret, *A State in Denial: British Collaboration with Loyalist Paramilitaries* (Cork: Mercier Press, 2016)

Newspapers

Belfast News Letter
Belfast Telegraph
Down Recorder
Irish Independent
The Anglo-Celt
The Cork Examiner
The Irish News
The Irish Times

Websites

GAA.ie
www.thedetail.tv

Acknowledgements

Writing a book such as this is a very solitary experience but only realised through sacrifices made by others. This one is no different and has only come into the world due to the unflinching support of so many people I am very fortunate to have in my life.

From the moment Conor Graham committed to *Shooting Crows*, a wide range of those involved in this story or simply those around me, personally or professionally, have made some kind of compromise. For this, I will be eternally grateful.

At home, my wife of almost twenty-five years, Sheila, has been unremitting in her support. It fell across a time of great change and immense pride for our family as two of our daughters, Ella and Mia, graduated from their respective London universities to both work in the film industry. Our youngest, Freya, is now a teenager with a sharp sense of sarcastic wit that keeps us entertained. I'm forever indebted to Sheila and the girls for their unstinting love and support.

There would be no book without the families of those who died and were injured in the Loughinisland massacre on 18 June 1994. Their proud stand for truth and justice has been nothing less than inspirational to all of us lucky enough to get to know them. Throughout their campaign, they have acted with great integrity.

I have worked with Michael Fanning for almost twenty-five years. He has become a close confidant and reliable source of sage advice and guidance in challenging times. Nothing in my professional life would be possible if it wasn't for his ability to chart a course that always brings us home without fuss or fanfare. He is simply peerless. The assiduous head of our Irish language department, Maire Breathnach, and colleagues Sabina Cherek and Carol Murphy, were all impacted by the searches on our offices but showed grit and determination in keeping the show on the road.

Eimhear O'Neill was integral to the production of *No Stone Unturned* and a constant source of editorial inspiration. Her ferocious tenacity in pursuit of the truth put fresh information and insight into the hands of the master storyteller Alex Gibney, who crafted a groundbreaking film that told the world of the horror of Loughinisland. This book only benefits from their fastidious talents.

If it wasn't for the self-sacrifices and inestimable talents of Andrew Tully at Fine Point Films, this book would never have been finished. He handles significant production pressures, usually caused by the author, with an even, gracious manner, which means no drama becomes a crisis. Since I first met him, when he was a teenager with a dream, he has become one of the finest journalists and producers working in the industry today.

Following our arrest in August 2018, Barry and I met with many people from across the political divide. On behalf of Barry and myself and our families, we thank you. Thanks also to my brother Ian, the inspirational marathon runner who travelled from Enniskillen to join protests outside police stations and the High Court on several occasions.

In London, Sarah Kavanagh has been there for us throughout the past six years with advice and guidance. We owe her a huge debt of gratitude. Others, such as Patrick Corrigan at Amnesty International and Daniel Holder at the Committee for the Administration of Justice, stood with us and our colleagues through bail appearances and court hearings.

The Amnesty International campaign was crucial in raising awareness in Britain of the PSNI's vicious attack on press freedom. The NUJ in Belfast, particularly Kevin Cooper, Gerry Carson and Kathryn Johnson, embodied the fraternal benefit of union membership at a time of personal pressure. Thanks also to the solicitor for the Thierafurth families, Gavin Booth.

There were benefits to our arrest. Not every conversation with Barry McDonald QC was easy, but it was always enriching. It was an honour to be represented by one of Belfast's leading legal figures. Barry's junior during our judicial review is now a senior barrister. Stephen Toal KC faced down the police in Fine Point's offices on the morning of our arrest, earning immediate respect from all present. Underneath that calm, steely exterior is a passionate lawyer who never misses a beat.

Away from the frontline, there were two people who never allowed us to lose perspective while providing us with humour and nourishment of every possible kind. Stuart and Linda. Nothing would be the same without their friendship. Thanks to Fearghal, Marcus, Brenda, John and Eamon for great company and pints of Guinness.

It was great to work again with editor, Noel O'Regan and with Wendy Logue at Merrion. Noel Doran, former editor of the *Irish News*, read the manuscript, bringing a South Down perspective and lifetime of experience in journalism to the task. Oscar winner Terry George also brought his local knowledge to bear and provided important notes. Thanks to them all.

There would never have been a book, never mind a career, if it wasn't for the journalistic legend that is Denzil McDaniel. He has been a constant in my life since I was a child trying to kick a ball on the Broadmeadow in Enniskillen. He was quick to appreciate I was never going to be a footballer, but he did change my life. The editorial decisions he took as editor of the *Impartial Reporter* in Fermanagh in the mid-1980s were groundbreaking and many years ahead of their time. He read a draft of the book and provided typically clear-sighted notes. Nothing I can do will repay the faith he showed a seventeen-year-old rookie, nor the counsel and friendship he has given me since.

I have said once or twice that if you are going to be arrested, having Barry McCaffrey as a co-accused is a significant upside. Ever since the moment I saw his walking boots outside a cell in the Terrorism Suite at Musgrave Street PSNI station in Belfast, I knew I couldn't be locked up with a better man. And so it has proved. There has never been a moment when Barry couldn't find a smart-arse quip to lighten any dark development. His wife, Véronique, brings passion, colour, homemade spirits and much more to our lives. Barry hasn't just been a friend to me. Sheila, our daughters, even our dogs, have all benefited from his unique ability to make connections.

It was purely instinctive to call Niall Murphy as the PSNI tried to get through our front door. We had worked together on *No Stone Unturned*, but having such a strong, able advocate by your side when being questioned by detectives determined you should go to prison was comforting, to say the least. Niall is a man who leaves you in no doubt of his loyalties and of his determination to succeed.

And, finally, thanks for the patience and support shown by my mother, Jean, whose energy and social life remain an inspiration.

Index

Abbey Hospital, Whiteabbey, 142
Abrams, J.J., 284–5
Adair, Johnny: attempt on his life, 125; opposes peace, 139–40; runs C Company, 88; ruthlessness, 122, 124
Adams, Gerry: carries Begley coffin, 128; Milltown cemetery attack, 60; talks with Hume, 96, 115, 122–3, 192; urged to declare ceasefire, 133; US visa, 136–7
Adams, Private Michael, 93
Ahtty, Vicky, 102
Aiken, Thomas, 57
Aldridge, John, 69
Alexander, Bill, 176
Allen, Detective Constable Andy, 4–6
Allister, Jim, 260
Altglas, Véronique, 259, 294, 300
Amnesty International, 291, 299, 304, 306
An Claidheamh Soluis, 15
Anderson, Sir John, 30
Andrews, Irene, 57
Anglo-Irish Agreement, 36, 38, 41, 96, 115
Anglo-Irish Treaty, 20
Angolan war, 81
Annalong, 25
Annesley, Sir Hugh, 84
Apprentice Boys, 26
Arbuckle, Victor, 27
Ardglass, 48
Armscor, 51, 53, 220
Arsenal FC, 130
Asquith, Herbert, 12, 13–4
Atlantic Philanthropies, 213
Atria, 55

Attfield, David, 252

B-Specials, 26–7, 30
Baggott, Chief Constable Matt, 224
Ballykinler, 30, 47, 65, 84–5;
Ballynahinch, 67, 83
Ballyshannon power station, 26
Balmoral, 14
Banbridge, 12, 20, 191
Barrett, Ken, 70, 74, 86
Barron, Justice Henry, 33
Barry, Bill, 140
Barton, Chief Constable Mike, 294–5
BBC: and IPT, 311; fears re Loughinisland documentary, 230, 246–7, 252–3, 256; Maguire on PSNI obstruction, 237; Paisley financing UVF, 24–5; Patrick Kielty documentary, 71; reduced current affairs coverage, 208
Begley, Thomas, 125, 128
Belfast City Hall, 38
Belfast pogrom, 20
Bell, William, 70, 75, 76, 79–80, 191
Below The Radar, 208, 213, 219, 277, 286
Berlin Wall, 89, 98
Bernhardt, Douglas, 51–2, 80–1
Best, George, 64
Beyers, Mick, 217
Bingham, Billy, 131
Binns, Jimmy, 182–3, 184–5, 194–5, 204, 205, 210, 245
Birch, Private John, 93
Birney, Mia, 2, 5, 286
Birney, Sheila, 1–3, 6, 265, 286, 294, 300
Blaney, Fr Michael, 71

Blaney, Greg, 95, 143, 188
Bloody Sunday, 29, 30, 199
Boal, Desmond, 103
Bodenstown, 27
Bogside, 24, 26
Bonner, Packie, 94, 152, 158, 178–9
border campaign, 21, 22
Boutcher, Chief Constable Jon, 305, 306
Bowman, Timothy, 13, 15, 16, 17
Boyle, Congressman Brendan, 285
Boyle's Bar, Cappagh, 139
Bradley, Lance Corporal John, 93
Brady, Gerald, 148
Brecknell, Trevor, 33
Breen, Suzanne, 189
Breslin, John, 71, 72
Brewer, John D., 21
Brighton bombing, 36
Brolly, Joe, 95, 143
Brooke, Peter, 96, 97, 122
Brown, Detective Jonty, 204
Bryansford, 29
Bucharest, 149, 174
Bull, William, 16
Buncrana, 69
Byrne, Chief Constable Simon, 299, 305
Byrne, Eamon, 150, 155–6, 157, 159, 172, 181, 307
Byrne, Marie: background, 150–1, 155–6; hears of atrocity, 163–4, 172; impact on children, 180, 193; ombudsman report, 238; stalled investigation, 197; at The Heights Bar, 157, 159

Cairns, Eamon and Sheila, 128
Cairns, Gerard and Rory, 114, 127–8
Cairns, Liam, 128
Cairns, Róisín, 127
Cambridgeshire Constabulary, 84
Cameron, David, 44, 244
Cameron, Jimmy, 126
Cameron, Margaret, 127

Campbell, Sheena, 128
Cappagh pub attack, 97
Carlingford Lough, 12
Carmichael, Lady, 304
Carr, Ross, 95, 96, 188
Carroll, Detective Albert; arrests Hilary Hawthorne, 250–1; John Smyth attempted murder, 117–8; Loughinisland investigation, 184, 186; meets author, 247–51; Peter McCormack murder, 106–8, 120; Police Officer 4, 244; retires to France, 247–9; 'turns off' Hawthorne, 250–1
Carson, Sir Edward, 13–15, 38, 61
Casement, Moira, 150, 155, 164, 166, 187, 193, 196
Castlewellan, 28, 48, 115
Ceasefire Massacre 130, 133, 153, 158, 172, 199, 223, 225, 226, 229, 231
Celtic Park, Derry, 143
Charlton, Jack, 64, 68–9, 89, 94, 128, 129–30, 131
Chicago Cubs, 135, 136
Chichester-Clark, James, 26
Churchill, Winston, 13, 183
CIA, 210
civil rights movement, 23–4, 28
Clinton, Bill, 121, 123, 133, 136, 137, 177
Clinton, Jim, 138
Clinton, Teresa, 138
Clough, 11, 65, 66, 68, 70, 74, 75, 76, 77, 78, 86, 104, 116, 190–1, 233, 235, 236, 245, 250, 281, 309
Clyde Valley, SS, 17
Coalisland, 23
Cobain, Ian, 220–1
Coll, Peter, 286–7, 289
Collins, Peggy, 136
Colmer, Phil, 68
Committee for the Administration of Justice, 217, 304, 306
Connolly House Group, 133, 136, 140, 141

Cook, Roger, 69–70
Cooper, Ivan, 30
Corey, Judge Peter, 212
Corrigan, Patrick, 291, 304
Corrigan, William, 148
Coupland, Jim, 211
Coventry, 183
Craig, Colin 'Crazy', 145–7
Craig, James, 13–14, 21
Craig, Jim, UDA leader, 71, 72
Craig, William, 24
Crawford, Frederick, 16–17
Crawford, Lucy, 208
Crawley, William, 299
Croke Park, 63
Cromwell, Oliver, 68
Crossgar RIC station, 19
Crowne Plaza Hotel, Belfast, 242
Crumlin Road Gaol, 91
Cultúrlann McAdam Ó Fiaich, 206
Cunningham, John Pat, 297
Curlett, David, 75, 79
Cusack, Jim, 146

Davis, David, 284, 286, 290–92, 299
de Silva, Sir Desmond: Ballykinler base break-in, 84–6; Nelson investigation, 45, 46, 50–1, 56, 91–2; Pat Finucane murder, 44; South African Arms, 52; Teresa Clinton murder, 138
Delaney, John, 221
Democratic Unionist Party (DUP), 36, 37, 41, 51, 61, 67, 93, 97, 103, 123, 134, 176, 260, 301, 306
Dennison, Phil, 245
Denvir, Fr Charles, 106
Derry Housing Action Committee, 24
Detail, The, 5, 44, 151, 193, 213, 214, 217, 219, 277, 286, 301, 302
Devine, John, 100
Devlin, Bernadette, 23–4
Dickenson, Rev. John, 67–8

Dodds, Nigel, 41
Doherty, Paddy, 63
Donadoni, Roberto, 94, 153
Donaldson, Jeffrey, 67, 260
Donard Demesne, 104
Donnelly, Michael, 33
Donnelly, Patsy, 33
Donnelly's Bar, Silverbridge, 33
Dooley, Seamus, 292
Dornan, Eamonn, 288
Dougherty, Cecil, 148
Downe Hospital, 29, 164, 171, 172, 184
Downing Street Declaration, 134
Downpatrick, 11, 12, 48
Drogheda, Siege of, 68
Drumaness, 39, 40, 150, 155, 156, 194, 201
Dublin and Monaghan bombings, 32–3, 57
Dundrum, South Down, 65, 70
Dungannon, 23–4, 113
Durham Constabulary, 5, 16, 257, 262, 266–72, 274, 277, 280–2, 283, 284, 286, 288, 289, 294–5, 296, 302, 304

Easter Rising, 15, 17, 22
educational apartheid, 21
Elizabeth II, Queen, 177
Ellis, Detective Darren, 5, 7, 277, 282–4, 288–92, 293, 296, 303, 309–10
Ellwood, Alison, 208
Enigma code, 183
Enniskillen bombing, 54
Erne, Earl of, 16
Escobar, Andrés, 223
Escobar, Pablo, 223
ESPN, 223

Fairfield, Terry, 184–5, 204–5, 210
Fanning, Michael, 277
Fanny, SS, 17
Farouzi, William, 55
Farrell, Mairead, 60
Farry, Stephen, 304

Faulkner, Brian, 26
Feeney, Chuck, 138, 213
Ferguson Smith, Lt Col. Gerald Bryce, 20
Ferguson, James, 48
Ferguson, Raychel, 208
Fine Point Films, 130, 222, 223, 279, 286, 300
Finlay, Billy, 48
Finucane, John, 273–4, 279, 287, 291, 292, 300, 302
Finucane, Pat, 44, 74, 91, 199, 203, 212
Fisher, Michael, 71
FitzGerald, Garret, 36
Fitzpatrick, Sean, 116
Fitzsimons, Harry, 46
Flanagan, Chief Constable Ronnie, 145, 198, 202
Flanagan, Jim, 177
Flynn, Bill: background 135–6; ceasefires, 192; fears about atrocity links, 225–6; Loughinisland connections, 140–2, 165–6; World Cup game, 152, 156–7
Force Research Unit (FRU), 44–47, 50, 51, 54, 56, 59, 62, 81, 84, 90, 91, 92, 102, 147
Fox, Charles and Teresa, 114, 139
Fox, Sean, 126
Frankel, Glenn, 83
Fraser, Nick, 229–30
Free Presbyterian Church, 51
Frenchies pub, Clough, 245
Frizzell, John, 125
Frizzell's fish shop atrocity, 125

GAA security force ban, 100
Gadaffi, Colonel, 65
Gallagher, Gino, 147
Galway Film Fleadh, 246
Garda Síochána, An, 87, 130
George V Hotel, Paris, 80, 82
Giants Stadium, 152, 165
Gibney, Alex, 5, 209–10, 222–3, 224, 225, 226, 229, 230, 251–2, 284, 287

Gibraltar, 60
Gilford, 48
Girvan, Peter, 279
Gladstone, William, 12
Glasson, Jonathan, 301
Glenanne gang, 33–4, 55
Glenarm, 15
Glengormley, 2, 126, 220
Good Friday Agreement, 198, 214
Gordon, Kevin, 161–2
Gough Barracks, 73, 186
Gould, Matilda 'Tilly', 22, 23
Gracey, Jim, 177–8
Gracey, Tim, 236
Gray, ACC Barbara, 296
Green, Barney, 142, 150, 155, 158–9
Green, Brigid, 142
Greysteel massacre, 129–30

Hagen, Chris, 105
Hamilton, Chief Constable George, 224–5, 228, 257, 260, 293, 294–5
Hamilton, Davy, 146
Hamilton, George, 157, 161–2
Hammersmith Inn, 16
Hancock, David, 25
Harris, Deputy Chief Constable Drew, 87, 253–4
Harris, Divisional Commander Alwyn, 78, 87
Harrods, 16
Haughey, Charles, 37, 89
Hawthorne Inn, Annaclone, 188–9
Hawthorne, Hilary, 67, 192, 233–6, 238, 246–7, 249–56
Hawthorne, Ronnie: arrests and release, 78, 192; background, 66; Charles Watson killing, 67; chief Loughinisland suspect, 7, 226–7; 'hurt and pain', 273–4, 278, 281–2; Jack Kielty murder, 75; Martin Lavery murder, 108–9; O'Rourke shooting, 74–5; Person A, 244; recruits Delbert Watson, 74; rat exterminator,

256, 281; UDR discharge, 79, 249–50; warned ahead of arrest, 240
Hawthorne, Trevor, 191
Hayes, Maurice, 100–1
Hazzard, Chris, 304
Heath, Edward, 29
Heights Bar, The, 148–66, 169, 173, 179, 201, 204, 215, 219–20, 275, 307
Henderson, Detective Sergeant Arnold, 278–9, 282, 293
Henderson, Deric, 79
Higgins, Gerry, 44–5
Hill, Private Robert, 39, 87
Hillen, Rosemary, 189–90
Historical Enquiries Team, 139
Hogan Cup, 64
Holder, Daniel, 304
Holmes, Paul, 245
Home Rule, 12–14
Hood, HMS, 135
Houghton, Ray, 69, 131, 153, 157, 178
Hume, John, 30, 96, 115, 122, 123, 129, 192
Humphreys, Justice Michael, 52, 56, 58
hunger strikes, 36
Hunt, Baron, 26
Hurst, Ian, 54–5
Hutchings, Dennis, 297
Hutchinson, Al: background 205; calls for resignation, 218; controversial report, 212, 217; denies collusion, 215–7; deputy, 211; malicious attacks, 214; meets families, 215–6; report quashed, 221–2; requests for information, 227–8
Hutchinson, Billy, 26

Imperial Defence College, 30
Inniskilling Dragoons, 30
internment, 27, 30
Investigatory Powers Tribunal (IPT), 300–2, 304–5
Irish National Liberation Army (INLA), 37, 146–7, 171

Irish Parliamentary Party (IPP), 12
Irish Republican Army (IRA): attacks Downing St, 97; attacks on RUC, 28; attacks on soldiers, 27; attacks on UDR, 39, 92–3; attempts to kill Adair, 124; bombing in England, 102; border campaign, 22; ceasefire, 192; Enniskillen atrocity, 54; Frizzell bombing, 125–6; Gibraltar bomb plot, 60; kills Charles Watson, 66–7; Libyan arms imports, 65; peace talks, 122; Teebane bombing, 102; urged to declare ceasefire, 133
Irish Volunteers, 15
Irwin, Denis, 153
Italia '90, 69, 89, 94

Jackson, Robin, 33, 35, 57, 88, 97, 101, 128, 139
Jaffey, Ben, 300, 302, 304–5, 306
Javeline missiles, 81
Jenkinson, Ann, 151, 156, 164, 172, 181
Jenkinson, Louise, 151, 156, 163, 172
Jenkinson, Malcolm, 151, 152, 156, 158, 160–1, 164, 172, 179, 181, 187
John Ferguson & Co., 16
John Paul II, Pope, 177
Johnston, Ken, 170–1
Johnston, William, 22
Jones, Prof. Greta, 142
Jones, Tom, 70
Justice Group, 198

Kavanagh, Sarah, 283, 300
Keane, Roy, 153
Kearney, Vincent, 218, 261, 304, 305, 311
Keefe, Patrick, 284
Keegan, Judge Siobhan, 283, 291, 298
Kelly, Dolores, 295
Kelly, Gerry, 295
Kelly, McEvoy & Brown, 70
Kelly, Sean, 125

Kennedy Smith, Jean, 123
Kennedy, Robert, 140
Kennedy, Senator Ted, 137
Kerr, Brian, 102
Kerr, Colonel Gordon, 102-3
Kielty, Jack, 70-2, 73-4, 75, 76-7, 78, 79, 86, 88
Kielty, John, 64
Kielty, Patrick, 64, 71-2
Kilkeel, 25, 41
Kincaid, ACC Sam, 200
Kincaid, Laurence, 59
King, James, 82
King, Trevor, 145-6

Larne, 17
Lashmar, Paul, 290
Lavery, Danielle, 109, 111
Lavery, Danny, 109, 110, 118
Lavery, John, 101
Lavery, Martin, 108-10, 115, 120, 191, 282
Lavery, Sean, 110
Lavery, Teresa, 108-9, 111, 118
Law, Andrew Bonar, 14
Law, Michael, 293
Lawrenson, Mark, 177-8
Linden, Mickey, 143, 144, 188
Little, Noel: approaches Armscor, 51-2, 53; arms buyer, 80-1, 220-1; arrests, 58, 82; stolen Shorts blueprints, 81; UDR and Ulster Resistance member, 51
Liverpool Club, Belfast, 109-10, 111, 119
Long, Naomi, 306
Loughgall RUC station, 66
Loughran, Neil, 96
Lowry, Lord Chief Justice, 33
Loy, John, 189
Loy, Valerie, 189
Loyalist Prisoners Association (LPA), 124, 125
Lyttle, Tommy, 50

Mac Brádaigh, Caoimhín, 60
MaCartan, James, 143
Macauley, Conor, 100
MacDermott, Lord Chief Justice, 23
MacDonald, Barry, 279, 287-9, 290, 294, 298, 300
MacNeill, Eoin, 15-6
MacRory Cup, 64
MacVeagh, Jeremiah, 12-13
Madden, Peter, 199
Magee, Canon Bernard, 174, 181
Magee, Fergus, 101
Magee, Rev. Roy, 146
Maginn, Loughlin, 83-4, 85, 86, 91, 92, 214
Maginnis, Ken, 176
Maguire, Dr Michael: accuses RUC of collusion, 239-44; arms shipments, 55-6, 59; confronts PSNI in court, 227-8; criticises OPONI, 218; issues Loughinisland report, 238-44; Jack Kielty murder, 72-4; Loughinisland investigation, 52-3, 186; Martin Lavery murder, 110; ombudsman, 219, 221; Peter McCormack murder, 106-8
Maguire, Laurence, 113, 114, 128
Major, John, 122, 123, 133, 134
Mallon, Christopher, 138
Mallon, Martin, 138
Mallon, Roseann, 138-9
Mallon, Seamus, 83
Manchester Trader, 55
Marks, Colum, 93-4
Martin, ACC Stephen, 253-5, 257, 262, 272, 279, 281, 285, 287, 299
Mason, Gary, 179-80, 188
Mason, Roy, 42
Mayhew, Patrick, 133, 174, 175
Maze Prison, 66, 139-40
McAuley, Mandy, 114, 128
McAvoy, Brian, 95
McCabe, Ciaran, 143-4

McCaffrey, Barry: arrested with author, 263–5, 273–4; background, 213–4; bail conditions, 283; collusion accusations, 44; court victory, 291–2; hospitalised, 236–7; marries, 259; NUJ support for, 286; police corruption investigation, 301–2; police hacking, 301–4, 306; Policing Board meeting, 295–6; probed by PSNI, 4–5; release from jail, 275–6; retrieving materials from PSNI, 293–4; *Talkback*, 299; Toman letter, 234–5; US lobbying, 285; vigil for, 275; whistleblower documents, 229–31
McCann, Dan, 60
McCann, Eamonn, 24
McCartan, James, 63, 64
McCarthy, Peter, 104
McClements, James, 165
McCloskey, Justice Bernard, 260, 280
McCord, Raymond, 203, 210
McCormack, Peter, 105–6, 108, 111, 117, 120, 184, 243, 244, 282
McCreanor, Dan, 150, 158, 164, 181
McCreanor, Patrick, 150, 164, 238
McCullough, Angus, 306
McCullough, James, 57
McCusker, Fergal, 143
McDonald, Alan, 132
McDonald, Henry, 146
McDonnell, John, 283
McDowell, Thomas, 25, 26
McEntagart, Mgr Liam, 113
McEvoy, John, 105–6
McGleenan, Tony, 227
McGrady, Eddie, 174–5, 176, 190
McGrath, Paul, 69, 133, 153, 157, 158
McGrath, Pete, 64, 71, 72, 95, 99, 143, 179, 180, 188
McGuinness, Martin, 60, 175–6, 291
McGurk's bar, Belfast, 28
McKay, Susan, 256, 284, 298
McKenna Hall, Kircubbin, 99

McKibben, Paul, 75
McLeigh, Brian, 157, 171
McLoughlin, Alan, 131
McMichael, John, 37, 40, 49, 51–2, 70
McMullan, Gorman: arrested, 190; avoids arrest, 192; car theft, 104; getaway driver, 233; identification as suspect, 245, 254–5; link to South Down UVF, 117; Liverpool Club, 110–1; marriage, 309; Person 1, 244; relationship with Hawthorne, 250; Special Branch awareness, 120–1, 185; Thierafurth Inn atrocity, 104, 106–7
McMurray, Constable Colleen, 5
McNulty, Peter, 28
McVeigh, Joe, 277
McVicker, Detective Constable, 6
McWilliams, David, 89
Metropolitan Police Service, 302
MI5: allows arms imports, 55–6; blueprints thefts, 81; collusion, 44; Ulsterisation policy, 42
Miami Showband, 101
Millar, Gavin, 279, 300
Millbrook Hotel, 200
Milligan, Andy, 171
Milltown Cemetery, 60, 79
Mitchell, James: arms from South Africa, 55–6; Dublin and Monaghan bombings, 32–4, 57; inspired by Paisley, 42
Moloney, Ed, 37, 41
Molyneaux, James, 36, 41, 122–3,
Molyneaux, Jim, 192
Moore, Chris, 43, 83, 214
Moran, Martin, 126
Morgan, Ray, 64
Morgan, Sir Declan, Chief Justice, 283, 287, 290–1, 296, 298–9
Morris MP, Grahame, 283
Morrison, Bruce, 123
Mowlam, Mo, 226
Moy, 102

Mullan, Kathleen, 40
Mullan, Terry, 39–40
Mullan, Tommy, 40
Murphy, Danny, 179
Murphy, John, GAA player, 63
Murphy, Niall: background, 199–201; contact from Fairfield, 204–5; Covid coma, 297–8; documentary, 219; granted injunction, 274–5; legal costs warning, 286; meets Lavery family, 118–9; ombudsman report, 222, 238–9, 241, 261–2; police interrogation, 265–72; press conference, 206–7; PSNI investigates journalists, 257; UVF decommissioning, 211
Murray, Sean 'Spike', 145
Musgrave Park Hospital, 29

National Union of Journalists (NUJ), 272, 279, 282, 283, 286, 291, 292, 299, 300, 306
Neal, Congressman Richard, 285
Nelson Diaries, 91
Nelson, Brian: arrest, 91; arms imports, 50–2, 59; background, 44; Ballykinler break-in, 84; British agent, 45–7, 91; immunity, 175; in court, 102–3; mental instability, 45; proposes target victims, 46, 62, 85, 103; UDA torturer, 44; witness protection, 103;
Nelson, Rosemary, 212
New York Film Festival, 255
Newcastle, Co. Down, 25, 75
Newry, 12
Newtownards TA base, 81, 82
Newtownards, 25
Niblock, Thomas, 179, 180
No Stone Unturned, 3, 5, 73, 86, 182, 184, 186, 219–20, 232, 236, 237, 249, 256–7, 258, 259, 267, 270–2, 274, 280, 284–5, 287, 289, 290, 300
Northern Bank, Portadown, 53

Northern Ireland Office (NIO), 202, 205, 219

O'Brien, Gay, 24
O'Brien, Martin, 213
O'Connell monument, 27
O'Donnell, Lord Justice, 79
O'Dowd, Niall, 132–3, 141, 152, 156–7, 165
O'Hare, Anne, 172
O'Hare, Pat, 143
O'Hare, Patsy, 150–1, 155, 172–3
O'Hare, Willie, 159, 172–3
O'Hehir, Michael, 142
O'Kane, Maurice, 144–5
O'Leary, David, 94
O'Loan, Nuala, 201–3, 205, 261
O'Neill, Eimhear, 230, 238, 254, 280
O'Neill, Patrick, 258
O'Neill, Sean, 63
O'Neill, Terence, 21, 25
O'Reilly, Ruth, 208–10, 302
O'Rourke, John, 49, 65, 74
O'Rourke, Paddy, 99
O'Toole, Aidan, 155, 159, 161–3, 171
O'Toole, Hugh, 149, 154, 158, 174, 190, 192, 225
Office of the Police Ombudsman (OPONI), 198, 202–5, 210–12, 215, 253, 254, 281, 303
Official Secrets Act (OSA), 3, 266, 289, 290
Omagh bomb, 196, 202, 261
Operation Aristocrat, 170
Operation Ballast, 202, 215
Operation Demetrius, 28
Operation Flavius, 60
Operation Yurta, 4
Orbison, Roy, 70
Orde, Chief Constable Hugh, 139
Oscar Wilde Awards, 284

Páirc Seán Ó Caoilte, 72

Paisley, Ian: ambivalence to terrorism, 24-5, 26, 37; attends Watson funeral, 67; bombings, 25; ejected from Commons, 133; opposes civil rights, 24; opposes O'Neill, 21, 24; talks with Major, 123; Ulster Clubs, 40-1; Ulster Resistance, 41, 96; UVF and UDA links, 24-5, 37
Paisley, Rhonda, 97
Parachute Regiment, 29
Pat Finucane Centre, 33-4
Patton, Chris, 198
Pauley, Mervyn, 115
Payne, Davy, 57
peace process, 123, 128, 139-40
Peacock, Paul, 75
Plunkett, Oliver, 21
Police Ombudsman of Northern Ireland, 5, 118-9,
Police Service of Northern Ireland (PSNI): alerted about film, 252-3; apology, 299; creation, 198; data harvesting, 305-6; destroys evidence, 212-3; Historical Enquiries, 139; investigates document 'theft', 257; monitors victims' families, 206; obstructs ombudsman, 224; pays compensation, 300
Policing Board, 198
Pollock, Sam, 211, 214-5, 218
Pomeroy, 19, 22
Porter-Porter, J., 17
Potter, John, 30
Prague Spring, 23
Protestant Action Committee, 36
Protestant Action Force, 36

Queen's Film Theatre, 257
Queen's Island, 144
Queen's University Belfast, 15
Quinn, Jimmy, 131
Quinn, Niall, 130-2, 153, 178, 307
Quinn, Peter, 99, 100
Quinn, Samuel, 82

Rae, Oliver, 28-9
Rafferty, Judge Neil, 278-9, 291, 302
Rathfriland, 83
Real IRA, 196
Reavey brothers, 33
Red Hand Commando, 97, 123
Redpath, Jackie, 141
Rees, Merlyn, 42
Reid, Fr Alex, 61
Relatives for Justice, 56, 61-2, 226
Retired Police Officers Association (RPOA), 258-61, 280
Reynolds, Albert, 121-3, 134, 152, 156
Rice, Francis, 48
Rice, James, 115-6
Rice, Joe, 162
Rice, Willie, 143, 144, 160
Rising Sun Bar, Greysteel, 129
Ritchie, Margaret, 176, 206, 244
Robinson, Mark, 278-9, 286
Robinson, Peter, 41, 51
Rodgers, Mark, 127
Rogan, Adrian 'Frosty', 98, 143, 144, 158-60, 163, 173
Rogan, Clare: Down supporter, 143-4; Heights Bar, 154-5, 162-3; 180; press interview, 206; stalled RUC investigation, 187-8, 193, 195, 199-200; tells her children about atrocity, 173
Rogan, Emma: father's funeral, 181; Justice Group, 198; OPONI meeting, 215-6; ombudsman report, 239, 260; persistence, 197; press interview, 206
Rogan, Mick, 162
Rogan, Tony, 181, 197
Rogers, Desmond, 101
Royal Irish Rangers, 97
Royal Ulster Constabulary (RUC): Ballykinler break-in ignored, 84-5; blamed for Loughinisland, 166; expansion, 29; ineffective

investigations, 192–4; Reserve, 32; Newcastle G Division, 72; Shorts blueprint thefts, 81; Special Branch, 43, 46, 53, 56, 147; summoned to Loughinisland, 170
RTÉ bombing, 26
Russell, Detective Superintendent David, 186

Salvation Army, 37
Sands, Bobby, 36
Savage, Sean, 60
Sayers, Eddie, 70
Schillaci, Salvatore, 95
Scullion, John Patrick, 22, 23
Seapark Complex, 90
Shankhill Butchers, 35, 248
Shannon, Jim, 93–4
Sharman-Crawford, Colonel Robert, 15
Shaw, Stephen, 304
Shields, Dabheoc, 113
Shields, Diarmuid, 113
Shields, Patrick, 113
Short Brothers, 53, 81
Shorts Aerospace, 53
Silent Valley, 25
Simpson, Charlie, 52–3
Singh, Sir Rabinder, 304, 311
Small, John Francis, 12
Smart, Private Steven, 93
Smithwick, Judge, 241
Smyth, Colm, 151–1, 156, 158–61, 164–5, 171
Smyth, Hugh and Muriel, 67
Smyth, John Henry, 116–8
Smyth, Robin, 67
Social Democratic and Labour Party (SDLP), 30, 48, 57, 83, 96, 115, 123, 174, 176, 206, 218, 232, 295, 304
Solemn League and Covenant, 14, 16
Sons of Ulster Accordion Band, 39
Special Air Service (SAS), 60, 66

Spence, Gusty, 23, 111, 141, 192
Spiro, Bruno 'Benny', 17
St Angelo base, 54
St Colman's College, Newry, 64
St Macartan's church, Loughinisland, 181, 307
Staunton, Steve, 153
Step Inn pub, Keady, 33
Stevens, Sir John: inquiries obstructed, 90–2, 103; Pat Finucane investigation, 203; RUC collusion, 84; UDR arrests, 87–8
Stevenson, Samuel, 25
Stewart, ACC Bill, 174
Stone, Michael, 60, 79
Stormont, 26, 29
Strain, Adam, 208
Sullivan, Richard, 174
Sunningdale Agreement, 32

targeted killings, 43–4, 45–7,
Taylor MP, John, 100
Taylor, Alan, 74–5, 104, 109, 190, 233, 244
Taylor, Peter, 146
Teconnaught, 180
Templeton, Darwin, 190–1
Thatcher, Margaret, 36, 37, 38, 39, 42, 54–5
Thierafurth Inn, 104, 105, 107, 117, 120, 184, 233
Thompson, Mark, 226
Titanic, 14
Toal, Stephen, 280, 291
Toman, Mick, 162
Toman, Patsy, 176, 192, 232–5, 246
Tone, Wolfe, 27
Torney, Kathryn, 277
Treacy, Judge Seamus, 283, 291, 298
Tripoli, 65
tuberculosis, 142

Ulster Clubs, 13, 38, 41
Ulster Day, 14–5
Ulster Defence Association (UDA): arms

from South Africa, 50–4, 55, 58; attacks on Catholics, 31, 45–6; Ballykinler break-in, 84; Kielty murder, 86; Maginn murder; 86 Mullan murder, 86; recruits, 31; targets pan-nationalist front, 115
Ulster Defence Regiment (UDR): Ballydugan Road bomb, 92–3; first commandant, 30; loyalist violence, 27; merged with RIR, 97; recruitment, 27, 29–31; structure, 30; targets IRA suspects, 47, 48; UDA/UVF collusion, 31, 47, 49
Ulster Division, 36th, 17
Ulster Freedom Fighters (UFF), 40, 45, 83, 97, 100
Ulster Resistance, 41, 49, 51, 53, 57, 58, 61
Ulster Unionist Council, 13
Ulster Volunteer Force (UVF): admits to Loughinisland atrocity, 171; arms purchases, 16; bombing campaigns, 26–8; decommissioning deal, 211; Dublin and Monaghan bombings, 33; early history, 13, 15, 16; First World War, 17; Glenanne gang, 33; Harold Wilson's assessment, 23; imports arms from South Africa, 58–9; INLA attack, 146; Paisley's support, 23; recruits from UDR, 31; revival, 19, 22; terrorism, 22; targets Catholics, 22–3; threatens IRA, 22
Ulster Volunteers, 13
Ulsterisation, 42

Valentine, Brendan 'Brenny', 158, 160–1, 165, 171–2, 180; death, 307; interview with, 225; misses funerals, 180–1; ombudsman report, 238–9

Walker Report, 43, 83, 110, 121
Walker, Sir Patrick, 42
Walsh, Bishop Patrick, 145, 174

War of Independence, 19
Ward, Peter, 23
Ware, John: arms imports, 51, 55–6, 58; meeting with PSNI, 253; Nelson murders, 103; South African arms imports, 59; Stevens inquiry, 90; summarises Maguire report, 260–1
Warnock, Ian, 106
Warrenpoint, 12
Watson, Charles, 65–8, 79
Watson, Delbert, 66, 67, 70–1, 73–7, 79, 181
Watson, Doreen, 74, 79
Watson, Tom, 284
Watson, Trevor, 104, 110, 191, 244
Whelan, Ronnie, 69
White, Ray, 261
Wildcard Distribution, 258
Williamson, Detective Chief Superintendent Derek, 200
Wilson, Detective Inspector, 201
Wilson, Gordon, 54
Wilson, Harold, 23
Wilson, Marie, 54
Wilson, Paddy, 57
Wilson, Sammy, 41, 61
Windsor Park, Belfast, 130
Winters, Kevin, 127, 199
Withnell, Peter, 95
Wood, Ian, 38
Wright, Alan, 37, 38, 41, 51
Wright, Billy: attempts to kill, 144–5; Cairns murders, 114; claims success against IRA, 139; killed in Maze, 212; King Rat, 88; MI5–Special Branch agent, 97, 114, 140; opposes peace, 139; religious faith, 139; reputation, 101; Shields murders, 113
Wright, Dick, 51

Young, David, 292